W9-BZV-794

Making the Software Business Case

Improvement by the Numbers

Donald J. Reifer

Addison-Wesley

Boston • San Francisco • New York • Toronto • Montreal
London • Munich • Paris • Madrid
Capetown • Sydney • Tokyo • Singapore • Mexico City

The publisher offers discounts on this book when ordered in quantity for special sales. For more information, please contact:

Pearson Education Corporate Sales Division
One Lake Street
Upper Saddle River, NJ 07458
(800) 382-3419
corpsales@pearsontechgroup.com

Visit AW on the Web: www.awl.com/cseng/

Library of Congress Cataloging-in-Publication Data

Reifer, Donald J.
    Making the software business case : improvement by the numbers / Donald J. Reifer.
        p. cm.
    Includes bibliographical references and index.
    ISBN 0-201-72887-7
    1. Computer software—Development—Management.   I. Title.

    QA 76.76.D47 R445 2001
    005.1'068—dc21

                                            2001027937

ISBN 0-201-72887-7
Text printed on recycled paper
1 2 3 4 5 6 7 8 9 10 — CRS — 0504030201
First printing, August 2001

Contents

Foreword

Some of the most frustrating and helpless feelings I've had in my career are associated with reviews I've done of software projects that are about to be terminated. Frequently, the people involved have been working hard as a closely knit team. They've come up with creative solutions to difficult problems. Their product has good modular structure and has been carefully tested. But when it's provided to potential users, nobody is very interested in it. They say, "Those are nice capabilities, but they address only about two percent of my operational problem." Or "That would help some of my operations, but I can't afford the time it would take to keep its database up to date." Or "You've got a great way to access all that information, but it's not the information I need to make decisions."

At those times, I have wished that I had been able to do the review at the beginning of the project rather than at the end. Problems like this can generally be identified and avoided with a relatively straightforward business case analysis. A good business case analysis estimates the proposed initiative's development, transition, and operational costs and relates these costs to the estimated benefits, both quantitative and qualitative. Such business cases also provide a framework for tradeoff analysis, enabling you to determine the conditions under which the benefits realized will be worth the investment. And it enables you and your fellow stakeholders to distinguish between the situations in which there is a good chance of success, from the situations in which there is virtually no chance that the benefits will be worth the investment, and where it's healthier to drop the project early rather than pursue it to an expensive and frustrating failure.

Business case analysis is often perceived to be an esoteric art practiced only by financial wizards. But its essentials involve relatively simple and intuitive algebraic formulas and concepts such as compound interest.

Fortunately for us in the software and information technology (IT) field, Don Reifer has packaged these essentials into ready-to-use approaches and procedures covering the most frequent situations in which business case analyses are needed. Don has had decades of experience in helping large and small commercial and government organizations develop and learn to apply business case analyses for software and IT strategic decisions. In this book, he has distilled this experience into tailorable business case analysis approaches and representative case studies, which show you how to apply the approaches in typical decision situations.

Chapter 1 is an overview of the rapidly moving IT field and how business case analysis can help you and your organization to cope with the socioeconomic challenges of rapid change. Chapter 2 summarizes how and where business case analyses fit into the software and IT life cycle, including a tailorable outline for business plans. Chapter 3 provides clear and simple explanations of the most common business case analysis tools and techniques: present value analysis, return-on-investment analysis, breakeven analysis, cost/benefit analysis, value chain analysis, cost estimation tools, and others. Chapter 4 presents frameworks and guidelines for using these business case analysis techniques for improving software and IT productivity and delivery time.

Chapter 5 through 8 provide worked-out case studies about decision situations involving software process improvement, new venture investment, architecting product lines, and acquiring an existing company. Each case study includes representative scenarios for preparing business case analyses and effectively presenting them in terms convincing to management decision makers.

A particularly nice feature of the case study scenarios is that they include some false starts and incomplete analyses and show you how to diagnose and fix them. Chapter 9 then brings everything back together into a set of critical success factors and strategic guidelines for whatever type of business case analysis you may want to pursue.

As a bottom line, though, this is much more than a book about business case analysis. Don Reifer has drawn on his wide array of consulting and research experiences to create a wonderful socio-techno-economic picture of the IT world we live and operate in. Just the understanding and insights you will pick up about how people encounter and cope with the combinations of technical, social, political, and economic opportunities and challenges make the book a joy to read and worth much more than its price alone.

Barry Boehm
University of Southern California

Preface

For years, I have watched software engineers struggle to justify investments of every kind and examine cost-effectiveness issues. Although they know how to present the technical issues and alternatives crisply and simply, they just can't seem to pull the numbers together. Those who try never seem to paint a convincing picture. While they fumble, the opportunity slips away. Or they are eaten alive as they pitch their ideas because they cannot answer the hard questions posed about costs/benefits, which typically involve the financials and business justifications. For example, engineers frequently fail to factor the cost of money and/or tax implications into the consideration (depreciation, R&D tax credits, and so on). If they had examined these considerations, they might have recommended a different course of action.

WHY WRITE THIS BOOK?

The failure of engineers to adequately address the business aspects of decisions has created opportunities for me throughout my career. I have built a profitable business and a national reputation by showing my clients how to make the numbers sing for management. I have also learned many lessons and developed many tricks of the trade, which have enabled me to repeatedly help my clients win the battle of budget. The primary purpose of this book is to communicate these lessons to other people who need them so that they can take advantage of what I've learned. Because of their importance, I believe that every engineer should be taught how to prepare business cases as part of their undergraduate and graduate education.

After 30 years in the field, I have an endless supply of case studies that I can use to illustrate why this important topic needs to be taught to everyone involved in an organization, from the top executive to a new recruit. For example, can you envision the CEO of a major international firm standing on a chair to see the charts from the back of the room? That's exactly what happened when I projected the results of a productivity analysis to executives. The numbers were so important to the CEO that he almost fell over backward as the chair he stood on wobbled in his effort to see them. The moral of this story is that, independently of whatever you say, *your numbers will do your talking for you when executives are in the room.*

The primary goal of this book is to help you understand how to develop a successful business case. To help you learn, I present principles and case studies. Because of its importance, the book focuses attention on the process of business case development, not the case itself. After reading the book, your task is to generalize and apply what you have learned in your own work environment. As part of this effort, you will have to figure out what will work for you and adapt the advice offered accordingly.

Business cases are typically prepared throughout the software development life cycle. Some are prepared along with the business plans used to justify new projects and product developments. Others are devised on the spot to justify changes and improvement activities. My focus in the book is on the latter because they tend to be the most difficult to pull off. Because such initiatives ask for money, the expenditures involved must be justified quantitatively in terms of the costs/benefits. When you finish this book, you will understand how to quantify the numbers. But using them effectively in your organization will be up to you.

FOR WHOM IS THIS BOOK INTENDED?

I wrote this book primarily for software engineers and managers, who frequently don't seem to have the foggiest idea of what it takes to prepare a business case. They may have great technical ideas, but most find it difficult to package the concepts to make the costs/benefits associated with pursuing them appealing to management. To do this, they need to highlight the cost savings, reduction in time to market, cost avoidance, and/or productivity improvement. Justifying expenditures for some good technical idea in terms of its return on investment is something that they haven't been taught in their university training or their opening stint in industry. To sell their ideas, they need to learn how to package them so that they are convincing to management.

My underlying assumption is that software engineers will be tasked to justify the improvements that they and their bosses recommend. If this is not the case, don't read any further. Instead, give your copy of this book to someone who needs help in preparing business cases.

As well as software engineers, I think people in the following positions could benefit from this book:

- *Managers and executives*   Those who act as sponsors and champions of a change when they're convinced that it has both technical and business merits

- *Buyers of products and services*   Those who use the technical and business data presented to justify a variety of purchasing decisions (equipment, tools, training, and so on)

- *Entrepreneurs*   Those who package the technical ideas in such a way that they stimulate investment by stockholders or venture capitalists

- *Process group leaders*   Those who seek to justify continued investment in process improvement (based on the returns, competitive reasons, and so on)

- *Programmers*   Those who use the architectures, processes, tools, and techniques that software engineers generate or select to develop and/or maintain software products and systems

- *Students*   Those pursuing undergraduate or graduate degrees in either computer science or information management. Both have a need for a book that shows them how to prepare and execute a business case.

- *Researchers*   Surprisingly, many researchers don't know how to prepare business cases aimed at soliciting industry sponsorship. This book will help them acquire the support they need to put their ideas into practice.

In other words, anyone interested in the topic could get a few pointers from the material presented, especially in the case studies.

WHAT'S IN THE BOOK?

If you are looking for a general-purpose textbook on business plans and cases, look elsewhere. This book isn't written for you. There are general management textbooks on the subject that will address your need for structure and guidance. Instead, this book addresses software improvements and what you need to do to justify them in terms of their costs/benefits. Yes, it treats the business case and provides instructions on how to build one. But it also provides examples of what it takes to succeed with the business case in the form of case studies. Most of these cases are taken from real life; I've embellished them to hide identities and illustrate lessons learned. However, software improvements involve more than just process. They might entail justifying capital investments, moving to product line architectures, or valuing the purchase price to be paid for a firm.

This is not a cookbook on business cases. Cookbooks by their nature infer that results are repeatable. Put a pinch of this and an ounce of that together and bake the mixture at 400 degrees for 10 minutes and a similar result will be generated almost every time. However, the improvement opportunities I've been associated with, even when conducted within similar organizations, are by their nature different almost every time. That's because there are so many factors involved that it is almost impossible to develop a generic formula for improvement. In response, I provide a process framework, not recipes, for making improvements.

The underlying message of this book is that there needs to be some compelling reason for making organizational changes or proposed improvements. Otherwise, why pursue them? Within this context, business cases are used to gather and present the facts needed to show that your proposals are worth the effort involved.

WHAT IS A BUSINESS CASE?

In this book, I use the term *business case* to refer to the materials you would use to show decision makers that the idea under consideration is a good one and that the numbers that surround it make financial sense. The focus is primarily on the numbers. Topics encompassed include breakeven, cost effectiveness, and cost/benefit analysis. That's where I got the idea for the subtitle, *Improvement by the Numbers.*

ORGANIZATION OF THE BOOK

The following table shows you the organization of the book and summarizes the emphasis provided in each of its nine chapters and two appendices.

Organization of the Book

Part	Chapter	Emphasis
I Fundamental Concepts	1 Improvement Is Everybody's Business	Justifying improvements by the numbers
	2 Making a Business Case	The business case process
	3 Making the Business Case: Principles, Rules, and Analysis Tools	Knowledge of principles, rules and tools surrounding the process
	4 Business Cases That Make Sense	Sets the stage for the case studies
II The Case Studies	5 Playing the Game of *Dungeons and Dragons:* Process Improvement Case Study	Justifying process improvement activities
	6 Quantifying the Costs/Benefits: Capitalizing Software Case Study	Justifying capital improvements within a firm
	7 Making Your Numbers Sing: Architecting Case Study	Justifying the move to use of architecture
	8 Maneuvering the Maze: Web-Based Economy Case Study	Determining the price to pay for knowledge capital
III Finale	9 Overcoming Adversity: More Than a Pep Talk	Final thoughts and key points summary
	Appendix A: Recommended Readings	
	Appendix B: Compound Interest Tables	

The Unifying Glue

I use the Goals-Question-Metrics framework and the business case development process that I explain in Chapter 2 as the glue to hold this book together. This framework emphasizes the use of quantitative methods throughout the software life cycle to select technical improvement options under consideration by their quantitative costs/benefits. It also helps those making improvements to identify the feasible options that will solve the organization's real problems, not the symptoms. This is important because many organizations treat the symptoms, instead of the root causes of their problem, with action.

Unique Features

Addison-Wesley hosts a Web site at *http://www.awl.com/cseng/titles/0-201-72887-7* so that I can provide updates and additional resources as they become available. For example, I plan to put a set of more detailed discount tables on line so that you can use them to compute present value and future worth of money. If I have the time and energy, I will put these tools on the Web site in spreadsheet format. I also plan to use the site to address errata, identify changes in technology, and update the Recommended Readings list between editions of this book. Please feel free to recommend improvements to the book and/or the site via e-mail (dreifer@ earthlink.net). I want you to use it as a resource to help build business cases.

User Road Map

The following table provides you with a suggested reading road map through the book. An X designates chapters I suggest various individuals read. Of course, read more if you want to. Use the materials at the back of the book as you apply what you have read to projects you're working on.

User Road Map

Reader	1	2	3	4	5	6	7	8
Software engineers	X	X	X	X	X	X	X	X
Managers	X	X	X					X
Buyers	X	X	X			X		
Entrepreneurs	X	X	X			X		X
Process group leads	X	X	X	X				X
Programmers	X	X	X		X			
Students	X	X	X	X	X	X	X	X
Researchers	X	X	X			X	X	X

Acknowledgments

I would like to acknowledge the many people and organizations I have worked with over the years that have helped me to perfect the concepts I share with you in this book. The list is so long that I cannot thank them all by name. However, three had a profound influence on the development of my ideas and me.

First, I would like to acknowledge the contributions of my dear departed friend Fred Joh. He taught me how to use numbers to win the battles that counted at Westinghouse. He also acted as a role model when it came to dealing with adversity.

Next, I would like to thank Dr. Robert Tausworthe of the Jet Propulsion Laboratory. He made working with the numbers fun. He also taught me to use cost estimating models well before it was popular to do so. Finally, I would like to thank my mentor, Dr. Barry Boehm. He taught me the ropes when it came to making the software business case and graciously agreed to write the Foreword of this book.

Finally, a special thanks goes to my wife and best friend, Carole. She proof-read the manuscript, helped me rewrite the rough sections, and made the document readable. Her attentiveness and attention to detail are deeply appreciated as are her many suggestions for improving the manuscript.

I would also like to thank my reviewers, Dr. Sunita Chulani of IBM and David Seaver of Fidelity Investments, and my editor, Peter Gordon, for their support, encouragement, and good humor. And I would like to express my appreciation to the Addison-Wesley reviewers. They helped me pull the book together and offered some insightful suggestions about the organization and flow of this final version.

Last but not least, I would like to thank my children, Joseph and Jessica, for their understanding and input.

This book is dedicated to everyone who inspired and helped me during the years to pull together the body of knowledge contained in it. My hope is that my experiences with numbers will serve you well.

Part 1

Fundamental Concepts

Understanding what *a business case is,* why *it is important,* who *should get involved, and* when *and* how *you would build one that will sell*

1

Improvement Is Everybody's Business

*Today change is so swift and relentless in the technosocieties
that yesterday's truths suddenly become today's fictions, and
the most highly skilled and intelligent members of society
admit difficulty in keeping up with the deluge of new
knowledge—even in extremely narrow fields.*
—Alvin Toffler [1971]

VIEWING SOFTWARE AS A BUSINESS

Everyone knows that software is the business to be in today. As Table 1.1 illustrates, it's where the jobs are projected to be in tomorrow's economy. It is also the business where fortunes are being made and lost seemingly overnight. Daily hundreds of employees become millionaires as new dotcom companies are brought to market. The value of these entrepreneurs swings back and forth depending on how the market reacts to earnings and product offerings. Fortunes are made and lost when firms are agile and quick to market.

Most people would agree that the software industry is a great place to be in today's computer-driven economy. However, the industry is still cloaked in a veil of mystery. Although computer literate, most users don't understand the intricacies associated with building quality software products. Instead, they focus their attention on the features and functions the software provides. Most people view

Table 1.1: *Fastest-Growing Occupations*

Profession	1998	2008	Percentage Change
Computer scientists	97,500	212,100	118
Computer engineers	299,300	622,100	108
Computer support specialists	429,300	868,700	102
Systems analysts	616,900	1,194,200	94
Database administrators	87,400	154,900	77
Paralegal personnel	136,000	220,400	62
Medical assistants	252,200	398,000	58
Human services workers	268,400	409,900	53
Residential counselors	189,900	277,800	46
Engineering managers	326,200	468,000	44
Medical records technicians	92,400	132,900	44
Dental assistants	228,900	325,400	42

Source: Bureau of Labor Statistics, 1999.

software as the mysterious thing that makes the machines do what you want them to do.

Thirty years ago, when my airplane seatmates asked about my job, I would say that I was a software engineer. They would ask what a software engineer did. When I told them about the job of building software, they would say, "Oh," and leave me alone so that I could read my book. They didn't pretend to understand what tasks a software engineer performed. Working with computers was beyond their comprehension.

Today, when I provide the same answer, I am deluged with questions about Windows and PCs. But although they are more computer literate, the general population still doesn't really understand what a software engineer does for a living. They still find the profession mysterious and unfathomable. I find it safer to tell my seatmates either that I am an IRS tax auditor or that I sell used cars. These are safe answers if your goal is to avoid a conversation so that you can read your book or watch the movie. But watch out for seatmates who are in the professions you name. Once, I sat next to a used car salesperson who became so excited when he found out that I was in the same profession that he talked the entire trip about car auctions and recent deals he'd made.

Obviously, the field of software has changed. Just 20 years ago, software was considered obscure. Few used computers, and even fewer understood what software was all about. Those who did viewed dealing with software with disdain. Firms had to have it to sell their hardware. Computer companies focused on selling machines, not software, because hardware was expensive and the profit margins associated with it were large. Software staffs were put to work developing system software and packages that acted as marketplace differentiators. Universal applications were considered a thing of the future, as was building for portability and widespread use outside the technical community.

Times have changed. Firms that were predominantly hardware-oriented in the past, like IBM, now consider themselves software companies. Hardware profits are derived from volume sales because computers are viewed as just another appliance. Network servers and communications gear are where equipment profits are being realized as firms move to the Web. Software firms, such as Microsoft, Oracle, and Rational, are the darlings of the market because of their large profit margins. ISPs whose focus is on exploiting the Web for electronic commerce dominate the new offerings on Wall Street. Software is now viewed as a money-making business by investors. Dotcoms may be dropping, but established enterprises in many industries still expect their Web-based revenues to grow over the next five years [Rice, 2001].

While software firms have been making noise since the early 1980s, they didn't take off until the early 1990s. Around that time the general public became computer literate. PC sales took off as nontechnical users embraced the computer as a tool in business, education, and commerce.

Current times are volatile from a business point of view. To survive, executives must be nimble and quick to market. They must look for better ways to do business. They must continually seek to improve their capabilities and capacity to get the work done. To survive, they must be able to institute changes that make both good technical and good business sense when faced with large risks and uncertainties. Such changes need to be justified; otherwise why make them? How do you justify change and the risks involved in making it happen? You do so by adding a business case to your technical story. To do this, any of the viewpoints shown in the improvement framework illustrated in Figure 1.1 provide a compelling reason for making the change.

Figure 1.1 illustrates the four dimensions of improvement, each of which can be used to justify an initiative. Each dimension's importance is a function of corporate goals and strategy. For example, you would use reductions in time to

Reduce	Avoid/Cut
Time to Market	Cost
Productivity	Quality
Increase	**Improve**

Figure 1.1: *Improvement Framework*

market to justify your proposed changes if your firm were focusing on this objective as a strategic goal.

What's needed to sell these improvements is a sound argument for the change; for example, the change cuts costs by a third or shaves three months off the production cycle. When the change is properly introduced and managed, improvement results. Not surprisingly, that's why I use "improvement by the numbers" as the subtitle of this book. To get approval to make the improvement, you need to develop a persuasive business case. To realize the improvement, you have to manage the change involved in rolling it out and making it happen.

A word of caution. Executives are like elephants when it comes to numbers. Their memories are long, and they rarely forget a number once they hear it. They may look as if they are sleeping in the back of the room, but beware. I remember briefing the president of a major telecommunications firm not so long ago about benchmarks I had developed for assessing his quality improvement program progress relative to industry norms. The president stated: "I'm surprised at the defect rates you are quoting. Three years ago in June you stated that the industry standard for the switching system domain was 1.31 errors per thousand lines of code versus the 1.33 that you are now saying we will have after the system is placed in the field."

CHANGE IS THE NATURE OF SOFTWARE

Although tricky, dealing with the changes made as part of any improvement program is a normal part of the job in a software organization for three reasons. First, the primary function of software is to accommodate change. That's why we put features and functions in software, not hardware. With hardware, functions are static. Although its performance can be optimized, its functionality is hard to change. In software, the same functions can be configured, extended, updated, and tailored to accommodate a wide range of client, architecture, or domain needs.

Second, the information technology (IT) marketplace is rapidly changing. As computers assume a greater and greater role in society, the role of the software engineer is becoming different. Figure 1.2 portrays the future marketplace model that Dr. Barry Boehm developed to guide technology development [Boehm et al., 2000]. The model is similar to that distributed by the phone industry during the last century. As telephone usage climbed after World War II, leaders in the industry alarmingly noted that if trends continued, everyone in the country would soon be a telephone operator. That's exactly what happened when the paradigm changed and self-dialing telephones were put into service in the 1940s.

Boehm's model in Figure 1.2 identifies a similar paradigm shift with users assuming the role of application developers and developers assuming the role of infrastructure providers. It portrays a large upper "end-user programming" sector of 55 million practitioners in the United States by the year 2005, a lower "infrastructure" sector of about 750,000 professionals, and three intermediate sectors involved in the development of application generators and composition aids, the development of systems by applications composition, and system integration of large-scale systems of about another 2 million.

Computer science jobs aren't going away. Instead, those who work these jobs will provide infrastructure products (operating systems, database managers,

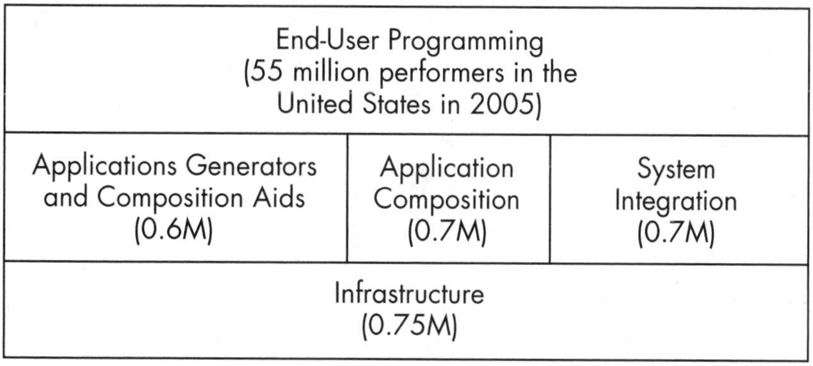

End-User Programming (55 million performers in the United States in 2005)		
Applications Generators and Composition Aids (0.6M)	Application Composition (0.7M)	System Integration (0.7M)
Infrastructure (0.75M)		

Figure 1.2: *Boehm's Future Software Marketplace Model*

Source: Adapted from Boehm/Abts/Brown/Chulani/Clark/Horowitz/Madachy/Reifer/Steece, *Software Cost Estimation with COCOMO II,* © 2000. Reprinted by permission of Pearson Education, Inc., Upper Saddle River, NJ.

middleware, and so on) and tools. These tools are the packages users employ to generate the applications they are closest to and understand best. These tools allow the user to focus on the application, not the computer technology that mechanizes it.

Third, software organizations have to cope with rapid change in the technology they use to make, market, and manufacture their products. Development methods, tools, and paradigms dominate this technology. The rate of technology change in the software industry is dizzying. Each time you think you have a handle on the technology available, you read about something new that causes you to lose confidence in your grasp of the situation. That's why many organizations have put a chief technology officer (CTO) in place to facilitate change. This person

- Acts as the enterprise's chief technologist, principal architect, and spokesperson.
- Develops a vision and strategy aligned with business goals that supports improvement.
- Identifies and oversees the implementation of new and emergent technologies.
- Applies extensive knowledge of business drivers, technology strategies, architecture goals, and infrastructure as new products are developed and fielded.
- Works closely/coordinates with technology providers, internal development teams, senior management, and department leaders to implement changes without negatively impacting project scope, budgets, and time lines.
- Ensures the scalability of products to accommodate rapid growth and expansion.

Software engineers need to keep eye on changes that occur due to the nature of the product, industry trends, and the technology used to make, market, and manufacture software-intensive products. These three factors greatly influence strategies and tactics for improvement. To facilitate improvement, you need to put in place a set of defined processes that lets you manage the introduction of change. You also need to develop process ownership and change sponsorship throughout the organization. The processes that I think are important include the seven activities in the new, staged version of capability maturity model integration (CMMI™) organizational process technology innovation level-5 practice [Ahern, 2001]:

- *Establish improvement objectives.*   Establish and maintain quantitative process improvement objectives for the organization.
- *Improvement proposal collection and analysis.*   Collect and analyze process improvement proposals.
- *Identify innovations.*   Identify innovative improvements that would increase the organization's process performance.
- *Perform cost/benefit analysis.*   Analyze the costs and benefits of potential process improvements and their effects on organizational process performance.
- *Perform pilot.*   Make pilot-selected process improvements.
- *Select candidate improvements.*   Select process and improvement proposals that are candidates for deployment across the organization.
- *Provide feedback.*   Provide feedback to the organization on the status and results of the organization's process improvement activities.

These CMMI processes represent a model of the practices that an organization can put into place to manage the selection and deployment of technology to make broader improvements than those associated with just process improvement. "Broader" in this sense refers to changes that have major organizational impact. For example, moving to either new processes or an architecture-first development paradigm requires changes to be made in how the firm is organized, its reward structure, and its culture.

However, the challenges associated with implementing any type of organizational change are mostly psychological and political, not technical and managerial. The challenges in Table 1.2 tend to be the ones that cause those championing change the most heartburn. I'm sure that those of you who have been involved in change have faced these obstacles. They are the most common.

MAKING THE GIANT LEAP FORWARD

As we've discussed, adopting improvement strategies that involve organizational change can turn out to be difficult. Making a leap forward is neither simple nor straightforward in most situations. Business conditions and lack of people, funds, and other resources may force you to take many side steps. In addition, people resist change especially when there are no rewards for risk taking. It takes skill, leadership and perseverance to overcome the many barriers that impede change. Because such changes are pervasive, implementation of them sometimes requires

Table 1.2: *Challenges Associated with Implementing Organizational Change*

Challenges	Explanation
Lack of incentives	Because the change makes the job smaller, cheaper, and more manageable, it can influence perceived importance, promotions, raises, and prestige. In response, the reward system must be changed to show that management is 100 percent behind the initiative.
"Good of the firm" versus "good of the project"	Doing something on a project for the good of the organization is counter to the prevailing attitude in many firms. Managers are rated on their ability to deliver what was promised on schedule and within budget. Improvement initiatives that can interfere with achieving this goal are viewed as a risk and avoided. Again, the reward system needs to be changed to address this problem.
Infrastructure shortfalls	In many firms, there is too much to do and not enough talent, time, and money to do it. If there are management shortfalls, these organizations rightfully invest in fixing them because success with other initiatives will falter if the infrastructure used to plan, organize, staff, direct, and control projects is broken.
Few meaningful metrics	Many firms don't collect the data needed to quantify improvements associated with change as part of their standard processes. Prioritizing the initiatives and tackling metrics issues first reduces the confusion.
Limited cash available	This is the old chicken-and-egg problem. To make improvements, we have to spend money. But to get the money, we have to make improvements. Incremental adoption provides a way out of the box. Do what you can with what you can get. Then use the returns to justify an increase in your budget.

a shift from a project-based culture to a culture that rewards sharing across the organization. Such changes by their nature are the hardest to accomplish.

Geoffrey Moore has developed a well-regarded technology adoption life cycle model that illustrates the difficulty in moving the technology from early adopters to the early majority [Moore, 1991]. This transition reflects the difficulty in moving technology from pilot projects to widespread use within most firms. This model (Figure 1.3) illustrates the willingness of organizations to put

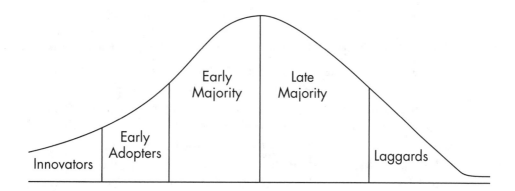

Stage in Life Cycle	Organizations' Characteristics
Innovators	Risk takers Develop new technology Push the envelope Nimble and quick to market
Early adopters	Trend setters Advance technology Will take high risks when justified
Early majority	Innovators Harness technology Take moderate risks
Late majority	Followers Exploit technology Conservative Take limited risks
Laggards	Critics Use proven technology Ultraconservative Risk averse

Figure 1.3: *Moore's Technology Adoption Life Cycle Model*

technology to work. Those who have tried to jump from one of his five stages to another realize that the most difficult task is enabling transition with proper management and product support.

For example, it took the Unix operating system 15 years to make the transition from the early adopter (internal use within in Bell Labs) to the early majority (external use by third parties who had adopted the operating system because of its merits) stage [Redwine, 1996]. I believe part of the reason for this was the failure of the technical community to provide the business community with the justification needed to invest in commercializing Unix and moving it from research and development (R&D) to the practitioner community via established marketing channels.

Those of us who have tried to make such changes in the past have learned the following eight useful lessons:

1. *Tie improvement to organization and/or business goals.*   Plan to make improvements because it makes good business sense to do so. Tie improvements to organizational goals. Using this approach, you will find it relatively easy to demonstrate the effectiveness of your investments in terms of things that matter to your management.

2. *Plan to emphasize product-oriented improvements.*   To succeed, focus your energy on making improvements that are visible and matter (i.e., that have a direct bearing on realizing your organizational and business goals). This approach will enable you to solicit support from those who really matter in the organization—the shakers and influence makers. It will also make it easy for you to make the worth of what you are pursuing observable.

3. *Plan to justify improvements by demonstrating their value.*   Prototyping is the best way to quell criticism and show your critics that the improvement idea works in practice in your organization. Rely on pilots to prove the concept and pathfinder projects to show other projects the right way to implement the idea in the constraints of your operational environment. Conduct periodic demonstrations to show management what you've realized. Plan demonstrations so that they are in step with the budgetary cycle. Gather hard data as you progress, and use it to tell your story in quantitative terms.

4. *Put processes in place that make product-related improvements a natural part of the way you do business.*   Changes in management infrastructure (organization, policies, processes, practices, and so on) are needed to support putting changes in place quickly. To increase your chances of success, address the people, process, and technology transition issues when you change the way you do business. Make it easy for your people to adopt and use new and better technology to do their jobs simply, quickly, and better.

5. *While technical issues will exist, recognize that the major barriers to any change will primarily be psychological and political.*   As we have already noted, most of the barriers to improvement stem from cultural, managerial, psychological, and political problems. Prepare your people for the change. Bring in needed education and training. Deal with the people and their fears, and you will be successful.

6. *Focus on changing the culture to one that rewards risk taking.*   As you change your management infrastructure, address the processes and rewards given for risk taking. Make it profitable for your people to try something new, especially if the results provide you an advantage. Don't penalize failure. Instead, make failure a learning situation. Recognize that the larger the risk involved, the bigger the reward.

7. *If you don't have the talent to reap the projected benefits, buy it.*   Improvement often revolves around tapping new technology. New skills, knowledge, and abilities must be developed to succeed. If you don't have the talent, hire people who do, and have them impart their knowledge to your people as part of a planned technology transition exercise. If you can't hire them, make them a deal that they can't say no to.

8. *Use the numbers to overcome postdecision dissonance.*   Managers wonder whether or not they have made the right decision. Your job is to convince them that they have. Convince them that they did the right thing by periodically briefing them on your progress. Use the hard data you've collected to convince them that they made the right choice. When you submit your next year's budget request, you will be glad you did this because you will be rewarded with funds to continue with your improvements.

SUCCESS IS A NUMBERS GAME

Many worthy improvements are never implemented. That's because most are cloaked in technical jargon and the real impact on the bottom line is rarely identified. To be successful with change, you must play the numbers game. You need to arm those who support you with the ammunition they will need to realize their corporate goals and win the battle of the budget. In addition to highlighting the technical merits of your approach, the information you supply must address the following business-oriented questions:

- Will this idea result in improvements that will save us money, defer costs, increase productivity, speed development, and/or improve quality? If so, by how much compared to industry averages? What are the alternatives? Why pursue this option?

- What is the impact of pursuing the innovation on the organization's bottom line?

- Who are our customers for the change and what are their expectations? Is the proposed change compatible with their corporate culture?

- How do we rate competitively? Have our primary competitors pursued similar initiatives? If so, what did they spend and what were the results?

- Will organizational changes have to be made? Will capital investments be required? Will the management infrastructure have to be updated?

- Do we have the talent and other needed resources to pursue these innovations? If not, how will we acquire them and at what cost?

- What are the tax and financial implications of pursuing the idea? Will we be able to claim depreciation and/or R&D tax credits on our returns? Will there be liabilities?

- Why should we invest in this idea rather than in others that are on the table?

Not surprisingly, every day management turns down ideas, some good, some bad, and some ugly. That's because they have only so much time, talent, and money to bring to the table. Projects compete for sparse resources. To win the game, you will have to use the numbers at your disposal to paint a pretty business picture. And because most of the time a pretty picture is not enough, you need to develop other arguments to gain approvals. You need to use the picture as a sales tool. You need to sell the merits of your idea up the chain of command. You need to present a cogent reason why management should invest in the proposed innovation now and not at a later time.

I have seen many good ideas shelved because the people presenting the concepts did not know how to show management their true value in terms of dollars and cents. Their arguments may have been too technical or too shallow. Often, this was, because they did not either provide or properly package the right information. The response they got when they presented to management was,

"We will have so and so [accounting, legal] look your proposal over and get back with you later." Avoid this kiss of death by precoordinating your presentation with everyone you think is important. Ask for help, and more than likely you'll get it. Take the advice offered, and you will get the support you desire when you need it. As a final suggestion, be prepared to execute your recommended plan of action the moment you get approval. Get any authorized funds committed quickly, and you won't lose support for your initiative as other complications arise.

IMPROVEMENT CYCLES AND TRICYCLES

You can implement an improvement in many different ways. You can adopt improvements using either a sequential or a staged improvement cycle, like the seven-phase model shown in Figure 1.4. If time were of the essence, you most likely would opt for an incremental improvement paradigm to take advantage of the parallelism, deploying your innovation in stages as pieces were developed. If risk were your major concern, you would use a spiral cycle to mitigate issues. Each spiral would attempt to address risk via prototyping, simulation, or other means.

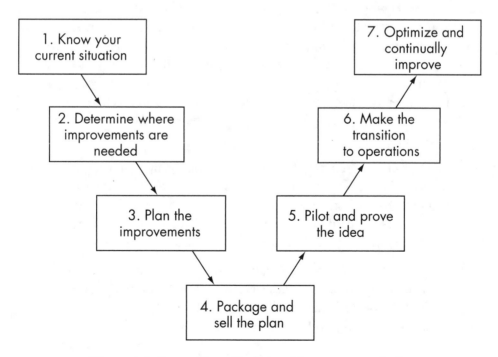

Figure 1.4: *Seven-Phase Traditional Improvement Cycle*

The choice of paradigm for modeling the improvement process will be a function of your goals and the obstacles you anticipate facing after you embark on your adventure. If you are seeking to speed introduction, you would pursue phases in parallel (bicycles and tricycles). If you are focusing on reducing risk, you would adopt some form of spiral process. The five keys to success with any of these selections follow:

- Identifying the players and their "win conditions" for succeeding with the improvement
- Knowing what you are trying to accomplish in each phase (including having a list of the phase's products, its input and outputs, and precedence conditions)
- Defining the entry and exit conditions for each improvement cycle phase prior to entering it
- Identifying the risks associated with each phase and how to address them
- Getting the resources committed to get the job done as promised

This book touches on each of the seven stages of the improvement process illustrated in Figure 1.4. But unlike most management textbooks, it focuses on what you have to do to pull your numbers together to build a business case that compels management to move forward with your idea. It also provides the guidelines and support material you will need to take the concepts and put them into action.

I have adapted the six basic principles of software process change identified by Watts Humphrey [Humphrey, 1989] to fit the classical improvement cycle outlined here:

Major changes must start at the top.   Senior management sponsorship is needed to launch a change effort and ensure that it receives the resources required to make it successful. The best advice I can offer is for you to get your seniors on board as early as possible. Then they will be positioned to help you win the political and budgetary battles that will follow.

Everyone impacted by the change must be convinced that it makes sense. You need to develop support at all levels of the organization. If you don't, those who fear change will resist it, especially if they don't understand that the change will help them do their job better.

Improvement can take place only when you have a baseline against which you can make a comparison. Maintaining momentum requires you to demonstrate that the change will make life better for all concerned; you must establish a yardstick to measure benefits against. Without a yardstick, your critics will argue that the money would be better spent elsewhere—typically on their initiatives or pet projects.

Improvement is a continual effort. Because information technology is changing rapidly, opportunities for improvement occur frequently and unexpectedly. To take advantage of these opportunities, you must be nimble and quick to market. You must be able to learn, grow, and exploit opportunities as they occur.

Improvement must be sold continually; otherwise, you will lose your support. Within most organizations, changing things for the better is not enough. You need to show those who represent your support base your worth. This is best done using a sales approach where you let those who influence others in the organization know of your accomplishments.

Improvement requires serious investment. To succeed with your initiatives, you will need time, talent, and capital resources. Time is required to plan the effort and develop a management infrastructure. Talent is needed to make things happen according to the plan.

If you are interested in changes that might be more radical, consider one of the more modern process models. In these models, work is performed in parallel. That's why I call them tricycles instead of improvement cycles. For example, as Figure 1.5 illustrates, you could execute improvements in parallel on the fly as you identify opportunities and plan your initiative using the iterative plan-try-learn-do process. The figure stresses the iterative nature of the improvement process. When building business cases, you would assume that your numbers would change using such a model. Of course, iterative processes like these require you to adopt tighter controls to ensure that effort isn't wasted as your priorities shift over time.

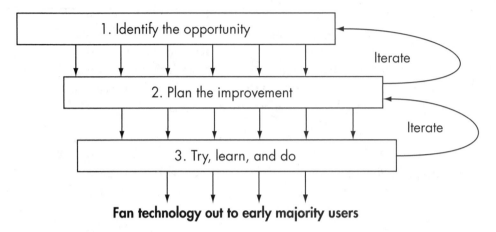

Figure 1.5: *The Plan–Try–Learn–Do Improvement Process*

IMPROVEMENT BY THE NUMBERS

This is not a book about managing change. However, it emphasizes change because that's often where the numbers come into play. For example, you would justify change with numbers as you build your technical and business cases. Many times, numbers provide the compelling motivation for change. But this may not be true in all cases. For example, you might need to make a change for competitive or other reasons (e.g., Y2K). There are many good references on the topic of change and change management (see [Betz, 1997] and [Levy, 1998] as examples). In addition, the Software Engineering Institute (SEI) and Software Productivity Consortium (SPC) in the United States have developed technology adoption models, processes, and training materials (visit their Web sites at *http://www.sei.cmu.edu/* and *http://www.software.org/* for details). These sites provide technology transition frameworks and guidelines aimed at accelerating technology adoption primarily in software engineering organizations (see [Christie, 1994] and [Fowler, 1993] as examples).

Instead of focusing on adoption models and processes, I have elected to share with you the pragmatics associated with developing the numbers you can use to sell change in your organization. Numbers form the basis of the business case as defined here.

> **Business case:** Materials prepared for decision makers to show that the business idea under consideration is a good one and that the numbers that surround it make financial sense

Throughout the book, I peel the onion using this definition as my starting point. I focus on specifics but emphasize software improvement in the most general sense. For many, software improvement has a broader scope than process improvement. However, because of the topic's popularity, many textbooks confine their improvement focus to process. I take a different tack. Besides process improvement, I use case studies to show how to develop the numbers for the following other types of initiatives:

- Capitalizing software—justifying the purchase of tools, equipment, and facilities
- Architecting software—migrating the transition to the systematic reuse of components and commercial off-the-shelf (COTS) software
- Moving to a Web-based economy by acquiring a firm with needed resources

After introducing you to the fundamentals in the first four chapters, I move to case studies in the next four. The case studies provide a blow-by-blow description of how an organization succeeded in tackling each of the four initiatives. Each case communicates lessons that the organization learned, often the hard way. Each is presented so that you can generalize the results. The final chapter summarizes the key points and provides some unifying thoughts for people trying to put the materials in this book to work in their organizations.

When the smoke clears, the thing that really matters to senior management is the numbers. They view your propositions in light of their business goals and priorities. Because there are many options, they want to know why they should spend their limited resources on your proposal instead of others. They want insight into the costs/benefits. They want to make sure your story is believable and achievable. They want to feel confident that you can pull off what you propose. If they don't feel assured, they will vacillate and procrastinate before making a "go/no go" decision. What you need to do is figure out how to get their support. Again, you will need their help in winning the battle of the budget.

You have similar goals. You want to be successful. Otherwise, why take on this venture? You want to be confident in your estimates and in your plans. You need to attract talent and staff your initiative with the right mix of people. You need to build teams and keep them focused on the tasks that need completing. You need to identify risks and keep them under control. You want to be able to track progress and deal with problems in advance of their occurrence. You want to work with early adopters to pilot improvements and show that they work in the large as well as in the small. You want to use pathfinder projects to get the rest of the organization involved. This will help you smoothly integrate the changes into your existing management infrastructure (e.g., established organizations, processes, and decision logic). That's probably why you bought this book.

BUSINESS VERSUS TECHNICAL CASES

Working with engineers is fun. They pay attention to the most trivial details. When you ask them to assess the options, they develop the most detailed comparisons. They start by devising evaluation criteria based on needed capabilities. They then assess each option using these criteria and portray the output in the form of a table or spreadsheet. I wish I had a dime for each time my friends have asked me for my matrix when shopping for some big-ticket item like a car or TV they know I have recently purchased. They know I did extensive research and want to share my analysis. But beware the results that engineers come up with, because they may lead you to purchase a microwave with four levels of memory when all you want to do is heat water.

To succeed, you must address the engineering mind-set. Let me illustrate the depth of detail that software engineers go to using the language tradeoff study illustrated in Table 1.3. To set the context for this example, assume that your firm is considering moving from C/C++ to Java. The reason behind the move from one language to another is that they will soon be bringing Web-enabled products to market that could benefit from Java's client-server features. This is especially true because they are planning to use Java's virtual machine concept to address portability. Notice that the table focuses on the technical features and functions. Although it fully addresses the merits of the language and the compilers available for target platforms, it neither visits the business considerations nor addresses the risks associated with moving to Java.

To complete the study, your firm needs to look at the business factors. Table 1.4 shows some of the business items that need to be considered when making the decision. They focus on the costs to develop core competency in the language and the costs of tools, training, and transition. Because Java's score is lower than that of C/C++, the people recommending the move to Java will need a strong business reason to compel senior management to take the risk. The reason could be provided either in an investment in Web infrastructure or in a productivity justification. If the need to invest is used, some form of cost/benefit or return-on-investment analysis will be needed to justify the recommendation.

Table 1.3: *Language Comparison Study Results (with "5" being "best")*

Factors	Java	C/C++
Core features (strong typing, exception handling, inheritance, polymorphism, etc.)	2	4
Degree of standardization and portability	3	4
Object-oriented support	3	5
Reuse facilities (library, search engine, etc.)	3	4
Web programming support	5	2
Optimizing compilers available for current host/target platforms	4	5
Optimizing compilers planned for future host/target platforms	3	5
Bindings to existing systems software available (POSIX, Windows 98, etc.)	5	5
Bindings to future systems software available (Linux, Windows 2000, etc.)	4	5
Bindings to GUIs and generators available	3	5
Rich libraries available (run time, math, class, building blocks, etc.)	3	4
Compiler support tools available (syntax-directed editor, symbolic debugger, etc.)	4	5
Inexpensive visual toolset available for target platforms	3	3
Oriented toward your future Web-enabled product offerings	5	2
Score	50	58

You will also need to get management to approve your capital budget and spending plan.

I use this example again in Chapters 2, 3, and 4 to help you to understand more fully what goes into a business case. As you will see, you will be able to use the numbers to justify either side of the argument. The real trick is to package the numbers so that they make business sense to those who will make the decision. Because the decision makers are often not software people, packaging the numbers will force you to learn new languages and skills. For example, you may have to compute the tax benefits of the investment options to appease the accountants on your boss's staff or prepare a breakeven analysis showing those in charge of

Table 1.4: *Business Factor Comparisons (with "5" being "best")*

Factors	Java	C/C++
Popularity—will the language enable the staff to improve their resumes?	5	5
Training opportunities available—public seminars, local college courses, etc.	5	4
Literature and textbooks readily available	5	5
Consultants and subcontractors with skills in language available for hire	5	3
Staff maintains core competency with the language and associated toolset	2	4
Retooling and retraining costs budgeted	1	5
Transition costs budgeted in terms of time needed to bring staff up to speed	1	5
Subtotal	24	31
New score	74	89

the financials that the change pays back in less than three years. You might also have to look at capitalizing the option instead of expensing it because of tax implications. You might also have to show the financial impacts on operational costs. Don't worry; you will get help in understanding these options in the remaining chapters of the book.

Of course, engineers don't have to learn everything lawyers, accountants, and other business analysts know. Instead, they must understand how to communicate to them the benefits of what they are trying to accomplish in nontechnical language that these professionals understand and can relate to. Engineers don't have to become either financial analysts or accountants, but they must be able to discuss things such as depreciation and present value of the benefit stream. Otherwise, the merits of the changes that they are proposing might not be fully understood.

WHY CHANGE?

As the language example illustrates, there needs to be some business reason for change. In this case, change is needed to enable you to better support future products. But improvements always have a price tag. In addition, the risks asso-

Table 1.5: *Primary Barriers to Change*

Barriers to Change	Amplification
"Not invented here" (NIH) syndrome	Many software people I have worked with especially resist changes that are modeled on changes that work outside the organization. You'll hear "They won't work here!" a lot when they are exposed to new ideas.
Limited investment capital	While the change has merit, management believes that there just aren't enough time, talent, and dollars available to successfully implement the improvement.
"Why change, we're successful" attitude	When people don't understand the motivation for change, you will often hear "If it isn't broken, why fix it?" Your response should be a promotion campaign aimed at enlisting support from the uninformed.
Limited senior management support	As we have already said, change starts at the top. Experience shows that you need management advocacy and support to win the battle of the budget and ward off political attacks.
Technology immaturity issues	Many initiatives fail because they put their faith in immature and/or unproven technology. Instead of managing the risk associated with the technology insertion, they charge ahead with blinders on. Often, the technology fails to scale, and so do they.
Readiness to change	Many firms are just not ready to make a change. Their infrastructure may be in shambles, and they need to address basic management issues before they can proceed with the change.

ciated with change need to be factored into the decision. The costs could be more than just the monetary price tag. For example, you might have to take schedule hits as you are developing skills with the new language, which could influence your ability to bring new products to market. Or worse, you might adversely affect existing projects as you adapt the infrastructure to support the Java distributed computing paradigm. That's why I opened this chapter with a discussion on change management. You need to understand that change in organizations requires business justification. That's why you need to understand the process of change and the barriers related to making it happen.

Table 1.5 lists some of the key barriers to change. Resistance to change becomes formidable when you couple the challenges listed in Table 1.2 with the points made in the "Change Is the Nature of Software" section. The reasons organizations pursue change in spite of barriers are as follows:

1. *Keeping up with the competition*   Playing catch-up is a great motivator. If you can show that your competitors have embraced an idea that might increase their market share, you can justify an initiative even if the numbers don't support it.

2. *Achieving economic benefits*   A better approach would be to quantify business reasons for change (see improvement rectangle in Figure 1.1). This makes any investment palatable because it justifies improvements in terms of dollars and cents.

3. *Supporting new product needs*   Often, changes may be stimulated by a need to support a product or product line or a new technology (like the Web). These changes are often considered investments (written off as research and development) and are sold on the basis of some perceived customer requirement (customer support, 7/24 operations, and so on).

4. *Avoiding legal entanglements*   Sometimes changes are needed to comply with new laws and/or accounting rules. These changes can represent targets of opportunity because they allow you to piggyback improvements on requirements that must be made. Legal changes are mandatory and not subject to debate, argument, and political infighting. But, as always, you still have to fight for a budget.

5. *Achieving efficiencies*   Changes are often identified when firms implement programs to improve the efficiency and effectiveness of the workforce (e.g., workflow analysis, process streamlining). Such efforts typically net improvements in productivity and, as a result, derive some tangible economic benefit. To sell the initiative, you have to quantify the costs/benefits and show the impact of the proposed improvement on the balance sheet.

In light of these barriers, the first question any organization should ask itself is "Are we ready to change?" If it isn't, it should get ready. If it doesn't, it will probably be caught and perish in the quicksand that surrounds change.

ARE YOU READY TO CHANGE?

The key question you should answer before mounting an improvement initiative is, "Is my firm ready to change?" To make your determinations and finding, you should examine the following criteria:

Consistent with business goals   Change should be directly aligned with your organization's business goals. This positioning provides a compelling reason for approving the change and justifies the headaches and heartburn. For example, being leaner can be equated to developing products quicker and better. As another example, being more efficient can be linked to trimming development, production, and/or distribution costs.

Compatible with level of process maturity   I strongly believe that an appropriate management infrastructure must be in place before you can succeed with change. I have witnessed organizations fail repeatedly because they didn't have the processes, organizations, and decision logic in place to manage the change and the turbulence that it creates.

Consistent with corporate culture   Sometimes radical changes are needed to move organizations ahead. But implementing such changes is tough because of the turmoil created. My best advice is not to make giant waves if you don't have to. Pursue changes in such a way that you don't alienate people on whom you must rely to be successful.

Compatible with investment strategies   Many problems can be avoided if you time and package proposals so that they support current business investment strategies. Realize that timing is strategy. Make sure proposals for change are synchronized with your organization's budget submission processes and time lines. Otherwise, you might not be able to get the approval and funds you need until the budget cycle repeats itself.

Achievable within desired timetable   Tell management what it will really take to be successful. Don't mince words and set unrealistic expectations. Establish aggressive but achievable targets and time lines. Discuss how you will manage the downside risks. Tell management the straight story, not what they want to hear. You'll be glad you did.

I have always been somewhat amazed by how risk averse some organizations can be. I find such an attitude self-defeating. To succeed in today's rapidly changing market-driven economy, you must adopt an entrepreneurial culture. The characteristics of an entrepreneurial culture are summarized and contrasted with the more old-fashioned style in Table 1.6. It is easy to see why such cultures are nimble and quick to market. They encourage their people to experiment with and pursue new ideas. They are pliant and flexible and reward risk taking and teamwork.

If you have the opportunity, you should develop a management infrastructure that takes full advantage of the entrepreneurial model. Unfortunately, this advice seems to be considered only as a new company starts up or when an older

Table 1.6: *Characteristics of Corporate Cultures Contrasted*

Entrepreneurial Culture	Old-Fashioned Culture
Seeks opportunities for improvement	Prefers the status quo
Action-oriented and willing to take risks	Avoids change and risk
Team-oriented	Territorial by nature
Rewards innovations	Rewards followers, not innovators
Learns from failures	Penalizes failures
Creative, imaginative, pliant, and flexible	Persistent, authoritative, and rigid

one has to be bailed out of trouble. I remember arguing with an executive that the optimum time to invest in making changes was when the firm was doing well. I was admonished and told that I was out of my mind. "Showing maximum profit to the stockholders is what business is all about," I was told. In a chance meeting three years later, the same executive told me that he wished he had taken my advice. His firm had lost its technology edge and was now a candidate for acquisition by a competitor. I was careful to offer my regrets instead of telling him, "I told you so."

GETTING YOUR BOSS TO COMMIT

All this preparation is focused at providing the structure and the numbers you will need to support your business case for change. The change cycles, barriers, elements of success, cultural characteristics, and guidance are all aimed at the same thing: developing a compelling reason for change.

We haven't yet talked about the human element. Engineers are logical by nature. They evaluate the options and base decisions on facts. They love a good technical argument and are prepared to defend their recommendations with references, figures, and so on. However, they don't seem to fare well when emotion and illogic become involved. When I think of the original *Star Trek,* I think of the battle between logic (Mr. Spock) and emotion (Dr. McCoy). In every story, it seemed that Captain Kirk had to choose between them. Sometimes he sided with logic. Other times he sided with emotion.

When I deal with executives, I think of Captain Kirk. I come armed with the facts and figures. But I carefully augment them to address the nonquantitative issues (the emotional side of the argument). These typically fit into my list of qualitative arguments for the proposed change. I package my presentation to show the quantitative arguments first. I strongly believe that the numbers carry a lot of weight. However, I recognize that the qualitative arguments can swing commitments, so I package my material accordingly.

I have had many bosses over the years, some good and others not so good. Most have not been engineers. Some have come from the sales side; others have been administrators, lawyers, and accountants. What characterizes all of them is their genuine concern for image, competitiveness, core competencies, profitability, and customer satisfaction. These are the concerns I address whenever I prepare a briefing proposing an improvement to management. While I can in most cases quantify competitiveness, efficiency, and profitability, I find I also have to address image, core competencies, and customer satisfaction through perceptions.

Recognize that 80 percent of a firm's business generally comes from 20 percent of its customers. What they think therefore means a lot in terms of future sales. Survey them to find out how they view your change proposition. Then use their opinions to seal the proposal. Also recognize that you need sponsorship to survive the battle of the budget. This means that you must presell your ideas and get seniors to champion your cause. At a minimum, a sponsor can help you package your change proposal so that it is palatable to those who make the "go/no go" decisions. A sponsor can also identify people you need to go to for help and will fight for you and enlist others in your cause.

When developing sponsorship, don't go around your immediate supervisors. Enlist their help, advice, and support, and keep them apprised of your movements. Make them part of the process, and most important, make them look good. Share credit with them if you have to. If you are successful, there will be plenty of praise to go around. Take care and recognize that bypassing your boss in most organizations is the kiss of death because your boss, not your sponsor or champion, writes your performance appraisal.

Finally, avoid the use of jargon when dealing with executives. Because they are from different backgrounds, they won't know what you are talking about. For example, most executives I deal with haven't the foggiest idea what object-oriented techniques are and why you would want to use them during software development. These same executives probably don't know how many software people are in the organization and how large a contribution software makes to their bottom line. All they see is the expense. You need to educate them about the importance of software and the flexibility it brings to the table in language that they understand.

You need to package your change proposal so that it talks to executives in their language. For example, you should differentiate between accounting and engineering arguments when dealing with executives who have an MBA instead of an advanced engineering degree. Accounting profits are the difference between the total revenue and the cost of producing goods and/or services. Accounting profits are what shows up on the bottom line of the firm's income statement. You may need to explain "sunk costs" to the same executive because the idea is something that is taught in engineering school, not business school. Sunk costs are expenditures that have already been made. Therefore, they don't enter into decisions involving future expenditures. What is important in decisions involving sunk costs is what a project will cost to complete, not what has been spent to date. You should look forward, not backward, when deciding on future courses of action.

HOW THIS BOOK CAN HELP YOU

This book was written to arm those interested in making improvement and change happen with the ammunition needed to:

- Understand why business cases are important and how they can be used to package and sell change organizationwide.

- Help you build a business case that can be used to substantiate the investments required to make product-oriented improvements.

- Increase your sensitivity to the business issues associated with technology choices.

- Develop an appreciation for the numbers and the insights they provide into the merits of alternatives.

- Provide you with metrics and measures of success that you can use to show your management that their expectations have been realized.

- Address the issues associated with changing the culture to one of risk taking instead of being risk averse.

- Provide examples, facts, hard data, and case studies to use as source material as you prepare winning business cases for your management.

- Address the qualitative aspects as well as the quantitative merits of a change or improvement proposal.

The specific goal of this book is to help you understand how to develop a successful business case. To help you learn, I present principles and case studies in the next seven chapters. Because of its importance, I also focus attention on the process of business case development.

After reading the book, your task is to generalize and apply the principles and the lessons presented in the case studies within your own work environment. As part of this effort, you will have to figure out what might work for you.

SUMMARY

This book helps you sell improvements and change by building business cases that provide compelling justification for organizational change. It broadly scopes improvement activities to encompass much more than just a process focus. Its emphasis is putting numbers into proposals so that you can sell change to those affected by it.

KEY POINTS

- ✔ Software is the fastest-growing business in the world.

- ✔ To survive in this fast-paced business, software practitioners must continually search for better ways of doing business.

- ✔ Change is natural in the software business as firms seek to put improvements to work in the way they make, market, and manufacture their products.

- ✔ The major barriers to implementing change are psychological, political, and managerial.

- ✔ Making change successfully is a numbers game. Businesses change when the numbers justify a reason to do so.

- ✔ Improvement can be implemented using one of the life cycle models for change, all of which consider risk as an integral part of their processes.

- ✔ To sell change to senior management, you need to develop both a good technical case and a good business case for the improvement.

- ✔ You need a sponsor to help champion the change and win the battle of the budget.

- ✔ Before making any change, you need to address your readiness to handle the change.

- ✔ To succeed, you must tie the change to your future business goals and ensure that the improvement is achievable within your culture per the advertised timetables.

- ✔ This book will help you build business cases that address the issues raised and build on the lessons early adopters learned when dealing with changes.

References

[Ahern, 2001] Ahern, Dennis M., Aaron Clouse, and Richard Turner. *CMMI Distilled: A Practical Introduction to Integrated Process Improvement.* Addison-Wesley, 2001.

[Betz, 1997] Betz, Frederick. *Managing Technological Innovation: Competitive Advantage from Change.* John Wiley & Sons, 1997.

[Boehm, 2000] Boehm, Barry, Chris Abts, A. Winsor Brown, Sunita Chulani, Bradford K. Clark, Ellis Horowitz, Ray Madachy, Donald Reifer, and Bert Steece. *Software Estimation with COCOMO II.* Prentice-Hall, 2000.

[Christie, 1994] Christie, A. *Practical Guide to the Technology and Adoption of Software Process Automation.* Software Engineering Institute, Report CMU/SEI-94-TR-007, 1994.

[Fowler, 1993] Fowler, P., and L. Levine. *Conceptual Framework for Software Technology Transition.* Software Engineering Institute, Report CMU/SEI-93-TR-031, 1993.

[Humphrey, 1989] Humphrey, Watts S. *Managing the Software Process.* Addison-Wesley, 1989.

[Levy, 1998] Levy, Nino S. *Managing High Technology and Innovation.* Prentice-Hall, 1998.

[Moore, 1991] Moore, Geoffrey A. *Crossing the Chasm.* HarperBusiness, 1991.

[Redwine, 1996] Redwine, Samuel. Personnel communications.

[Rice, 2001] Rice, Valerie. "Recession? What Recession? Many Enterprises Up E-biz Spending," *eWeek,* Vol. 18, No. 6, February 12, 2001, pp. 49–57.

[Toffler, 1971] Toffler, Alvin. *Future Shock.* Bantam, 1971.

2

Making a Business Case

It's important to step back from an industry that is full of people announcing new widgets every day—faster widgets, smaller widgets, more widgets. What I'm learning from customers is that there is an excess of technology out there. The real pressure is "How do I use this stuff to achieve something important for my business?"

—Louis V. Gerstner, Jr.
CEO of IBM [1993]

THE *WHATS, WHYS,* AND *WHENS* OF BUSINESS CASES

In this chapter, we define a business case as follows:

> **Business case:** Materials prepared for decision makers to show that the idea being considered is a good one and that the numbers that surround it make financial sense

This definition suggests that business cases are prepared to justify investments in technology. As the trend line in Figure 2.1 illustrates, investments in information technology are an increasing percentage of overall capital spending for the three identified industrial segments. Business cases provide you with the means to justify such investments. Without justification, spending in information technology can easily get out of control.

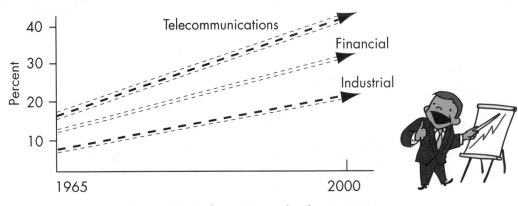

Figure 2.1: *Information Technology Investment as a Percentage of Overall Capital Spending*

Let's take software tools as an example of investments in technology. Engineers love them. They are like toys for software engineers. It seems that engineers always want to get a copy of the latest and greatest products right after they read about them in one of the popular software engineering magazines. Unfortunately, many tools end up on the shelf because these engineers just don't have time in their schedules to play with them and become proficient in their use. The expense could be avoided by having the engineers justify their purchases beforehand. There is also a good chance that engineers will use tools when they spend time and effort to obtain them. However, justification can't be too difficult. If it is, the engineers will get so turned off that they will never try to use something new and innovative.

Why buy tools? What's the justification? Will they help you get the job done more quickly and better? If so, can you quantify benefits in terms of increased productivity and reduced time to market? Why use the money for your improvements and not other worthwhile ones? Without justification, you are going to have a hard time convincing your management to spring for the tool purchase (or lease).

Software engineers in actuality prepare business justifications throughout the software life cycle. However, few of them really comprehend how to package a proposal in order for it to sell. For example, they might ask for capital funds to purchase the tools when such money is not available if they don't understand the restrictions placed on the money used to pay for such items. In most organizations, engineers acquire assets (tools, equipment, and so on) for software development using both capital and project budgets. Capital budgets fund improvements that are made for the enterprise as a whole and can be expensed, depreciated, and/or carried as a tax credit. Typical spending is for equipment, facilities, software, and R&D that benefit the entire enterprise. Because capital budgets have tax consequences, many accounting rules govern them. For example, firms are currently allowed to write off $20,000 of capital purchases without depreciating them. However, depreciation may be preferable to write-offs because it offsets taxes over several years.

In contrast, project budgets encompass expenditures made to develop, maintain, and sustain a specific product or service that appears as a line item charged against a specific engineering or R&D portfolio. Typical project spending is for the specific people, tools, equipment, and facilities needed to generate a product or service. Project budgets are typically prepared before the start of a project when software engineers forecast what resources are needed to meet their deadlines. The budgets are updated periodically to reflect changes in requirements and past performance. Because they are under their direct control, project managers find that they have more flexibility when using project instead of capital budgets [Royce, 1998].

Many games are played in the capital and project budgeting process. Capital budgets are limited in most organizations. Most are based on how much was spent last year. This motivates organizations to spend whatever funds they are given to preserve their budget, not seek economies. This situation occurred many times when I served in government. Equipment was upgraded annually because there was money to spend, not because better gear was needed. I remember asking: "Why upgrade? I don't need a new computer." The response I got was, "If you don't take it, our budget for capital equipment will be cut next year."

Project budgets are based on estimates of what it will take to generate a specific product per an agreed-to schedule. Typically, the only limitation on such budgets is available resources (cash, people, and so on). Of course, every effort is made initially to keep the budget lean. That's because projects with fat don't win contracts or approvals to begin work. To ensure delivery on time and within budget, organizations rank and rate project managers on their ability to deliver quality products (or services) on schedule and within budget. Their merit increases, bonuses, prestige, and promotions are therefore directly linked to their ability to deliver within budget and under deadline pressure. That's why project leaders tend to be so focused. They take performance personally because that's how the organization rates them.

Software engineers get involved in both capital and project budgeting processes. They use both budgets to fund work in their organizations. They try to fund shortfalls in project funds using R&D accounts and buy equipment using capital authorizations. There is no shortage of creativity when it comes to covering the expenses associated with getting the job done. In most cases, software engineers provide inputs to these budgets. They figure out what is needed and justify the expenditures. But having a budget doesn't mean that you will get to spend it. In many cases, the money might just not be available. For example, in an effort to address risk, management may keep funds in reserve. To spend reserve funds, software engineers might have to justify the importance of planned project expenditures.

THE BUSINESS CASE PROCESS

The process of justifying expenditures is never-ending. That's because major events occur throughout the software life cycle that force business cases to be prepared over and over again. The framework I have selected to represent such interactions is called Model-Based (System) Architecting and Software Engineering (MBASE). This framework was developed at the University of Southern California to provide a structure for life cycle planning and tradeoffs using any of several popular life cycle models (Rational Unified Process™ [Kruchten, 1998], Spiral [Boehm, 1998], WinWin [Boehm, 1996], and so on). As shown in Figure 2.2, four milestones anchor the primary development phases within this framework. The most critical of these milestones are Life Cycle Objectives (LCO) and Life Cycle Architecture (LCA) because they represent the time when requirements and architecture are baselined. The milestones that anchor the construction and transition phases are Initial Operational Capability (IOC) and Full Release. Work can be done sequentially or iteratively in any phase.

As you might expect, budgets are prepared in the inception phase and updated thereafter. Expenditures are continual, as are changes to budgets. That's because requirements change as we learn more about what it is the customer or user really wants. In response, organizations often prepare themselves to address such change by allocating discretionary funds and schedule buffers to address known risks and handle the unexpected. Savvy software engineers know that they can tap these reserves if they come to the table with sound justifications for their ideas. Let's look at how to come up with justifications before digging deeper into the processes involved in developing business cases. Then let's tie the software development and business case processes together throughout the life cycle using the Goal–Question–Metric (GQM) paradigm.

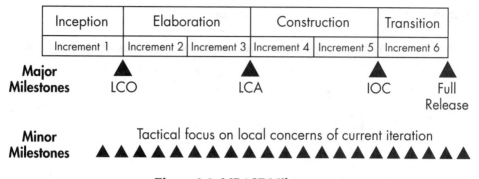

Figure 2.2: *MBASE Milestones*

Source: Adapted from Boehm, B. W., "MBASE Tutorial" presentation at the Los Angeles SPIN meeting, 2000. Reprinted by permission of the University of Southern California, Center for Software Engineering, and the author.

SETTING IMPROVEMENT GOALS USING THE GQM PARADIGM

The first question that must be answered when proposing improvements or changes is, "Why?" You would be surprised how many of us forget to answer this question in a way that relates to the organization's objectives. For example, you want the tools to increase productivity. The reason for their purchase is that they automate many of the tedious, labor-intensive activities that must be done before you can get the product out the door. Based on the feasible options, you must justify your selection. For example, have you considered what options could ease the situation? You should. If you don't, you might have difficulty getting management to fund buying a tool that you believe is necessary to make your job easier.

The approach I have used over the years to pull this information together and establish a context for my business cases throughout the life cycle is the GQM paradigm [Basili, 1988]. Using this informal mechanism, you first identify the relevant organizational goal. At a high level, you could use one of the four items in the improvement framework in Figure 1.1 (increase productivity, reduce time to market, avoid/cut costs, improve quality) as a start. To reach the goal, you identify the pertinent questions, which in turn leads to the metrics and models you will use to quantify your answers. Why buy a tool? What are the options? What are the costs and benefits? What metrics will you use to measure these cost and benefits? You could derive a business case using the GQM logic illustrated in Figure 2.3.

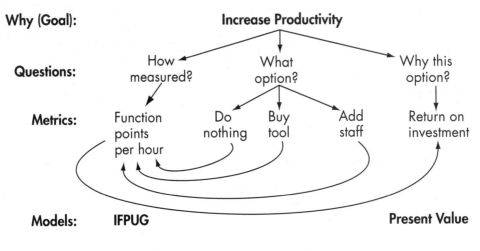

Figure 2.3: *GQM Example*

The GQM information you prepare guides you through how to justify your tool purchase. It provides the following information in a single glance:

- Your goal is to increase productivity for this labor-intensive task.
- You measure productivity using function points/hour using the International Function Point User's Group (IFPUG) guidelines to define your terms of reference.
- You have considered three options: do nothing, buy tool, and add staff.
- You justify selection of the best option using return on investment by taking the present value of the investment options.

Present value is an economic measure that uses today's value of money as the basis of decisions involving further expenditures. Because it is used extensively in business case preparation, I discuss it in Chapter 3 when we elaborate on the principles, rules, and tools that automate business case process.

Of course, you have to be careful when performing present value analysis. Often, the option that comes out ahead isn't what you thought it would be. Sometimes you have to be creative when developing your justifications. Otherwise, you might wind up doing something you hadn't planned on doing. This isn't so bad when the unexpected turns out to be the right choice.

DEVELOPING BUSINESS CASES: THE FRONT-END PROCESS

As already stated, a business case needs to provide management with a persuasive and sound reason for approving your idea or improvement proposal. The business case is important because it provides them with the financial, competitive, and/or other form of justification that they need to approve investments of time, talent, money, and other resources in your and not someone else's improvement proposal. But there is a lot of confusion about the business case process. Just because you've prepared one doesn't mean you won't have to prepare another. That's because business cases are used throughout the software development life cycle to justify purchases, decisions, and improvement initiatives.

In most cases, business cases assume that whatever you are proposing is technically as well as economically attractive. Organizations frown on investing in technology for technology's sake. They are in business to make a profit. They will approve pursuit of an idea when it makes good business sense. If they don't have funds available, they will find some if the business case is compelling enough. Therefore, your business case must convince management that the potential rewards justify the costs. To do this, you need to first relate your ideas to corporate objectives. That's what the GQM paradigm helps you accomplish. Then you have to examine the options you have identified and develop recommendations. Your recommendation will be approved if you have analyzed the options in detail and laid out a feasible, low-risk plan that allows you to deliver what you promised. The cliché "The devil is in the details" holds true. What you promise to deliver is important as well. The product of the effort needs to be packaged so that it is attractive to management. For example, you will have a hard time selling proposals for improvements in productivity when quality is currently on management's radar screen. Success in a software venture is a function of both content and packaging in equal proportion.

Over the years, I have been involved in numerous proposals that kicked off different types of improvement initiatives. In almost all cases, it was hard to get these ventures approved because of the organizational and culture changes that accompanied them. As discussed in Chapter 1, the resistance to change was fierce and had to be dealt with before the initiative could be successful. Luckily, lots of papers have been published by the process community on how to manage change. These publications and others [Grady, 1997] suggest that you need to address overcoming resistance to change as part of the business plan you develop to structure your improvement efforts. Yes, most experts agree that preparing a business plan is a necessary prerequisite for addressing change. Business cases should accompany business plans to convey the arguments that justify pursuit of the initiatives. As you develop your arguments for change, be sure that you align your proposal with your corporate goals. Otherwise, management may discard them because they have more important problems on their minds.

The GQM approach lets you establish a context for your business cases. Its outputs are used to start the seven-step business planning process shown in Figure 2.4 and described in the following sections.

Prepare White Paper

A white paper outlining your idea or improvement is an essential first step in the process. It allows you to crisply summarize what you are trying to accomplish and why it is important to your organization. A white paper is an excellent sales tool because it gets potential sponsors excited about the change. It should be short and to the point. If you can't say what you have to say in less than 10 pages, don't write it. It should use pictures and graphics to communicate concepts. The paper should

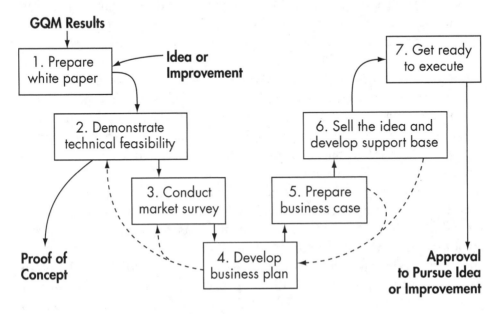

Figure 2.4: *Seven-Step Business Planning Process*

describe in high-level terms the opportunity, how you will take advantage of it, and the expected results if you are successful. You should be as specific as possible about your goals without going into the details. You should limit the scope and set realizable expectations. The white paper should be well written, compelling, and, most important, focused on the actions that the organization must take to realize the benefits described. In other words, it should discuss cultural changes.

Demonstrate Technical Feasibility

If you haven't already proved the idea's value, you should conduct a feasibility demonstration as your next step in the planning process. Demonstrations provide evidence of value through "show and tell." They force you to do something like pull a prototype together to prove feasibility of the concept. They help you gather support from the customers for the idea. The trick to being successful with prototypes is to focus on the essentials. You don't have to build a production article to convince skeptics that your idea is worthy. Instead, place a premium on what everyone considers the risks to be, and you'll reap the dividends.

Often, textbooks instruct you to perform a feasibility study first and pilot the idea next. I believe that takes too much time. Instead, develop something that management can touch, see, smell, and taste. For example, pull a simulation together to show how a new security algorithm might work instead of preparing a report about it. By playing with this trial product, they will be better able to visualize what you are trying do.

Conduct Market Survey

Determining the market for your idea or improvement is a long-lead item. You will need hard data to size the market, develop market penetration strategies, and generate reasonable sales forecasts. The hard data can either be acquired from market research firms or generated through benchmarking exercises, surveys, or focus groups. Digging out the data needed to size the market and determine its demographics takes time, money, and perseverance. Marketing in today's fast-paced economy is dynamic, not static.

To get your arms around the potential target opportunity you need to understand the following concepts:

- Competitive forces
- Core competencies
- Customer preferences

- Legal restrictions
- Market infrastructure/relationships
- Social trends
- Strategic relationships
- Technology trends
- Timing (of adoption)
- Windows of opportunity

I believe that successful organizations focus on market creation, not market sharing. They get to market first, are nimble, and take risks. They become the market leaders by seizing opportunities. They build the market and become the market leader through instinct, luck, and quantitative analysis. And when dealing with improvement opportunities, they need to provide a compelling reason to change the way they do business.

Develop Business Plan

Most organizations require some form of business plan or trade study before they will fund pursuit of a new idea or innovation. A business plan doesn't have to be big or extremely detailed. What it needs to do is cover the right stuff. The document should be short, focused, meaty, and written to communicate everything your sponsor needs to know to approve your proposal. In small organizations, the concept can be presented as a briefing so long as it has the right content—the business aspects of your idea. Although related, business plans differ from project plans.

As shown in the boxed text that follows, business plans summarize what you have to do to make or save money, not how you will get the job done. As seen in the box, the plan puts the pieces of the puzzle together to convince your sponsor that pursuit of the opportunity is sound for business reasons. I developed this outline to get venture funding for an idea I had several years ago. It worked, I was successful, and I used it again when called on to write another business plan.

If developing business and project plans separately bothers you, combine them when it makes sense. For example, two plans often don't make sense when dealing with small proposals. However, develop them separately when dealing with money people because they want to focus on the financials, not the development details.

BUSINESS PLAN OUTLINE

Table of Contents
Executive summary
1. Introduction
   1.1 Purpose and scope
   1.2 Background
   1.3 The opportunity
   1.4 Plan organization
2. Company description
   2.1 History
   2.2 Existing capabilities
   2.3 New products and services
3. Industry analysis
   3.1 Current situation
   3.2 Future trends
4. Target market
   4.1 Market sizing
   4.2 Targets of opportunity   Glossar
5. Competition
   5.1 Competitive position
   5.2 Market Penetration
6. Marketing plan
   6.1 Marketing tactics
   6.2 Sales strategy
7. Operations
   7.1 Production, inventory
       and distribution
   7.2 Order fulfillment and
       customer support
   7.3 Financial controls
   7.4 Security

8. Master schedule
9. Management and organization
   9.1 Organization structure
   9.2 Key staff and their vitae
   9.3 Executive and advisory
       committees
   9.4 Task management
   9.5 Risk management
   9.6 Facilities and equipment
   9.7 Communications
10. Long-term development
    10.1 Long-term goals
    10.2 Exiting the business
11. Financials
    11.1 Sales projections
    11.2 Cash flow
    11.3 Profit and loss
    11.4 Bridge financing
    11.5 Financial analysis
References
Appendix A: Financial Analysis
    A.1 Return on investment
    A.2 Breakeven analysis
    A.3 Investment opportunity
        analysis
    A.4 Other analysis
Appendix B: Backup materials
    B.1 Market survey
    B.2 Other data
Appendix C: Glossary

Prepare Business Case

As part of the business plan, you should provide analysis aimed at convincing potential sponsors that your proposal makes both good business and good technical sense. As noted in Chapter 1, this can be achieved by highlighting the costs/benefits, financial advantages, and/or competitive situation. As shown in the box, you should showcase your business case in the plan's executive summary and place the details in an appendix. The required return on investment and other forms of analysis should be placed in this appendix using the competitive, financial, and marketing data supplied in the body of the plan.

Don't be fooled by the fact that the business case appears as an appendix. Success or failure of the business plan often hinges on the justifications that are placed at the end of the document (and quoted throughout). Errors in the numbers can be damaging. Check the plausibility of your forecasts, and make sure that your math is accurate before you publish your results. I have seen proposals thrown out due to math errors. I remember a situation where two groups were competing for resources. Both sides had good ideas and justification. But the side with the math error lost as the other side used it to question their credibility.

Presell the Idea and Develop Support Base

Just developing a business plan is not enough. In practice, you must presell your ideas to develop the support you need to succeed. Support comes from all parts of the organization. As stated in Chapter 1, you need a champion at the senior management level to help win the political and budget battles. But that's not enough. You need support at the worker and middle levels of the organization as well. The best way to get sponsorship at those levels is to use your demonstration to sell your improvement ideas to them. They are the doers and influence-makers, the people who do the lion's share of the work within the firm. If they like your idea, everyone else will, too, because of the respect they command.

I remember trying to convince a software database firm to adopt complexity analysis tools some years ago. I encountered nothing but resistance until the most senior programmer loudly proclaimed how beneficial these tools would be in efforts to pinpoint error-prone modules. I had cornered him in the cafeteria, and we had looked through listings that showed the complexity ratings. By the end of the day, it seemed that everyone was downloading the tools and trying to use them for this purpose.

Get Ready to Execute

As your final step, get ready to start rolling the minute management approves the go-ahead for your initiative. To be ready, the following long-lead activities need to be completed as your proposal is reviewed by the powers that be:

- *Project planning*   Use your business plan to get your project plan in shape. Develop your task breakouts, and identify critical paths through the schedule. Solidify your budgets and your staffing curves. Tailor your institutional process as part of your plan, and get ready to start work. Prepare whatever paperwork is needed to open your charge numbers.

- *Staffing*   Start recruiting staff to fill positions once the work begins. Have your position descriptions prepared and cleared by personnel. Prepare the paperwork for transfers and contingent job offers. Work out the people transition issues beforehand so that you can maintain goodwill with peers.

- *Committee formation*   Identify the people you want to serve on your executive and advisory committees. Ask your champion to chair the executive committee, and get key people to sign up. Prepare organizational charts and charters before holding your initial meetings.

- *Equipment and tools acquisition*   Submit requests for long-lead equipment and tools when you have a chance. This is especially valuable when you can influence your capital budget.

- *Facilities*   Search out space to collocate your teams and for the demonstration. Work out plans with the facilities department for relocating people once you receive the go-ahead for the effort.

- *Operational concepts*   Prepare your operational concepts, and ready the infrastructure you will use to manage the effort in anticipation of the go-ahead.

I have seen too many projects stumble as they begin because they haven't worked these long-lead items. As a result, these projects had to play catch-up and were weeks behind schedule before they started. Facilities are often the cause of a lot of the heartburn. Even in good times, it can be harder to get collocated space for your people than anything else on your list. So be prepared to work this issue in earnest.

PUTTING THE PROCESS TO WORK

You are probably wondering when you would be required to use this process to justify pursuit of an initiative. It seems like a lot of work. Here is some guidance:

- If you are seeking to start up or acquire a business, you would use the business planning process to assess alternatives and justify how they would handle finance, marketing, and operations.
  - Such plans are required in order to secure financing for the startup or acquisition from either internal or external sources.
- You would use the business planning process to help plan for and justify major changes or expenditures. *Major,* in this sense, is defined in terms of the magnitude of the resources required and degree of organization change.
  - Most organizations require a business plan and business case when requested expenditures exceed certain thresholds. Check with your organization to see what these thresholds are, because they vary greatly from industry to industry.
  - Many organizations require a plan to show how organizational changes will be managed and cultures transformed (insertion of new organizations, training of those who will perform new job functions, and so on).
- You would use the business planning process when capital expenditures are being requested independent of thresholds.
  - In most firms, considerable justification is needed before management will approve major equipment, software, and/or facility updates.

The information needed to develop your business plan/case, along with sources, is summarized in Table 2.1. Much of this information can be gathered from internal sources. Internal sources tend to be more credible because they understand the firm, its culture, and the client base. No outsider can develop your baseline performance data. This data needs to be gathered at the source from those who do the work. If it isn't, its trustworthiness will be continually challenged.

TYING THE BUSINESS PROCESS TO THE SOFTWARE DEVELOPMENT LIFE CYCLE

You probably realize that few engineers actually go through the elaborate business process shown in Figure 2.4. That's because this process is primarily used to make big decisions (the ones involving lots of resources and culture changes). However, instances of the process are used throughout the software develop-

Table 2.1: *Business Plan/Case Information Needs/Sources*

Types of Information	Source of Information
Business cases	
■ Format for acceptable cases	This chapter provides all the information needed.
■ Process for preparing the case	Figure 2.4 provides a seven-step process.
■ Examples of analysis	Chapters 5 to 8 provide examples.
Marketing data	
■ Demographic information	Ask marketing or use a third-party market research firm.
■ Market position/competition	Ask marketing or use a third-party market research firm.
■ Sales forecasts	Ask marketing or use a third-party market research firm.
Financial data	
■ Accounting conventions	Ask accounting and finance.
■ Labor rates	Ask accounting and finance.
■ Past costs (by product, organization, or deliverable)	Ask accounting and finance.
■ Tax tables and rates	Ask accounting and finance.
■ Discount tables	Appendix C provides discount tables.
Benchmarks	
■ Competitive performance	Ask your customers, not your marketing people.
■ Productivity norms	Seek published data from credible sources.
■ Quality norms (defect rates, defect density, etc.)	Seek published data from credible sources.
■ Time-to-market norms	Seek published data from credible sources.

ment life cycle to justify improvements and change proposals. You would develop a GQM chart for just about any change proposal because it sets the business case context for justifying the selection of different technical options.

You can identify many possible uses for business cases just by looking at the MBASE life cycle we discussed earlier. Examples of the development and business activities that should be conducted between milestones are summarized for convenience in Table 2.2. These mappings between activities are important because they permit you to anticipate and plan for the work that needs to be

Table 2.2: *Mapping the Business and Development Process via MBASE*

Milestones	Development Process Activities	Business Process Activities
Life Cycle Objective (LCO)	Definition of requirements Definition of operational concept Development of top-level development plans Identification of life cycle process (spiral, incremental, etc.)	Identification/justification of capital budget items Results of cost-schedule-requirements tradeoffs Details of risk analysis Results of market analysis
Life Cycle Architecture (LCA)	Choice of architecture Solidification of detailed development plans Availability of software engineering environment Results of prototyping and simulation	Details of domain analysis and product line trade studies Results of make/buy analysis Identification/justification of project/product budgets Results of licensing agreements Details of updated risk analysis
Initial Operational Capability (IOC)	Design and development of software elements (per the selected life cycle process) Integration of software into increments Results of alpha and beta testing Generation of documentation and software versions	Quantification of process improvement ideas/proposals Results of continuing cost-schedule-requirements tradeoff exercises Cost-to-complete estimates based on actual expenditures and assessment of progress
Full Release	Integration and test of system Readiness and training of operational workforce Transition and turnover of system to operations Progression into maintenance phase	Results of repair versus replace analysis Details of maintenance budgeting exercises Results of sustaining engineering budgeting exercises Details of outsourcing analysis
Throughout the life cycle	Putting the process infrastructure and best practices in place Acquiring/maintaining the software environment Maintaining the workforce skills	Justification for process initiatives (see Chapter 5) Results of trade studies comparing alternatives (e.g., in-house versus external training)

done during these periods. You can then address the long-lead times associated with adequately preparing to perform these and other tasks without penalty.

Many business cases result from conducting trade studies. They are used by software engineers to justify expenditures for equipment, tools, and other technical apparatus to be used on a project. For example, to justify a tool purchase, you must do more than just compare the technical virtues of two competing products. You have to compare what features you get for what cost. You might also need to determine whether either package requires equipment upgrades (to provide more memory, disk space, and so on) and if training and consulting support is available to help your people get up to speed on the package quickly. Finally, you would factor the license maintenance and renewal costs into the evaluation. You would then develop your recommendation based on your assessment of these factors.

BUSINESS CASES: STEPPING THROUGH THE LIFE CYCLE

Let's step through a software example to illustrate how business cases can be used throughout the software life cycle to quantify alternatives and help make business decisions based on technical inputs. Let's assume that you are building a trading application in Java that runs on a client-server system 24/7. At each of the life cycle milestones identified in Table 2.2, you will encounter technical decisions whose resolution is driven by business. Referring to Table 2.2, let's look at some of the decisions you might get involved with as you step through the life cycle. The tools and techniques referred to will be explained in more detail in Chapter 3.

Life Cycle Objective Milestone

As you start your effort, you must develop a business model for your product. Based on your initial product features and functions list, you would develop a high-level cost estimate for the development. Then you would determine at what price you would sell your software and how you would go about marketing it. To answer these and other questions, you would conduct a market survey to determine the features users wanted and how much they would be willing to pay for them. Features not on the list would then be dropped. You would next assess the competition to determine what you must do to penetrate the marketplace. As part of this assessment, you would decide if it made sense to develop your own marketing organization or use a third-party dealer network to reduce your cost of sales. Finally, you would generate a sales forecast and use it to generate the business case to justify going ahead with product development for both your management and their venture partners.

Some of the business case tradeoffs you would investigate as you develop your business model include the following:

■ Examining cost-schedule-feature/function tradeoffs using cost as an independent variable (CAIV) analysis techniques

■ Pricing the product using breakeven and trend analysis to predict necessary sales volume

■ Requesting capital budgets using cost/benefit analysis to justify needed expenditures

The key focus of activities conducted in anticipation of this milestone is to baseline the requirements for the product (e.g., the features and functions list).

Life Cycle Architecture Milestone

As you solidify your requirements and finalize the architecture of your product, you must decide whether to make or buy the middleware that enables your applications to run on the Java virtual machine. Such a decision has major technical and business impacts on the overall viability of the product development effort. A poor choice of middleware could result in inadequate performance, which could in turn lead to reduced sales and user dissatisfaction. In contrast, building fully functional middleware might be too time-consuming and expensive based on your sales forecasts. To justify your decision, you must develop a business case to quantify the cost/schedule/performance tradeoffs.

Other business case tradeoffs that you might investigate prior to completing this milestone include the following:

■ Conducting make/buy analysis to determine how best to populate the architecture using payback and investment opportunity analysis techniques

■ Developing software cost and schedule budgets using models like COCOMO II [Boehm, 2000] for estimating the required effort and duration

■ Prioritizing risk by performing a quantitative assessment of the impacts of hazardous items

The focus of activities conducted in anticipation of this milestone is to baseline the product architecture (assuming the requirements are under control).

Initial Operational Capability Milestone

As a result of feedback from users of increments, you would conduct trade studies as versions of the product are released to look at the costs versus benefits associated with adding features and functions to the product as it is being generated. From the results of these studies, market windows, and available funding, you would decide on the configuration of the version you plan to release. For example, you might cut back on functionality to release the product at a particular trade show or industry event that was scheduled in the near term.

Other business case tradeoffs you might investigate prior to completing this milestone include the following:

- Determining whether or not to release an increment or version of the product based on trend analysis (e.g., looking at defects and associated quality levels)
- Developing cost and schedule-to-complete estimates using cost models to determine whether or not you can deliver as promised depending on actual rate of progress

The focus of activities conducted in anticipation of this milestone is on getting an acceptable product out the door.

Full Release Milestone

As you release the product, you must decide how many people must remain on the project. If you release the product prematurely, there will be lots of problems to repair and rework to do. This work is in addition to that which is needed to generate planned new versions. By forecasting the work based on past problem report frequencies and productivity rates, you plan on justifying the retention of a selective percentage of the software work force at least during the initial months of operation. Your goal is to make the product "industrial strength" by replacing error-prone models and making selective repairs.

Other business case tradeoffs you might investigate prior to completing this milestone include the following:

- Conducting replace/repair tradeoffs using techniques, such as the Pareto analysis, to determine defect-prone modules of the software
- Developing maintenance estimates using cost models to predict effort and duration based on projected change statistics

The focus of activities conducted in anticipation of this milestone is on getting ready to support the user once the product is placed in the field.

Business case analysis techniques are used throughout the software process to provide software engineers with the hard data they need to make difficult decisions. Most of these decisions involve technical-cost-schedule tradeoffs. For example, you might prioritize your risks based on their cost, schedule, and technical performance impacts. When the impacts are large, you can easily justify spending additional resources to address them.

SUMMARY

Business cases provide decision makers with compelling reasons to pursue implementation of either an idea or an improvement. This chapter summarizes the whats, whys, and whens associated with their use. It also provides insight into the business planning process and helps you understand when business cases are prepared throughout the software life cycle.

In the next chapter, I provide you with some insight into referenced analysis tools and techniques. Then I show you how to use them as part of the case studies that will be covered in Chapters 5 to 8.

Observations

During the past thirty years, I have made a business of developing business cases for software improvement. Friends have called me in repeatedly to help them package successful proposals for change. I have succeeded where others have failed by focusing attention on the numbers. I have used the processes briefly discussed in this chapter to get funding for major initiatives and win the battle of the budget. This chapter sets the stage. It provides you with the process that you will use to put business cases to work on the job. The remaining chapters reference this process and build on it to show you how to use it productively.

KEY POINTS

✔ Business cases are prepared throughout the software development life cycle to stimulate pursuit of good ideas and improvements.

✔ The GQM paradigm can be used effectively to establish a context for business case design.

✔ Both project and capital budgets are used to fund investments called out in business cases.

✔ The business planning process emphasizes use of business cases for justifying major expenditures on new initiatives to management.

✔ Software engineers put business cases to work for them as part of the tradeoff analysis they conduct throughout the life cycle.

✔ Paying attention to content and packaging is an essential ingredient for business case success.

References

[Basili, 1988] Basili, Victor R., and H. Dieter Rombach. "The TAME project: Towards improvement-oriented software environments," *IEEE Transactions on Software Engineering,* Vol. 14, No. 6, 1988, pp. 758–773.

[Boehm, 2000] Boehm, Barry W., Chris Abts, A. Winsor Brown, Sunita Chulani, Bradford K. Clark, Ellis Horowtiz, Ray Madachy, Donald Reifer, and Bert Steece. *Software Cost Estimation with COCOMO II.* Prentice-Hall, 2000.

[Boehm, 1998] Boehm, Barry W. "A Spiral Model of Software Development and Enhancement," *IEEE Computer,* May 1998, pp. 61–72.

[Boehm, 1996] Boehm, Barry W. "Anchoring the Software Process," *IEEE Software,* July 1996, pp. 73–82.

[Gerstner, 1993] Gerstner, Louis V., Jr. *Fortune,* November 1993. (From Ehrlich, Henry. *The Wiley Book of Business Quotations.* John Wiley & Sons, 1998.)

[Grady, 1997] Grady, Robert B. *Successful Software Process Improvement.* Prentice Hall, 1997.

[Kruchten, 1998] Kruchten, Philippe. *The Rational Unified Process.* Addison-Wesley, 1998.

[Royce, 1998] Royce, Walker. *Software Project Management: A Unified Framework.* Addison-Wesley, 1998.

3

Making a Business Case
Principles, Rules, and Analysis Tools

I think a lot of senior managers have lost their resolve and their ability to face up to hard work. Change is never easy and there are no special formulas, no quick fixes. You just have to roll up your sleeves and keep working at it without backing down.
–Arden C. Sims, CEO of Global Metallurgical [1992]

TOOLING THE PROCESS

This chapter provides the principles, rules, and analysis tools to put the process that was described in Chapter 2 into action in your organization. These tools are aimed at helping you quantify the costs/benefits of alternatives and develop recommendations that make sense for your organization throughout the software life cycle. In essence, the process forms the underlying framework for developing business cases. Nine principles or fundamental truths are added to the process to provide a solid foundation for quantifying costs/benefits. To help you to quantify the pluses and minuses of the alternatives under consideration, I discuss a wide variety of analytical techniques. As illustrated in Figure 3.1, the rules and tools discussed are sprinkled throughout the software development process along with guidance on how to apply them in practice to reenforce the principles discussed as you develop your business cases, do tradeoffs, and perform financial analysis.

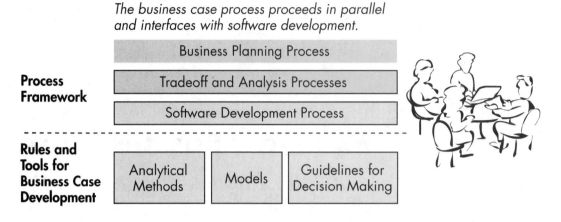

The business case process proceeds in parallel and interfaces with software development.

Process Framework

| Business Planning Process |
| Tradeoff and Analysis Processes |
| Software Development Process |

Rules and Tools for Business Case Development

| Analytical Methods | Models | Guidelines for Decision Making |

Figure 3.1: *Tooling the Process*

BUSINESS CASE PRINCIPLES

When developing business cases, several principles or fundamental truths can be applied. Unlike software development, these principles are based on decision theory rather than on software engineering dogma. The following nine principles provide the foundation for the quantitative techniques I use throughout the remainder of the book. To illustrate use of these principles, let's assume that you are thinking about running seminars to train your people in Java and component-based software engineering concepts.

   1. *Decisions are made relative to alternatives.* The options that are available to you include (1) do nothing and let your people learn Java at their own pace via the manuals, (2) implement an on-the-job training program, or (3) bring in training seminars taught hands-on by seasoned professionals in a just-in-time manner. If funds were not available for (3), you would disregard this option as unrealistic. The choice would narrow down to the first two options. If on-the-job training weren't feasible because you don't have the staff to put it together, your remaining option would be to let your people learn at their own pace.

   2. *If possible, money should be used as a common denominator.* When making decisions, the prospective consequences of each of the alternatives need to be expressed in common monetary units. The current value or worth of these funds is determined over time using today's value as the basis. To justify the investment, you need to determine whether training seminars reduce the time needed to become proficient in the use of the language. If they do, then you must determine how much time and effort can be saved via this option.

3. *Sunk costs are irrelevant.* It doesn't matter that you already ran a seminar in Java a year ago. That's a sunk cost and is irrelevant to this decision because your staff has changed and most of those assigned to this project are new and inexperienced. In this case, all events that took place prior to the decision being made have no effect on the resulting decision.

4. *Investment decisions should recognize the time value of money.* Money has value that increases over time due to inflation. Today's money is worth less tomorrow. Because you can put the money in a bank with a yield of 5 to 6 percent, this interest rate represents the minimum attractive rate of return. Any option you consider should yield more. If it doesn't, why pursue it? In addition, if you did nothing with the money, you would incur an opportunity cost of 6 percent—the interest you could earn, or the cost of money.

5. *Separable decisions should be considered separately.* You might be called on to recommend a training firm as part of the decision process. The criteria you would use to make this decision would be different from the criteria used to select the training option to pursue. It would be better to consider the two issues separately because it is possible that you would obscure the results if you tried to address them simultaneously.

6. *Decisions should consider both quantitative and qualitative factors.* Whenever possible, differences in alternatives should be viewed quantitatively. But it may not be possible to quantify all the costs/benefits associated with an option in this manner. For example, bringing in training might improve image and morale. These qualitative factors would then be used to swing the decision from one option to another if the costs/benefits were close.

7. *The risks associated with the decision should be quantified if possible.* All decisions are based on forecasts of the future. There is uncertainty or risk associated with predictions. This risk needs to be scoped and quantified if possible. For example, what is your plan should the training you desire not be available when needed? Do you have a fallback position? If so, what is the added cost of this contingency plan? Have you assessed the consequences of this risk and included a reserve in your budget to handle it?

8. *The timing associated with making decisions is critical.* As noted in Chapter 1, you need to make decisions in sync with your budgetary cycle. If you don't, you might have to wait until the cycle repeats itself before you can put in your request for funding approval. Time your decisions so that you can be ready to strike either when money is available or when budgets for training are being formulated and approved.

9. *Decision processes should be periodically assessed and continually improved.* Like any set of procedures, the procedures you use for assessing the business aspects of decisions can be improved. Look for ways to streamline your processes. Look for models and tools that you can use to improve the quality of your decisions and the quantity of options considered. Once decided, realize that you need to manage the actions needed to implement your suggestions.

As the principles illustrate, software engineers look to the future to determine the impact of options under consideration. They are more interested in cost at completion than cost to date. That's because they can influence the future with their decisions, not the past. I once asked a business school friend of mine what the difference is between an accountant and an engineer. He said that accountants look to the past to analyze expenditures; engineers typically look to the future to determine what it will take to get a job done.

To put these principles to work in a business environment, software engineers must understand the terminology that business professionals with whom they interface commonly use that is not part of their technical vocabulary. This terminology includes accounting, economics, investment, and tax-related terms. Software engineers must understand how to take the cost of money into account via discounting. They must also understand how to assess the tax implications of investment decisions. If they don't, they will have a difficult time communicating with the people involved in approving their requests for money.

PRESENT VALUE AND FUTURE WORTH

One of the most basic mathematical concepts used when business cases are prepared is "cost of money." This factor is used to normalize future expenditures using current-year dollars as the basis. The "cost of money" can be likened to the "interest" or the money that banks charge for use of assets. The interest rate, i, is the ratio of interest charged to the amount of money borrowed (the principal) during the interest period. Simple interest is merely the interest generated in the first interest period multiplied by the total number of periods covered by the decision. For example, the interest earned on $10,000 invested for 6 years at 5 percent would be computed as follows: $10,000 $\times$ 5% $\times$ 6 = $3,000. In contrast,

Table 3.1: *Effects of Periodic Compounding*

Period	Money Owed at Start of Period	Interest Accumulated during Period	Sum of Money Owed at End of Period
1	P	iP	$P + iP = P(1 + i)$
2	$P(1 + i)$	$iP(1 + i)$	$P(1 + i) + iP(1 + i) = P(1 + i)^2$
3	$P(1 + i)^2$	$iP(1 + i)^2$	...
4	$P(1 + i)^3$	$iP(1 + i)^3$	...
5	$P(1 + i)^4$	$iP(1 + i)^4$	...
6	$P(1 + i)^5$	$iP(1 + i)^5$	...
N	$P(1 + i)^{N-1}$	$iP(1 + i)^{N-1}$	...

compound interest is computed periodically on the amount owed at the start of each period, as illustrated in Table 3.1.

Present value (PV) is the value today of future cash flows. You use PV to normalize future expenditures using today's dollar as your basis. Table 3.1 lets you generalize a formula that computes the future worth (FW) of some investment decision at the end of N periods based on PV and some interest rate i:

$$FW = PV(1 + i)^N$$

We can use this formula and the interest tables that appear in Appendix C to determine the FW for our example as follows:

$$FW = PV(1 + i)^N = \$10,000(1 + 0.05)^6 = \$10,000(1.34) = \$13,400$$

As expected, annual compounding results in an increase in interest earned, in this case $400.

We can use the same formula to compute the present value PV of some future investment, again using the interest tables in Appendix C, by dividing both sides of the equation by $(1 + i)^N$ in the following formula:

$$PV = FW/(1 + i)^N$$

Present value is an important consideration in making business decisions. It allows decision makers to view future investments in terms of what money is worth today. It also lets them assess the impact of cash flow on their current operations. To illustrate its use, let's assume that management is seriously considering funding your training proposal. Your justification for the estimated expenditure is based on reduced personnel turnover of 3 versus 6 percent. You believe this will save $35,000 a year in lost productivity. As illustrated in Table 3.2, the PV is calculated on an annual basis, assuming that the cost of money is 8 percent per year, as follows:

$$PV = (\$10,000)/(1.08)^N$$

You would compute the PV annually and sum them instead of tabulating the value at the end of the fourth year. If you didn't, the PV would be computed as $29,400 because you would treat the calculation as a single and not a uniform cash flow series over four annual periods.

As an option, you could use the "Continuous" uniform series present value (SPV) tables in Appendix B with $N = 4$ to make this computation directly as follows: SPV = $10,000 (3.312) = $33,120. You would next compute the return on investment (ROI) by dividing the net benefits of $40,000 due to reduced turnover over the four years by the investment of $100,000, as follows:

$$ROI = net\ benefits/investment = \$40,000/\$100,000 = 40\%,\ or\ 10\%\ annually$$

Management often uses interest rates to establish a minimum attractive rate of return for their decisions. For our example, management might not consider pursuing your training opportunity because its yield is only 10 percent annually. They have set a minimum attractive rate of return of 15 percent for investments because they can put the money into an insured bank account that yields 8 percent a year with no risk. As a result, you will need to make your business case for training more attractive. Your justification is not strong enough.

This example illustrates why you need champions at the senior management level. They would coach you to increase your minimum attractive rate of return so that you could sell your training idea within your firm.

Table 3.2: *Present Value Calculation for Training Example*

Year	Training Cost	Benefits	Net Benefits	$(1 + i)^N$	Present Value
1	$25K	$35K	$10K	0.9259	$9,259
2	$25K	$35K	$10K	0.8573	$8,573
3	$25K	$35K	$10K	0.7938	$7,938
4	$25K	$35K	$10K	0.7350	$7,350
			$40K		$33,120

A SMORGASBORD OF ANALYSIS TECHNIQUES

So far, I've developed present value and rudimentary return on investment analysis. Along with these terms, business analysts and managers use a hodge-podge of other terminology and a smorgasbord of analysis techniques. Commonly used terms are defined for convenience in the Glossary. The following sections explain the types of analysis techniques that are commonly used within the business community. I use some of these to develop the numbers that make up the business cases in Chapters 5 through 8.

- Breakeven analysis
- Cause-and-effect analysis
- Cost/benefit analysis
- Value chain analysis
- Investment opportunity analysis
- Pareto analysis
- Payback analysis
- Sensitivity analysis
- Trend analysis

Breakeven Analysis

You would perform this type of analysis to identify the breakeven point where the benefits equal costs. Typically, this point is a function of volume. For example, unit costs that have fixed and variable parts go down as volume goes up because the fixed costs can be amortized across a larger sales base. For example, Poulin reports that the breakeven point for reusable parts is 3 [Poulin, 1997]. In other words, it doesn't make financial sense to build a software component to be reusable if you can't identify three potential uses for the part. Figure 3.2 graphically shows the breakeven point (where revenue = total cost), assuming that profit is a function of variable demand or sales.

In the training example, you would pay a fixed amount for the seminar. It wouldn't matter if 5 or 25 students attended the class. Assuming the cost of each seminar to be $12,500, the unit cost per participant would vary from $500 to $2,500 based on estimated attendance. To get the most for your money, you would maximize attendance. The breakeven point could be computed as a function of the savings that projects realize based on the training versus the costs (Year 3).

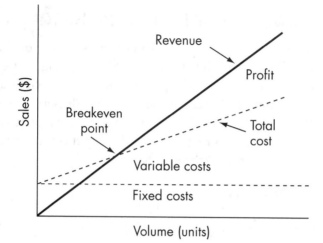

Figure 3.2: *Breakeven Analysis*

Cause-and-Effect Analysis

Another form of analysis that can be used to explore solutions to problems is what business analysts call cause-and-effect analysis. A cause-and-effect diagram—also called a fishbone chart and Ishikawa diagram [Ishikawa, 1982], like that displayed in Figure 3.3—is used to identify, analyze, and display all possible causes of a problem, event, or parametric variation. The diagram is usually prepared in a series of collaborative meetings where knowledgeable people brainstorm possible problems and then reach consensus on solutions. It is standard practice to weight the causes by their potential impact and the effects quantitatively. This weighting permits management to prioritize action plans aimed at resolving the causes of problems based on their potential cost and schedule impacts.

The fishbone diagram in Figure 3.3 is used to examine solutions to problems in the training example. Based on the diagram, steps could be taken to reduce the negative consequences of each of the problems. For example, you might have someone drive the instructor from the airport because the class couldn't go on without him/her showing up on time.

Cost/Benefit Analysis

The next type of analysis that is used extensively in Chapters 5 through 8 deals with costs/benefits. Justification for expenditures can be done using either cost

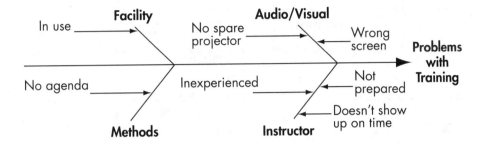

Figure 3.3: *Cause-and-Effect Diagram for Training Example*

avoidance or cost savings. As noted in Chapter 1, I prefer using cost avoidance because it deals with future, not current, expenditures. For example, increased productivity can be justified by cutbacks in future hiring. I try to avoid justifying ideas with cost savings because they often translate to more immediate actions such as layoffs, organizational cutbacks, and streamlining. I remember pitching a proposal involving cost savings not too long ago to a perceptive executive whose immediate response to my pitch was, "How many people do I lay off and whom do you recommend?" This response caught me totally by surprise. Needless to say, my customer—the software manager—wasn't happy.

Financial analysts use several approaches to determine the cost effectiveness of a business case proposal. The simplest of these looks at the cost/benefit ratio. This ratio is computed by taking the present value of the total monetary costs divided by the monetary benefits over the decision period. To develop the ratio for the training example, you would construct a worksheet like that shown in the box on the next page. The cost/benefit ratio would then be computed as follows:

cost/benefit ratio = PV(total costs ($)/total benefits ($))

The worksheet example in the box shows how the principles expressed earlier in this chapter can be used. First, costs are separated into nonrecurring and recurring categories. Nonrecurring costs are expenses that occur one time, while recurring costs are ongoing outlays. Second, benefits are classified as tangible and intangible. Tangible benefits are easy to quantify, while intangibles are not. However, a monetary value can be determined for intangibles if you put your mind to it. For example, lost morale translates into increased turnover and recruiting

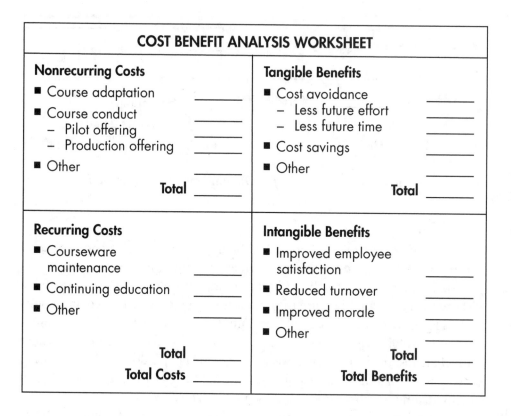

COST BENEFIT ANALYSIS WORKSHEET

Nonrecurring Costs
- Course adaptation _____
- Course conduct _____
  - Pilot offering _____
  - Production offering _____
- Other _____
  Total _____

Tangible Benefits
- Cost avoidance _____
  - Less future effort _____
  - Less future time _____
- Cost savings _____
- Other _____
  Total _____

Recurring Costs
- Courseware maintenance _____
- Continuing education _____
- Other _____
  Total _____
  Total Costs _____

Intangible Benefits
- Improved employee satisfaction _____
- Reduced turnover _____
- Improved morale _____
- Other _____
  Total _____
  Total Benefits _____

costs. Intangibles act as a swing vote. When the costs/benefits of two alternatives are close, the intangibles decide the selection by swinging the vote one way or the other. Third, the ratio uses present value to show the value of money as a function of time. The example also illustrates things we haven't done. Capital costs associated with the option are not included in the analysis because they are taken from a different budget. Last, the analysis doesn't look at the tax implications of the investment. For example, if there were tax credits available for retraining personnel, you would put them as a new line item under tangible benefits.

Value Chain Analysis

Value chain analysis is another approach that is useful in evaluating alternatives. This technique can be used to assess the impact of each option using a form of decision tree. This form of analysis should be appealing to software engineers because many engineers use decision trees to perform test coverage analysis. As

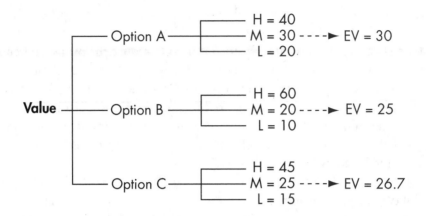

Figure 3.4: *Value Chain Analysis*

shown in Figure 3.4, the expected value for each option represented on the tree is computed using the formula

$$\text{expected value}_i \text{ (EV)} = (H_i + 4M_i + L_i)/6$$

where H_i = highest possible value for option i, M_i = the most likely value for option i, and L_i = the lowest possible value for option i.

Decision trees can be used to show the projected financial impact of each option at a glance. The formula used to compute the expected value creates a weighted average around the statistical mean of a bell-shaped curve, or normal distribution. The accuracy of the value chain is as good as the inputs used to quantify the financial gain associated with each alternative.

Investment Opportunity Analysis

Many financial measures can be used to assess the attractiveness of a range of alternatives. Two of the more useful of these are return on capital and after-tax rate of return. Both measures have the additional advantage that they make sense to financial people. Both measures also assume that the items acquired as part of improvement recommendations are carried as capitalized expenses by an organization on its books. I use both measures in Chapters 5 through 8 to take taxes into account in case studies.

Return on capital looks at the amount of money the investment makes over its useful life. It is computed by dividing the investment's cumulative return by the one-time investment. For example, the nondiscounted return on capital for software that costs you $50,000 would be 5:1 if it saved $250,000 in equivalent labor costs over its useful life.

The effective after-tax rate of return is used to reduce the projected benefit stream associated with an improvement option by its potential tax liability. The investment is divided by the resulting revenue stream to determine the effective rate of return. This rate is then compared to some minimum attractive rate of return to determine whether it is a good investment. For example, an investment that yielded a 12-percent after-tax return might be considered an excellent investment if the going interest rate was 5 percent.

Other financial performance measures like ROI can be used to assess the desirability of investment alternatives. I recommend that you select whatever measures your financial people use to establish credibility with them especially when your management asks them to perform an independent review of your numbers.

Pareto Analysis

This form of analysis is based on the Pareto principle, which states that a few of the problems are responsible for most of the effect, sometimes called the 80–20 rule. A notable contributor to the field of quality control, Joseph Juran, referred to this proportion as the "vital few and the trivial many" [Juran, 1981]. Pareto charts, such as the one shown in Figure 3.5, are the primary tool used to perform this type of analysis. This chart, a bar graph showing error sources by work unit arranged in descending order, displays the relative importance of the problems by category.

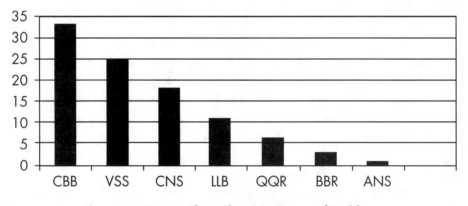

Figure 3.5: *Pareto Chart Showing Causes of Problems*
by Program Unit as a Percentage

Pareto charts provide insight into causes of problems. For example, Pareto analysis may identify a certain few error-prone models that are the source of most of the system's failures. From Figure 3.5, you can learn that the first three problem sources are responsible for about 78 percent of the errors. These sources appear error-prone, and therefore, the program units responsible for them should be your first targets for repair or replacement.

Payback Analysis

This analysis technique is used to determine the number of periods required to recover one's investment—the payback period. Options can then be compared using the payback period as a basis. For the training example, the payback period for the first year's investment would be computed as follows:

payment period = investment/net savings = \$25K/(\$10K/year) = 2.5 years

Unfortunately, using the payback period disregards the consequences of the investment beyond the end of the payback period, making comparing options with different useful lives difficult especially when there is an uneven pattern of annual cash flows. Some analysts use either return on capital or after-tax effective rate of return to address this deficiency. However, both measures assume that the improvement investment will be carried as a capital item on an organization's books.

Other decision makers may evaluate investment opportunities by estimating their impact in the first year. The investment may be accepted if the resulting benefits provide "added value" in terms of the intangibles.

Sensitivity Analysis

Sensitivity analysis techniques look at how the results change as small changes are made to parametric values. Typically, many variables influence your decisions. For example, when buying a car, you might look at the price/performance of the options as a function of choice of body style, engine, transmission, stereo, and options. However, your decision is sensitive to body style because you anticipate that you will need a four-door sedan to accommodate your growing family. Luckily, the training example is simpler. The effective price per participant for training drops as a function of number of courses ordered if the supplier offers a volume discount for their purchase. In this case, price is sensitive to order quantity.

Trend Analysis

This form of analysis looks at movement in the data as a function of time. Software engineers use trend lines frequently for technical purposes (e.g., to plot cyclomatic complexity as a function of size of a software component to look for targets for simplification during an update [Pressman, 2001]). Normally, trends are displayed graphically so that the tendencies of the data are visible to all who view them. For example, travel costs vary as a function of season. If prices are high in the summer, you might use trend data to anticipate increased prices and purchase tickets in spring when there is a discount.

In business cases, trends are heavily used in forecasting. For example, managers can consider future raises when estimating labor costs by inflating salaries based on trends in economic index data. They can plot buying trends as a function of their sales forecast. In software organizations during testing, software engineers can examine defect find-and-fix rates to determine whether they are removing defects more quickly than they are finding them. Software managers can plot their rate of progress in achieving milestones as a means to assess their programmatic performance to supplement concepts like earned value.

TOOLS OF THE TRADE

The three tools most software engineers and managers use to perform business case analyses are spreadsheets, financial calculators, and cost models. They don't need to use the more sophisticated tools and techniques that business analysts employ for statistical and financial analysts. That's not their job. Their goal is to make recommendations using credible numbers. For major decisions, business analysts take the numbers software engineers and managers prepare and turn them inside out and upside down as they examine their many tax, financial, and investment implications. That's why you should check that your numbers make sense before submitting them. If you make an error, your credibility will be questioned.

Spreadsheets are the primary tools used for financial analysis because they are simple, easy to use, and allow alternatives to be compared side by side. Financial calculators can be used to compute the present value and discount rates. These calculators can be called from any spreadsheet cell to perform these simple mathematical computations.

Cost models are more sophisticated tools and take some time, effort, and training to learn to use effectively. These software programs take heuristic relationships (e.g., average productivity of a programmer is 2 function points/staff-month of effort) and modify them to fit actual experience using a number of factors to which costs have been shown to be sensitive in the past (e.g., if staff experience is low, add 18 percent to the nominal cost to compensate for this problem based on our past experience).

Cost models can be used to perform business case analysis (quantify and compare costs of options, perform parametric analysis, and so on). One of the most popular of these models is the COCOMO II model [Boehm, 2000]. However, any of the popular packages on the market today can be used for this purpose. The COCOMO model estimates the effort and duration associated with a software job based on past experience using linear regression formulas. A variety of factors that have been shown to statistically influence the cost are then varied to adjust the resulting estimates according to such parameters as product complexity, applications experience, process maturity, use of software tools, and requirements evolution and volatility.

The COCOMO II software cost estimation model's mathematical formulas are currently derived from both expert opinion and actual data collected from 161 completed software projects. The projects in this database range in both size and complexity from simple management information systems to military command and control applications.

The COCOMO II software cost estimation model uses the following mathematical formula to predict the effort associated with developing software. A similar equation is used to estimate the duration for the software project.

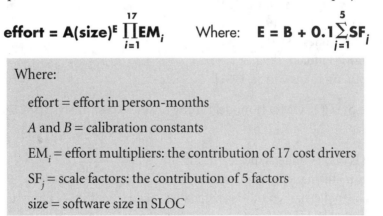

$$\textbf{effort = A(size)}^{\textbf{E}} \prod_{i=1}^{17} \textbf{EM}_i \qquad \text{Where:} \qquad \textbf{E = B + 0.1} \sum_{j=1}^{5} \textbf{SF}_j$$

Where:

effort = effort in person-months

A and B = calibration constants

EM_i = effort multipliers: the contribution of 17 cost drivers

SF_j = scale factors: the contribution of 5 factors

size = software size in SLOC

The cost drivers used in the COCOMO II model are described in Table 3.3. Scale factors in COCOMO II relate to organizational conditions such as how mature the processes used are and whether or not collaborative teams are built and employed as the norm during product development. The model primarily uses five scale factors to rate how well an organization can develop software systems. These five scale factors have a relatively large impact on the effort estimate because their sum forms an exponent to which size is raised. For example, the range of an effort estimate for a software program sized as 500 function points could vary by as much as a factor of 3:1 dependent on how these scale factors are rated.

Cost drivers assess the relative impact of a variety of product, process, platform, personnel, and project factors on effort and duration estimates. You can vary them to investigate the cost and schedule consequences of different technical and/or staffing decisions. For example, the effort estimate in person-months would vary from 0.81 to 1.22 based on applications experience (the experience of the staff assigned to the project doing similar applications with about the same complexity and size). In other words, your estimate would have to be increased by 22 percent if the average staff application experience were less than 2 months. In contrast, the effort would be reduced by 19 percent if your average staff experience with the application exceeded 6 years.

In Chapters 5 through 8, I perform a variety of analyses using the COCOMO II estimation model. In fairness, any of the following other popular cost-estimating packages could be employed to provide similar results:

- CostExpert [Roetzheim, 1997]
- KnowledgePlan [Jones, 2000]
- PRICE-S [Jones, 1998]
- SEER [Jones, 1998]
- SLIM [Putnam, 1992]
- SoftCost [Tausworthe, 1981]

I use the COCOMO II model for my business case analyses for the following reasons:

1. It is easy to understand, learn, and use.
2. Its mathematics is simple and in the public domain.
3. The model has recently been updated to address effects of life cycle paradigms like MBASE (see Chapter 2 for a discussion of such life cycle models).
4. It has been subjected to a broad public review and validation process.
5. I find it easy to explain the model to management.

Table 3.3: *COCOMO II Cost Drivers*

Scale Factors	Brief Overview
PREC - Precedentedness	Has the system ever been built before?
FLEX - Development flexibility	Must you strictly conform to requirements?
RESL - Architecture and risk resolution	Is the architecture stable and have the risks been mitigated?
TEAM - Team cohesion	How complicated are stakeholder interactions?
PMAT - Process maturity	How mature are the processes used?

Cost Drivers	Brief Overview
RELY - Required software reliability	How risky is the software to people and property?
DATA - Database size	How big are the databases relative to norms?
CPLX - Product complexity	How complex is the product to be built?
DOCU - Documentation match to life cycle needs	Is the documentation the right size for the project's needs?
RUSE - Developed for reuse	How much design for reuse is planned?
TIME - Execution time constraint	Is timing a constraint?
STOR - Main storage constraint	Is memory a constraint?
PVOL - Platform volatility	How volatile is the development platform?
ACAP - Analyst capability	How capable are the analysts?
PCAP - Programmer capability	How capable are the programmers?
PCON - Personnel continuity	How stable is the workforce?
AEXP - Applications experience	What's the team's average application experience?
PEXP - Platform experience	What's the team's average platform experience?
LTEX - Language and tool experience	What's the team's language and/or tool experience?
TOOL - Use of software tools	How sophisticated is toolset to be used?
SITE - Multisite development	Will team use multiple development sites?
SCED - Required development schedule	Will the development schedule be constrained?

Probably the most compelling reason for me to use COCOMO II is that it is available at no cost from the University of Southern California (*http://sunset. usc.edu/cocomoii*). For me, this price establishes a compelling business case. Even better, I don't have to prepare a purchase order or justify the expenditure. All I have to do is download the package from the Center for Software Engineering's Web site and install it on my PC.

PACKAGING THE BUSINESS CASE FOR MANAGEMENT CONSUMPTION

I can't stress how important packaging is when it comes to business plan preparation. It needs to catch the attention of those whose support you need to get a favorable decision. As noted in our business plan outline in the box at the end of Chapter 2, packaging the business case involves preparing (1) a short and enticing business case summary, and (2) detailed financial analyses that substantiate the findings stated in the summary. In most cases, the numbers will speak for themselves. By packaging them smartly, you can get management to make commitments promptly.

How do you package the numbers? The following eight tips can help you accomplish this task with a minimum of wasted effort:

- In case that's all that's read by seniors, clearly and convincingly summarize the business case justification for your initiative in the executive summary.

- Define your terms precisely. Use examples to communicate meaning whenever possible. Don't let management infer meaning. If you do, they'll infer the wrong one.

- Be conservative with your numbers, or you may be discredited for being too optimistic.

- Quantify tangible benefits in monetary terms. Then factor the intangibles in, if you can, to show how they provide added value for your recommended option.

- Don't mix capital expenditures with project budgets. Keep the numbers separate because they come out of different pots.

- Use ranges for costs/benefits whenever possible. This allows you to scope the risk associated with the numbers quantitatively.

- Portray the PV of your benefits in this year's dollars. This will impress managers and convince them that you understand the business issues.

■ Focus attention on the business, not the technical, issues. Executives often ask others to review and comment on technical desirability and details.

When packaging business cases, I try to make the numbers sing a tune that the audience wants to hear. I start by identifying the issues that the seniors are most worried about. More often then not, competition and customer satisfaction are at the top of their list. If the competition was gaining market share, I would try to find out why. I would start by talking to customers who recently switched to find out the cause. When you ask them, most people will tell you the truth. In most cases, the reasons given are obvious: the competition provides better price/performance, or their customer support is better. These findings can be used to make your business case stronger. In the case of price/performance, you could show how your recommendations make your products more appealing to your customer base. For improved customer support, you could show how the improvements proposed increase sales to both existing and new clients. An example of a business case summary packaged along these lines is provided in the accompanying box. I include an example that is broader than just software because it sells your software improvement initiative as a solution to a broader, more business-oriented challenge.

AVOIDING TAXES AND TAX PENALTIES

I have learned over the years that you will make enemies if management funds pursuit of your improvement proposals using taxes. For example, your boss likes your training idea. Your sales presentation was well received, and he wants to fund the training immediately. However, there is not enough money left in the training budget to do so. Your boss addresses the funding shortfall by reducing the travel budget for the entire engineering organization. He cuts everyone's travel budget to the bone to pay for your training. No wonder the other engineers and managers in your organization won't talk to you.

A better way to proceed might be tapping unspent budgets. Many groups don't spend all the money allocated to them for lots of reasons. For instance, the recruiting budget may be fat because the people hired during the last six months didn't need relocation assistance. Of course, the specialists in the personnel department might get angry if you take their budget to pay for your training. They might strike back by putting your hiring requests at the bottom of their in-baskets. But that's the price that you pay for success.

EXAMPLE BUSINESS CASE
IN THE BUSINESS PLAN EXECUTIVE SUMMARY

The market

The acknowledged largest growing market in the world for wireless products is the People's Republic of China. Current projections indicate that this market will grow by a factor of 100 within the next decade. If projections hold true, this market will account for one of every two new sales of wireless products in the year 2010.

Current situation

We have successfully penetrated this market by teaming with several leading Chinese telecommunications manufacturers, distributors, and retail establishments. We have invested over $500 million in facilities and equipment and have trained over 5,000 Chinese workers in modern engineering and manufacturing techniques. This strategy has enabled us to capture 40 percent of the market for equipment. However, we were late to the handset market and command only 10 percent of the marketplace.

The competition

The market for handsets is extremely competitive. Our two chief rivals have recently teamed with Chinese companies and have offered products with better price/performance than ours. They have brought new products to market more rapidly than we have and are encroaching on our market share. Their customer support facilities are also more extensive than ours, and their technicians seem better trained to handle problems endemic to China.

The opportunity

We can bring products to market quicker with improved price/performance for the Chinese and Asian marketplaces by setting up a software development and customer support facility within the new economic development zone the government has created outside Beijing. Besides having tax advantages in China, the facility will bring us closer to the marketplace. It will also enable us to create software for new low-end products that we can sell in volume through local distributors with better price/performance than our competitors.

Solution	We can develop competitive products by adapting our new [code name] handset architecture and our quick-to-market engineering process to the Chinese and Asian marketplaces. The architecture would enable us to rapidly replace software in our new low-end handset offerings for new markets. This quick turnaround would permit us to capture between 40 and 50 percent of the market for these products during the next five years. The process would enable us to introduce these new products every six months instead of on an annual basis.
The numbers	We estimate that it will take an investment of $50 million to put this plan into action. Based on our sales forecasts, we believe the breakeven point for this investment would occur in less than two years. The present value of the benefits that will accrue over our five-year planning horizon is estimated at between $100 and $150 million based on a very conservative income stream. The after-tax effective rate of return for this investment within the United States exceeds 48% per year based on these projections.
Your actions	We would like to approach potential partners and the Chinese government to determine whether the climate for pursuit of this initiative is timely. We have developed a four-phase plan of attack to minimize the risk associated with this investment. The first phase of this plan requires an investment of $3 million to assess feasibility of using the Chinese to develop our software. We solicit your approval of this funding to pursue this potentially rewarding opportunity.

When I went into government in 1993, the first thing I did was to research the budgets. There were so many types of money, each with different types of restrictions, that I was initially overwhelmed. However, I soon found ways of tapping one budget for another as I learned the intricacies of the money system. I also learned that you can find money in big organizations to fund anything when you put your mind to it. You just have to know where to look and be first in line when it becomes available. For example, software tools for my projects were normally funded using engineering dollars. But labor was at a premium, and I did not want to trade it for tools. I therefore defined my software tools as support equipment and took money from this line item in my budget to fund their purchase. Some people complained, but I got away with it because it made sense to the specialists in the purchasing department.

Following are some other things your organization can do to avoid using taxes to pay for improvements:

- Keep a contingency budget in reserve to fund good ideas and improvements. If you have to, keep this budget line hidden under another label because such budgets are often taken away to bail out troubled projects.

- Know when surplus funds become available and be first in line to claim them. In many organizations, mid-year and year-end money becomes available when organizations don't spend all the funds allocated to them. This money is often reallocated to worthwhile projects. Make it easy for others to redistribute this money to your project by having the paperwork ready to transfer available funds to your accounts.

- Find a sponsor who has cash to fund your idea or improvement. This isn't as far-fetched as it sounds. Many software firms work under contract to others. Many times the sponsor will fund an improvement proposal when you share the benefits with them (e.g., increase your profit margin when you cut contract costs). Your sponsor could be a client, a needy project, or the government. For example, the U.S. government funds value engineering and process-improvement proposals on many of its contracts. While primarily directed toward manufacturing, some funds have been used to sponsor software improvements.

- Initiate efforts in other areas to free up funds for your new idea or improvement initiative. For example, put processes in place to implement enterprise-wide licensing for packaged software used throughout the firm. This initiative can free up millions of dollars in firms that do their licensing on a project-by-project basis [Reifer, 1999]. This money can then be used to fund other initiatives as long as it will be spent during the same fiscal year as the original expenditures.

SUMMARY

Business cases provide decision makers with a compelling reason to pursue implementation of an improvement idea or initiative. Chapter 2 sets the stage by describing the business case process and how it is used throughout software development to perform tradeoffs and justify investment. This chapter summarizes the principles, rules, and tools that you can use to get the job done. It also introduces you to commonly used business concepts and terms.

Observations

When I moved into management earlier in my career, I took many business school courses to better understand what was involved. Because of my engineering and math background, my focus was analytical methods. Much of this business knowledge has proved valuable to me as I have moved to/from management positions in industry and government. As a result of this experience, I have tried to focus attention in this chapter on the principles and the methods that proved useful to me as I prepared business cases. I have used each of the analytical techniques summarized in this chapter to my advantage as I have prepared business cases. In Chapters 5 through 8, I use some of these techniques to show you how to develop business cases in the process framework I have established.

KEY POINTS

- ✔ Business cases are prepared throughout the software development life cycle to stimulate pursuit of good ideas and improvements.
- ✔ Nine principles serve as the foundation for business case formulation.
- ✔ These principles spawn many rules that are sprinkled throughout the text to provide you with guidelines for taking action.
- ✔ The monetary value of future investments needs to be assessed in terms of today's currency.
- ✔ A smorgasbord of analysis techniques can be used to assess costs/benefits and justify your pursuit of an improvement idea or initiative.
- ✔ The primary tools used in conjunction with these analysis techniques are spreadsheets, financial calculators, and cost models.

✔ The COCOMO II cost model is a simple and effective tool for developing estimates and analyzing the financial implications of variations in cost drivers.

✔ Whenever possible, paying for improvements by taxing others should be
avoided.

References

[Boehm, 2000] Boehm, Barry W., Chris Abts, A. Winsor Brown, Sunita Chulani, Bradford
K. Clark, Ellis Horowitz, Ray Madachy, Donald Reifer, and Bert Steece. *Software Cost
Estimation with COCOMO II.* Prentice-Hall, 2000.

[Ishikawa, 1982] Ishikawa, K. *Guide to Quality Control.* White Plains, NY: Quality
Resources, 1982.

[Jones, 2000] Jones, T. Capers. *Software Assessments, Benchmarks, and Best Practices.* Addison-
Wesley, 2000.

[Jones, 1998] Jones, T. Capers. *Estimating Software Costs.* McGraw-Hill, 1998.

[Juran, 1981] Juran, Joseph. *Management of Quality,* 4th Edition. Juan Institute, 1981.

[Poulin, 1997] Poulin, Jeffrey S. *Measuring Software Reuse.* Addison-Wesley, 1997.

[Pressman, 2001] Pressman, Roger S. *Software Engineering: A Practitioner's Approach,* 5th
Edition. McGraw-Hill, 2001.

[Putnam, 1992] Putnam, Lawrence H., and Ware Myers. *Measures of Excellence: Reliable
Software on Time, within Budget.* Prentice Hall, 1992.

[Reifer, 1999] Reifer, Donald J., George E. Kalb, and Tara Ragan. "Licensing: A Target for
Process Improvement." Acquisition Management Conference, Defense Systems Management College, 1999.

[Roetzheim, 1997] Roetzheim, William H., and Reyna A. Beasley. *Software Project Cost and
Schedule Estimating Best Practices.* Prentice Hall, 1997.

[Sims, 1992] *Harvard Business Review,* May–June 1992. (From Ehrlich, Henry. *The Wiley
Book of Business Quotations.* John Wiley & Sons, 1998.)

[Tausworthe, 1981] Tausworthe, Robert C. *Deep Space Network Software Cost Estimation
Model.* Jet Propulsion Laboratory Publication 81-7, April 1981.

4

Business Cases
That Make Sense

The true speculator is one who observes the future and acts before it occurs.
Like a surgeon, he must be able to search through a mass of complex and
contradictory details to the significant facts. Then, like the surgeon,
he must be able to operate coldly, clearly, and skillfully
on the basis of the facts before him.
—Bernard Baruch [1957]

This chapter introduces you to the case studies that follow in Chapters 5 through 8. It sets the stage and provides you with the necessary background information you need to understand what the case studies are all about.

The business planning process outlined in Chapter 2 (see Figure 2.4) will be the starting point for most of you. You will kick off your effort by writing a white paper justifying your idea or improvement using some tangible benefits. In it, you will set your goals and discuss how you will achieve them. The paper will allow you to set aggressive but realizable expectations. Because most of you will try to justify your proposals using productivity improvement, cost avoidance, or time-to-market decreases, I open this chapter with some additional guidance on what to do when using these measures. In the remainder of this chapter, I provide you with background material on the four case studies that follow (see Chapters 5–8) so that you will understand them more completely as we go through the remainder of the business planning process.

THE PARABLE OF THE CHINESE EMPEROR

Let's start by looking at software productivity and ways to improve it. When I think of productivity, I think of the parable of the Chinese emperor. The emperor wanted to optimize productivity as his subjects dug a tunnel through a mountain. He asked his chief advisor how to achieve this goal. This wise, old man said: "Form two teams, and have them dig toward each other from either side of the mountain." He then amplified: "Because they will meet in the middle, productivity will be increased." The emperor thought for a minute. Then, he stated in an alarmed manner: "What happens if the teams don't meet?" The sage quickly replied: "Productivity will increase as well because two tunnels will result." The emperor perceptively replied: "Building tunnels is a win-win situation."

This parable illustrates the dual nature of productivity. Because productivity is defined as the ratio of outputs to inputs used to generate them, implementing strategies aimed at either side of the equation can optimize it. To improve the input side of the formula, organizations try to get the most they can from their employees by arming them with good processes, methods, tools, and a modern workspace. To optimize the output side, they attempt to make large jobs smaller using application generators, reuse, and component-based software engineering strategies. Both techniques work. However, better results occur when both techniques are put into action at the same time.

In any case, productivity improvement requires a strategy. My advice is to start by tackling the simple and obvious targets of opportunity first. Productivity improvement in virtually all organizations is there for the taking. All you have to do is search for the untapped and underutilized resources to make a positive impact. The sum of many small individual improvements can add up to significant increases. That's why I recommend pursuing many small changes in parallel instead of a single big change all at once. While the net result is the same, small improvements are much more manageable. In addition, a relatively small increase in overall productivity can frequently have a large impact on profit as long as a proper perspective and a reasonable pace are maintained.

Most people use productivity to justify their initiatives. Guidelines recommending what to do and what not to do when using productivity as the basis of your justification for improvements are provided in Table 4.1. These guidelines assume that there is no mismatch between how your firm defines organizational productivity and software productivity. If there is, you need to fix this problem by somehow relating your definition to that used by your organization. Your goal

Table 4.1: *Productivity Improvement Guidelines*

What to Do	What Not to Do
■ Be prepared to deliver what you promise; you will be held accountable for results.	■ Don't forget to make sure you align your proposals with your firm's business objectives.
■ Use definitions for productivity that are accepted by your industry and your firm.	■ Don't make promises you don't think you can keep.
■ If you don't know what it is, benchmark your current software productivity.	■ Don't leave anything to chance. Do your homework when it comes to numbers and know what they mean and how they are derived mathematically.
■ Benchmark the competition's productivity. Ask customers to rate best of class if the data is not readily available to you.	■ Don't use terms and definitions that are foreign to your company and industry.
■ Plot a trend line to compare the current rate of software productivity improvement made by your firm to industry norms.	■ Don't assume that everyone knows what your current software productivity is and how it is measured. I can assure you that most don't.
■ Use ranges instead of discrete numbers to bound your productivity numbers.	■ Don't assume you can find out what your competition's productivity is. The best you can probably do is get customer perceptions about who is best in class.
■ Define what your numbers include and don't include.	■ Don't forget to double- and triple-check your numbers before you present them. A math error can lead to an immediate and irrecoverable creditability gap.
■ Prepare backup materials to defend your justification; if management is interested, they will ask you to supply details in a follow-up briefing.	

is to show management how proposed improvements in software productivity contribute to the bottom line using definitions they are familiar with and understand.

PROCESS IMPROVEMENT USING PRODUCTIVITY INCREASES AS JUSTIFICATION

In Chapter 5, I present a case study that justifies pursuing process improvement by productivity improvement. Process improvement in this case is defined in terms of the Software Engineering Institute's Software Capability Maturity Model (SW-CMM) [Paulk, 1995]. The SW-CMM provides a conceptual framework for improving how you manage and develop your software products. It is organized around five levels of maturity that you can use to prioritize the opportunities that exist for process improvement. Clusters of related activities that, when performed, achieve the goals established for improving process capabilities at each

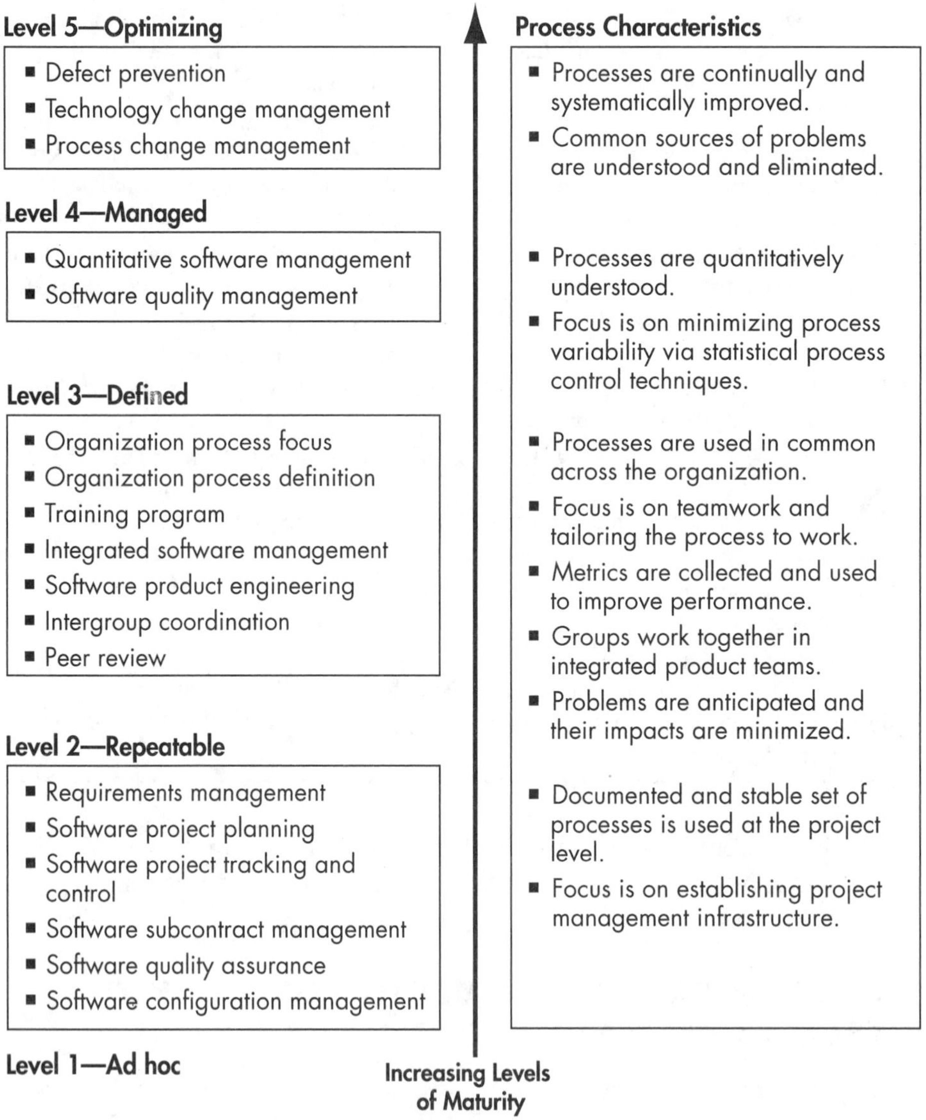

Level 5—Optimizing

- Defect prevention
- Technology change management
- Process change management

Level 4—Managed

- Quantitative software management
- Software quality management

Level 3—Defined

- Organization process focus
- Organization process definition
- Training program
- Integrated software management
- Software product engineering
- Intergroup coordination
- Peer review

Level 2—Repeatable

- Requirements management
- Software project planning
- Software project tracking and control
- Software subcontract management
- Software quality assurance
- Software configuration management

Level 1—Ad hoc

Increasing Levels of Maturity

Process Characteristics

- Processes are continually and systematically improved.
- Common sources of problems are understood and eliminated.

- Processes are quantitatively understood.
- Focus is on minimizing process variability via statistical process control techniques.

- Processes are used in common across the organization.
- Focus is on teamwork and tailoring the process to work.
- Metrics are collected and used to improve performance.
- Groups work together in integrated product teams.
- Problems are anticipated and their impacts are minimized.

- Documented and stable set of processes is used at the project level.
- Focus is on establishing project management infrastructure.

Figure 4.1: *Characteristics and Key Process Areas of Maturity Levels*

level of the framework are called key process areas (KPA). The five levels are illustrated along with their KPAs in Figure 4.1. Although the software framework is being incorporated into the new CMM integration (CMMI), this example represents an interesting case study because it shows how just a little productivity data can be used to justify the large investments in infrastructure needed to pull it off. I plan to replace this case with one that emphasizes the CMMI when a relevant example becomes available.

During the past decade, many organizations have provided reports documenting their use of the SW-CMM to structure the processes that software organizations use to generate their products. A process group conference sponsored by the SEI is held every year, and monthly Software Process Improvement Network (SPIN) meetings are held throughout the world. In addition, the number of organizations embarking on process improvement efforts seems to increase every year. Unfortunately, most of the experience reports I've read from these organizations, while informative and valuable, have been qualitative in nature. They discuss the experience and benefits that accrue due to the use of the CMM in soft rather than hard terms.

In the early days of process improvement, most of the organizations that adopted the maturity framework were aerospace/military. However, that tendency has changed in recent years; by far, most new organizations are commercial. The current demographics taken from 1,166 organizations who have conducted 1,512 assessments on 6,168 projects are illustrated in Figures 4.2 and 4.3 [SEI, 2000].

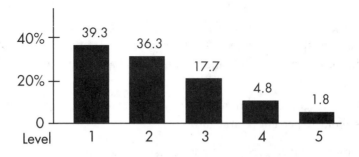

Figure 4.2: *Organizational Ratings by Maturity Level*

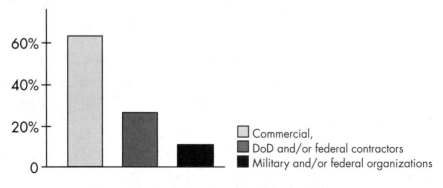

Figure 4.3: *Organizational Ratings by Industry*

The following compilation of hard data on benefits summarizes the facts that I have been able to find in the open literature relative to process improvement:

■ On average, it takes between 18 and 30 months to move from one maturity level to another. The median times to shift toward higher maturity are as follows [SEI, 2000]:
  – From Level 1 to Level 2: 25 months
  – From Level 2 to Level 3: 23 months
  – From Level 3 to Level 4: 36 months

■ The average investment to move up one such level in maturity rating is hefty, in the millions [Haley, 1995]. These costs often fund operation of a process group whose job is to write and deploy the process that fits in the CMM framework [Harp, 2001].

■ The gains attributable to early error detection and correction can be substantial, assuming that it is 20 times cheaper to fix an error found during the requirements and design phase than during test and integration [Harp, 2001].

■ The average increase in productivity attributable to process improvement is about 10 percent [Harp, 2001].

The most detailed study of benefits associated with the CMM that I have seen is in the Ph.D. thesis of Dr. Brad Clark for the University of Southern California. Using a 161 project database, he concluded that an increase in one process maturity level can reduce development effort by between 4 to 11 percent [Clark, 2000].

COST AVOIDANCE VERSUS COST REDUCTION

Many people equate productivity improvement with either cost reduction or cost avoidance. This is not always the case: in many situations, increasing productivity results in increased cost. Take the case of teams producing software to the wrong requirements. While they may be very productive, rework and false starts due to requirements evolution and volatility could force them to throw away much of what they produced. Taking one step backward to get their requirements right might be a better alternative.

As another example, consider the productivity of people who fail to devote effort early in the development to defect removal. Their productivity would seem high until the poor quality caught up with them either during testing or after the product was released. Because improvements in one dimension don't always lead to improvements in the other, I suggest separating cost and productivity when generating an improvement justification. I also suggest not including profit in your numbers when justifying an improvement using a cost avoidance. There are situations where you can take a loss on a job and still make a profit. You might, for example, simply price your product at less than its cost to capture market share (e.g., as a loss leader). Your market entry strategy would be to keep the purchase price low and make your money on maintenance or license renewals. Many software firms use this strategy to reap large profits. They sell their products cheaply and make their money on annual releases or updates.

There may be other sound justifications for taking a loss on a job. For example, the economics of the situation may show that doing the job reduces overhead and thereby results in increased profit. For example, let's say that your software department is working at 80 percent capacity (i.e., charging 80 percent of their work to projects). A job comes in that you can take for a loss that will allow you to charge the remaining 20 percent of the workforce to a project. This job could then result in a profit because it would take people off overhead and put them to work for a client. It could also help make the firm more competitive because reductions in overhead could reduce the price a client would pay for other goods and services.

This discussion suggests that things aren't always what they seem when looking at profits. But costs are costs. They have to be accounted for somehow in your ledgers. If they aren't, the auditors will be upset.

The most important thing to know when developing improvement justifications is the money system. As I stated in Chapters 2 and 3, knowing it enables you to know when surplus money will become available. In addition to being creative with how you allocate these budgets, you need to understand how your proposal affects them. Let me illustrate this point using the training example I introduced in Chapter 2. Unfortunately, the budget surplus that was found is no longer available. It was used to bail a project out of trouble. You examine other budgets and find a line item called university relationships funded at $250,000 per year. Its aim is to improve recruiting of new college graduates via grants to foster improved relationships with local colleges and universities. Further investigation indicates that half of this year's allocation has not been spent. Proposing to take $25,000 to fund your shortfall seems logical. However, when queried, your champion warns you against pursuing such use. He says that the president of the company has earmarked the money for his alma mater. You would probably ruin your career if you tried to grab it. But you have a brainstorm. Why not fund the university to provide the training you need with this money? The school would get the money, and you would get your training. Of course, you would have to check to make sure that the university could deliver the needed training. But, it's an opportunity that you can seize.

When justifying improvements, cost avoidance is preferable to cost reduction. That's because reductions occur now, while avoidance takes place in the future. Cost avoidance works best when you are in a growth mode because you can offset costs using increased demand or sales. For example, you could justify your training proposal based on decreased hiring instead of reduced turnover. Both are reasonable justifications. Both approaches look to the future. Both request additional funds without jeopardizing current budgets and staff retention.

I believe you need to focus your attention on controlling the cost drivers that are under your control. For example, you can control the experience of the personnel you assign to a project. However, you can't control the project's requirements because others define their content. While you can influence and manage the requirements, content is outside your control. This principle of controlling the controllables is important because it focuses your attention on things you can do to make things happen without someone else approving them. Management has a feel for the numbers. Their perceptions are often based on hearsay and folklore, not hard data. However, you need to respect their convictions to stay out of trouble.

I remember trying to convince executives at a semiconductor firm to capitalize their software development operation by increasing the per-seat investment in software engineering tools and equipment. My pitch was going fine

Table 4.2: *Cost Avoidance Guidelines*

What to Do	What Not to Do
■ Whenever possible, use cost avoidance, not cost reductions, to justify your improvement. ■ Separate cost considerations and productivity considerations. ■ Know your money system, including when budget surpluses become available and how to tap them. ■ Know how your current costs are normally allocated to different cost centers. Understand the sensitivity of your cost justifications to different cost drivers. ■ Know what costs you can control and who controls the others. ■ Offset costs against growth trends to get your proposals funded. ■ Package your numbers using the guidance provided in Chapters 1, 2, and 3.	■ Don't assume that your numbers will not be scrutinized. ■ Don't suppose that everyone knows what your current costs are and how they are allocated to different cost centers. ■ Don't confuse management by putting cost and profit considerations in the same proposal. ■ Don't pursue improvements that are outside your immediate span of control. ■ Don't mix cost accounts when justifying your improvement proposal. Keep labor separate from other costs; never mix project and capital budgets. ■ Don't assume that management will take your numbers at face value (i.e., respond to what they perceive the numbers should be even if they are wrong).

until I showed the dollar cost per seat for hardware versus software engineer. Management wouldn't believe the disparity. Their perception was that hardware and software capitalization costs were equivalent. Of course, they weren't. But I had to pull out my backup charts that showed the detailed cost breakouts per engineer before I could get past that point in the presentation.

Table 4.2 provides guidelines of what to do and what not to do when using cost avoidance as the basis of your justification for your idea or improvements. They assume that your numbers are sound and that those who review them will not find any mathematical errors.

SOFTWARE CAPITALIZATION APPROACHES

In Chapter 6, I present a case study that justifies capitalizing software using cost avoidance as the basis. Capitalization of software involves spending money to save money. To get the most from your people, like the Chinese emperor, you would provide them with a well-equipped and modern software engineering environment:

- *Equipment*   Servers, workstations, printers, scanners, test gear, and access to copiers
- *Facilities*   Personal workspace, meeting rooms, training rooms, and labs
- *Networks*   Local and wide area networks connecting equipment and facilities and tying them to the Internet to allow teams of geographically dispersed engineers to collaborate and build software products
- *Software tools*   An integrated collection of software programs that automate selected "best practices" and that make work products available from some repository under some form of access control to all the team members working on the project
- *Components*   Libraries of building blocks and COTS packages used to build applications
- *Communications gear*   Routers, switches, telephones (wireless, portables, and so on), fax machines, and specialized software that enable engineers to send/receive voice, data, video, and multimedia information to each other across networks

To develop such an environment, you must take into account the differences between yesterday's and today's corporations as highlighted in Table 4.3. I remember how fascinated we in America were when the Japanese built the first software factories as strategic resources for developing software [Cusomano, 1987]. They recognized well before we did that software should be capitalized. Capitalization in this sense means that senior management recognizes that a large part of their capital budget must be used to acquire a modern environment for building software. Without it, they cannot generate products for today's marketplace.

Software development in the twenty-first-century view of the corporation summarized in Table 4.3 will have a profound effect on software environment design. This distributed view of development assumes that the environment will include equipment and facilities that link geographically dispersed workforces, provide Web-based tools, support collaboration, address mobile code development, support distributed testing via agents, handle version control and documentation automatically, and provide support for prototyping and experimentation.

It is interesting to look at what it costs to acquire this kind of environment. Information displayed in Table 4.4 sheds some light on what the numbers,

Table 4.3: *Contrasting Views of the Corporation*

Characteristic	Twentieth Century	Twenty-first Century
Goals	Grow the business nationally	Grow the business internationally
Organization	Hierarchical	Collaborative
Markets	National	The World
Structure	Self-reliance	Global partnerships
Emphasis	Physical plant	Corporate infrastructure
Source of strength	People	Process and team
Strategy	Maximize efficiency	Be agile and quick to market
Tactics	High productivity and low cost	E-everything
Competition	Corporate teams	National groupings
Products	Product families	Product lines
Technology	Manufacturing-oriented	Consumer-oriented
Workforce	Domestic	International
Expectations	Security	Mobility
Major issues	– Capital costs (for growth) – Developing core competency – Motivating staff	– Conversion costs (to e-economy) – Maintaining core competency – Retaining staff
Marketplace discriminators	– Lowest possible cost – Highest possible quality	– Best value for the money – Best-of-breed in quality

Table 4.4: *Capitalization Costs for Common IT Jobs*

Job Category	Cost/Seat
Computer technician	$12,000
Digital designer	$35,000
Manager	$11,000
Secretary	$9,000
Software engineer	$24,000
System engineer	$20,000

expressed in dollars/seat capitalization cost, should be for representative information technology jobs. Software engineering needs seem quite modest compared to digital designers'. The requirement for laboratory space and expensive computer-aided design (CAD) tools increase the capital costs for digital designers. Managers and secretaries have very basic needs. Thus, their capitalization costs are relatively low.

DEPRECIATION CONCEPTS

It is important to note that capitalized items held for more than a year are normally depreciated. Depreciation is a system of accounting that lets organizations distribute the costs of a tangible asset, less its salvage value (if any), over its estimated useful life. From a tax point of view, depreciation lets the firm write off part of the cost of an asset for obsolescence, exhaustion, and wear and tear so that it can be replaced without undue tax consequences. Normally, the value or basis of the asset is its cost. The useful life of the asset is its expected service time. If the asset is held for more than one year, it is treated as a capital expenditure. The estimated salvage value is the amount that is expected to be realized when the asset is retired from service.

There are several commonly accepted depreciation methods. The method most often used is called straight-line depreciation. Under the straight-line method, the salvage value is first subtracted from the original cost. Then the result is divided by the useful life to compute the annual depreciation charge. For example, you would be able to write off $2,000 a year against depreciation if you capitalized a $10,000 server whose useful life is five years, assuming that there is no salvage value on retirement. Depreciation lets you write off your investment over several years. On the other hand, you can expense $20,000 in any single year with the United States if this is more beneficial.

From a tax point of view, it is to your benefit to depreciate the asset as quickly as possible. Methods such as the declining balance and sum of the years digits support taking larger amounts of depreciation earlier than the straight-line method. To prevent too much from being depreciated too quickly, the Internal Revenue Service (IRS) has established rigid accounting guidelines for computer equipment and software. The IRS dictates what depreciation method can be used and what the useful life is. For example, computers are normally depreciated over a period of five years using the straight-line method under the assumption of no salvage value. Printers are written off over a period of three years. To comply with current tax laws, you should consult your financial people or your accountant to get help with the calculations and the most current information on the tax codes.

Trade studies are often required when making capital decisions. Selection of equipment and software involves alternatives, and management will want you to justify your selections. They will also want to know the criteria you used for your analysis. Besides doing a complete and technically competent evaluation, they will want to make sure that you were fair and impartial in your judgments. One of the more critical trade studies (a focus in Chapter 6) is called make/buy analysis. Make/buy analysis answers questions such as these: Does your staff develop the product or do you employ a commercial product? Do you perform the function in house or do you hire an outside contractor to do the job?

QUICK-TO-MARKET STRATEGIES

Most commercial firms I have worked with are more interested in shortening their time to market than in cutting costs or increasing productivity. They want to rapidly create and build their business as new markets open and become viable. They want to bring their products to market ahead of their competitors. Time means money in such situations. But the time and effort required to generate the product in staff-months of labor aren't always interchangeable. As Fred Brooks said so aptly in his classic *The Mythical Man-Month,* "adding manpower to a late project often makes it later," and "just because a woman can have a baby in nine months doesn't mean nine women working together can have a baby in one month" [Brooks, 1995]. There are some underlying laws of nature that money can't change.

To speed the process, many organizations use rapid application development (RAD) and other lightweight methods like extreme programming [Beck, 1999]. They break the job into its parts and schedule the work so that it can be done iteratively, in parallel, or in spurts. They then streamline the process and improve efficiency by doing things such as eliminating tasks, reducing the time per task, reducing backtracking, and increasing the effective workweek. In pursuit of these strategies, they try to take advantage of the approaches that appear in the RAD opportunity tree illustrated in Figure 4.4 [Boehm, 2000].

Justifying ideas or improvements using quick-to-market strategies is difficult because comparative time-line benchmarks don't exist in most industries. How can you demonstrate increased speed and agility if you don't know how

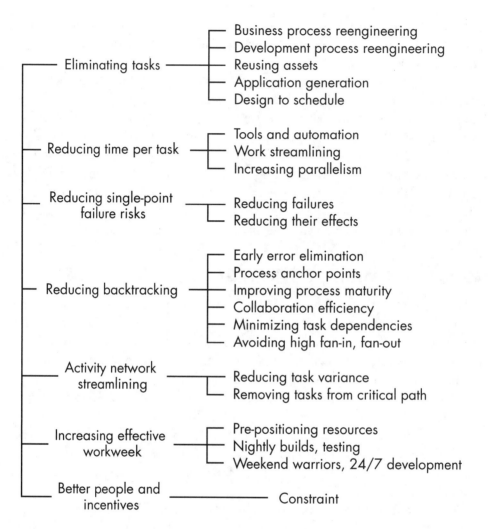

Figure 4.4: *RAD Opportunity Tree*

Source: Adapted from Boehm/Abts/Brown/Chulani/Clark/Horowitz/Madachy/Reifer/Steece, *Software Cost Estimation with COCOMO II*, © 2000. Reprinted by permission of Pearson Education, Inc., Upper Saddle River, NJ.

long it should take your staff to bring a product to market? You might try time lines for similar projects, but there may have been a lot of noise in the past performance data. For example, a project may have taken a year to bring a product to market. The forcing function for this schedule was an industry show that represented a major market window. If you didn't make this show, you missed your product launch opportunity because this is the only time all your customers gather in one place to view new product offerings (e.g., a consumer electronics show). In the rush to make the show, many compromises were made. As a result, the product was neither fully functional nor of the quality expected. While it looked good, performance was also slower than expected. Consequently, using such a project as a benchmark for other projects would be a major mistake.

I recommend using calibrated cost models to generate benchmarks for comparison. Calibrated cost models can generate duration estimates that are within 20 percent of your actual experience 80 percent of the time when they are properly calibrated [Boehm, 2000]. Of course, calibration is not an easy task in most organizations. However, the credibility it adds is worth the effort.

Guidelines of what to do and what not to do when using time to market as the basis of justification for your improvements are listed in Table 4.5. They

Table 4.5: *Quick-to-Market Guidelines*

What to Do	What Not to Do
■ As your first option, be prepared to streamline the work and plan your work tasks so they can be done in parallel.	■ Don't promise the impossible; relate your schedules to desired capabilities instead of delivery dates set in stone.
■ Determine a realistic schedule before you negotiate your time line for delivery.	■ Don't assume that the past is predictive of the future; there are often biases in the data that make it unreliable in establishing benchmarks.
■ Increase management's flexibility by keeping profit-and-loss responsibility as low as possible in your organization.	■ Don't schedule a death march project [Yourdon, 1997]; people burn out and leave when confronted with unreasonable expectations and continuous adversity.
■ Avoid backtracking and false starts; these two culprits are a major cause of schedule delays.	
■ Use calibrated software cost models to generate comparison benchmarks.	■ Don't streamline tasks on the critical path without fully analyzing the impacts.
■ Recognize the biases associated with your past performance data.	■ Don't forget to seek major improvements via simple changes.
■ Minimize the bureaucracy to maximize the organizational efficiency.	■ Don't rely only on efficiencies to achieve desired improvements; corporate culture and personal preferences need to be taken into account as well.
■ Manage the risks associated with your actions to increase the probability of success.	

assume that you are pursuing one of the strategies listed in the RAD Opportunity Tree in Figure 4.4. For example, you could speed things up by doing noncritical path tasks in parallel. Although this will increase your risk, you may be willing to tolerate it because it makes shorter schedules achievable. As a preventive measure, you decide to put proven risk management techniques to work on the project to improve your chances for success [Reifer, 1997a]. These techniques focus your attention on tracking and controlling the many variables that can adversely affect schedule performance (vacation schedules, task startup delays, and so on).

ARCHITECTING PRODUCTS USING TIME TO MARKET AS JUSTIFICATION

In Chapter 7, I present a case study that justifies the move to product lines, architectures, and systematic software reuse using shortened time to market. Many firms are adopting architecture-centric strategies because, when adequately populated with components, they reduce the amount of work that is required to get a product out the door. The technology, best processes, and experience associated with software reuse are proven, available, and well documented in the open literature (see [McClure, 1997; Reifer, 1997]). As Figure 4.4 shows, architecture-based software reuse allows you to cut time to market by eliminating tasks and making the job easier.

Moving to product line management and architectural concepts is an extremely difficult task to accomplish in project-based organizations. As I stated in Chapter 1, the primary reason for these difficulties is that it is hard to share assets across projects because of the way work is budgeted and people are rewarded. In project-based organizations, software engineers and mangers are rewarded for their contributions to the project, not a product line. "Are the benefits worth the effort?" you are probably asking. Most experience reports on the topic say, "yes" [Lim, 1998]. The organizations involved have reported substantial savings in time and effort with architecture-based software reuse when these barriers have been overcome [Jacobson, 1997]. In addition, software defect rates have been reduced by a factor of up to 10 compared to industrywide benchmarks when reuse technology has been brought into use [Reifer, 1997b].

To take full advantage of product line and architectural concepts, you must make changes in your management infrastructure. Figure 4.5 summarizes the

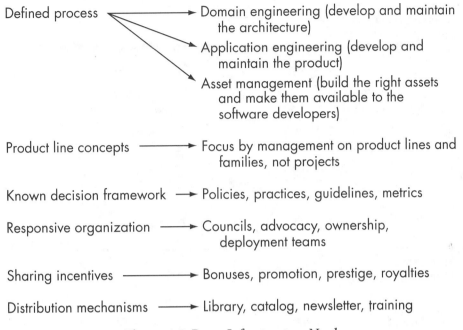

Defined process → Domain engineering (develop and maintain the architecture)

Application engineering (develop and maintain the product)

Asset management (build the right assets and make them available to the software developers)

Product line concepts → Focus by management on product lines and families, not projects

Known decision framework → Policies, practices, guidelines, metrics

Responsive organization → Councils, advocacy, ownership, deployment teams

Sharing incentives → Bonuses, promotion, prestige, royalties

Distribution mechanisms → Library, catalog, newsletter, training

Figure 4.5: *Reuse Infrastructure Needs*

changes needed to put reuse concepts to work. The resulting process (Figure 4.6 [Reifer,1997b]) is what people in the software reuse business call the "dual life cycle paradigm." Based on this paradigm, the domain engineering process (it includes the activities of domain analysis and implementation) develops/evolves the architecture to serve as a framework for product line and family development. The applications engineering process is pursued in parallel to take advantage of the architecture and develop products that take full advantage of the repository of reusable software assets built to support it. Assets in this sense are any product of the software development life cycle that can be potentially reused (architectures, designs, code, tests, and so on). They include both new and COTS components.

The asset management process is established to manage the assets that are put into the repository so that they can be made available to potential users in an acceptable form. The paradigm is called dual life cycle because the architecture is refined in parallel as applications are developed.

The software reuse library is the mechanism that is used to manage the assets and handle their distribution. The beauty of this approach is that specialists can perform architecture activities without adversely affecting the applications

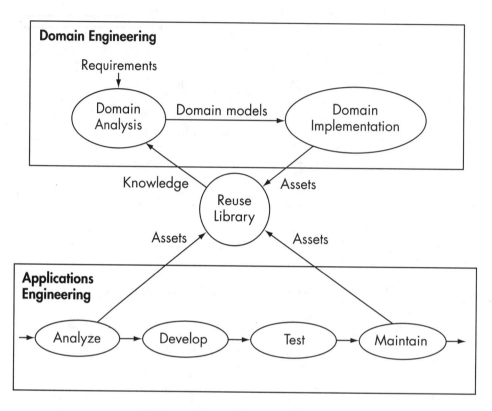

Figure 4.6: *Dual Life Cycle Paradigm*

Source: Adapted from Reifer, D. J., *Practical Software Reuse.* Copyright © 1997. Reprinted by permission of John Wiley & Sons, Inc.

engineering process. In addition, each process can select the development approach it believes is best for the situation. For example, architecture could be developed iteratively as applications are developed using any modern approach.

This paradigm puts a premium on architecture development. For the purposes of our discussion, architecture is defined as a structure describing the components, their interrelationships, and the principles and guidelines governing their design and evolution over time [Bass, 1998].

The following rules of thumb are extracted from my own and others' experience [Poulin, 1997]. They should help you estimate the effort and duration of a reuse program structured using an architectural basis and the dual life cycle paradigm.

- *20/80 rule*   Twenty percent of your assets will be responsible for 80 percent of the reuse; 20 percent of your users will be responsible for 80 percent of the results.

- *Design for reuse rule*   The additional cost to develop an asset for reuse will range from 35 to 50 percent of nominal costs.

- *Design with reuse rule*   The cost with reuse averages between 20 to 25 percent of nominal costs when the component was designed with reuse in mind.

- *Three strikes you're out rule*   The breakeven point for developing an asset to be reusable is three instances of use. In other words, don't develop an asset to be reusable unless three or more projects within the product line or family agree to use it within a specified time period.

- *Ten times the norm in quality rule*   Because of their extensive use, expect reusable assets to exhibit ten times the quality when compared to the norm.

- *Throwaway code rule*   Expect less than 10 percent of the code that is advertised as throwaway code to be thrown away.

- *Domain engineering rule of six*   It takes six experienced engineers an average six months to do a full domain analysis and a year to develop a reference architecture.

I share these rules of thumb with you because I use some of them in the case study in Chapter 7. If you are interested in additional references on product line management and architecture concepts, Appendix A provides annotated descriptions of several books on this topic that I feel are worth reading.

MAKE-VERSUS-BUY ANALYSIS

One of the key considerations covered in the case study in Chapter 7 is whether to make or buy the software. To make the software, you would deploy the resources (skilled people, equipment, facilities, tools, infrastructure, and so on) that are available in house to get the job done. If these resources weren't available, you might consider contracting for or outsourcing the work to qualified sources. As an option, you could obtain needed resources by hiring more permanent or part-time staff or by making selected acquisitions of firms with needed capabilities. In either case, you have to make sure that your future workload could sustain additional employees because you don't want to hire and fire them at the whim of fluctuations in the workload.

Table 4.6: *Make versus Buy: Difference in Mind-sets*

In-house Software	COTS Software
Developed to satisfy requirements.	Developed to satisfy market need or niche.
Engineered for development.	Engineered for evolution.
Internal forces drive content.	Market drives content.
Integration is a natural part of the overall development process.	Integration is often difficult; addressed via glue code and wrappers.
Maintenance is where money is made.	Maintenance is a nightmare for customer (new versions must be considered and evaluated).
Primary asset is the component design.	Primary asset is the product architecture.

The buy option should also consider the use of commercial off-the-shelf software. COTS software with most of the desired functionality is provided by some third party. It has the advantage that you don't have to maintain the software once it is deployed; the firm providing the software takes on this responsibility. While seemingly attractive, use of COTS software is risky because others are in control of its evolution. To take full advantage of COTS, you need to understand that it was developed with different goals in mind. See Table 4.6 for a summary of the differences between COTS and software developed in house.

To evaluate the financial tradeoffs involved in using COTS, you must consider the differences given in the table as you evaluate the alternatives. For example, many firms contrast the COTS licensing costs directly with their software development effort. For the comparison to be fair, the cost tradeoffs should consider the glue code or wrapper development effort. The comparisons also need to take operations and maintenance costs into account. For custom software, sustaining costs can be substantial, especially if the software is released with lots of bugs. In the case of COTS, maintenance involves license renewals and glue code repair.

MOVING TO A WEB-BASED ECONOMY

In Chapter 8, I present a case study that puts a value on an Internet startup firm you are considering acquiring. This kind of investment decision is difficult to make because you have to assess the worth of the firm's intellectual property.

Dealing with startups is extremely complicated, especially when you must deal with legal challenges inherent in a networked economy, determine the value of an Internet startup, and put a value on knowledge as capital.

We all know and use the Internet and the World Wide Web (WWW). Put in its most basic form, the Internet is a collection of interconnected networks of computers that communicate throughout the world via packet-switching proto-cols. The Web uses the Internet to provide its users with links to more than 100,000 networks, consisting of over 10 million host computers located in over 100 nations. The Web and the Internet have revolutionized business and created a new economy, new tools, and new rules. There are lots of money, people, and businesses on the Web. To thrive in the e-commerce world, organizations are changing their management infrastructures and adjusting the way they do busi-ness. They are learning to manage the flow of information and employ knowl-edge as capital as they throw away their often outdated business practices. They are being taught that they must be able to react quickly, innovate ceaselessly, pur-sue alliances, and handle change continually.

Capital Is Abundant

People are moving to e-business because that's where the markets are, and fortunes are being made and lost. Even though the failure rates for Web startup firms is high, more initial public offerings (IPOs) seem to be coming to market every day. Many liken today's e-business and e-commerce world to the days of the Gold Rush. Few prospectors actually got rich quick by striking pay dirt. Most of those who made fortunes did so by providing the prospectors with the tools, mules, and supplies they needed to start up. I believe that the people who provision firms making a transition with tools, training, and support will prosper as business on the Web expands.

As shown in Figure 4.7, the venture capital used to fuel new developments along these lines is still plentiful according to the U.S. Department of Commerce [DoC, 2000]. The challenge is bringing the idea to market first.

Concerns Associated with Electronic Commerce

The Internet also provides a conduit for many types of commercial and financial transactions. Consumers are utilizing on-line banking, brokerage, real estate, shopping, and countless other services. Business-to-business (B-to-B) sites have emerged whose primary function is to promote on-line bartering with suppliers

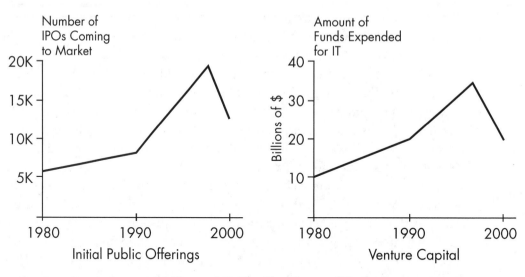

Figure 4.7: *The Abundance of Capital*

and create virtual warehouses. Contracts for goods and services are made on line without face-to-face meetings of participants. Most important, e-commerce is changing the manner in which firms use the Web. For example, General Electric and many other large organizations are cutting costs and improving customer satisfaction via the Web. They are using its capabilities to coordinate purchases, lever buying power, and tap on-line markets for goods and services.

In the case study in Chapter 8, a large firm decides to acquire a smaller Internet startup to secure e-business and e-commerce skills. The challenge the larger firm faces is deciding how much to pay for the smaller firm, whose only assets are people and intellectual capital. The case develops a unique framework for making such a determination. It builds on concepts taken from the knowledge management field to place a value on the intellectual capital of the Internet startup [Roberts, 2001].

Determining Value of Startups

In determining the value of startups, you must remember that knowledge by itself has no value. Knowledge by its very nature takes on value only when people use it to solve a problem. Therefore, as shown in Figure 4.8, for an organization to have value, its people, markets, and intellectual property must provide recognized expertise in a specialized domain. In other words, the startup must have the

Figure 4.8: *Value Framework*

human skills, intuition and wisdom to bring the right products (and services) to market before the competition.

How would you put a value on an Internet startup whose only assets were people, ideas, and venture funding? To assess the startup's investment potential, you would start by evaluating the factors that influence its ability to make a profit (many of these factors are listed in the business plan outline in Chapter 2). As you will see in Chapter 8, we use such traditional models to determine the return on investment and breakeven point associated with a startup. Many Internet startups don't make profits for years, but their principals can get rich if they catch the imagination of the investing public during their initial stock offering.

The more challenging exercise is determining a value for the firm based on the notions that software is knowledge and knowledge is capital. For the purpose of our discussion, "knowledge capital" refers to the ideas that facilitate production of goods and services. To put a cap on their investment, potential backers want to know how much the "knowledge capital" the firm owns is worth. Making the appraisal is especially difficult because bright people can generate great products that don't sell. This forces us to separate the ability to innovate from the facility to sell.

Although I don't get into appraising the worth of "knowledge capital" in Chapter 8, I share with you a framework I have developed for this purpose. This structure is displayed in Figure 4.9 and amplified briefly here:

- Recognition that people are the primary resource, not tools, equipment, and machinery
- Emphasis on investing in getting smarter, not stronger

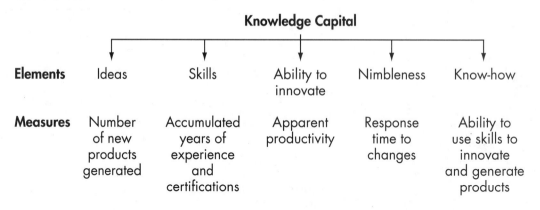

Figure 4.9: *Framework for Assessing Knowledge Capital*

- Focus on developing both the learning and the know-how needed to use available skills
- Realization that responding to changing markets is as important as being innovative
- Putting a premium on generating new products, not on developing new ideas

While all the factors in this framework are quantitative, most are hard to measure. In response, I have developed a more qualitative evaluation scheme that I use in Chapter 8.

If you are interested in a good book on this topic, read the delightful text by Sveiby and Lloyd about adding value by valuing creativity [Sveiby, 1987]. Most of the other books I have read on the topic of innovation discuss process, not measurement, because even though it is easy to measure the effect of innovation after the fact, it is hard to establish a value for it when it appears before your eyes. That's the purpose of the framework illustrated in Figure 4.9.

SUMMARY

This chapter serves as an introduction to the case studies that follow in Chapters 5 through 8. It summarizes the case studies and highlights how materials covered in the earlier chapters of the book will be used to build a business case. Besides providing necessary background information, the chapter prepares you to delve in the world of numbers.

Observations

The key point of this chapter is that it is almost impossible to separate software from organizational improvement activities. Factors that influence improvement in one domain impact the other. That's because few organizations generate software in a vacuum. Their goal is to use software to make a profit. For example, software in cellular phones provides functions and features that provide marketplace discrimination. As another example, packaged software sells well when the organizations buying it believe they are getting good value for their money and customer support will be above average. In response, software engineers need to understand how to relate what they are trying to accomplish to the broader organizational improvement goals. From my experience, I believe they will be better able to acquire senior management support when they are armed for the battle of the budget with sound business as well as technical cases. The case studies in Chapters 5 through 8 provide you with examples of how to accomplish this feat.

KEY POINTS

- ✔ Like the Chinese emperor, you can improve productivity by taking advantage of the dual nature of software productivity.
- ✔ Whenever making cost or productivity comparisons, develop industry benchmarks to serve as measurement yardsticks.
- ✔ Process improvement can cut costs by an estimated 11 to 15 percent when an organization jumps a level in the Software Engineering Institute's capability maturity model.
- ✔ Cost avoidance is preferred to cost reduction because it deals with future expenditures.
- ✔ Capitalizing software provides good people with the equipment, facilities, and tools they need to get the job done efficiently.
- ✔ Reductions in time-to-market strategies can be accomplished by streamlining the work, reducing backtracking, and performing tasks in parallel.
- ✔ Migration to the use of product line, architecture, and systematic reuse concepts requires major investments and infrastructure changes to facilitate sharing.

✔ The dual life cycle paradigm focuses on managing architecture and development tasks as they are conducted in parallel.

✔ Moving to a Web-based economy presents the community with many challenges.

✔ Determining the value of Internet startups requires us to develop new models and metrics.

References

[Baruch, 1957] Baruch, Bernard M. *Baruch: My Own Story.* Holt, 1957.

[Bass, 1998] Bass, Len, Paul Clements, and Rick Kazman. *Software Architecture in Practice.* Addison-Wesley, 1998.

[Beck, 1999] Beck, Kent. *Extreme Programming Explained.* Addison-Wesley, 1999.

[Boehm, 2000] Boehm, Barry W., Chris Abts, A. Winsor Brown, Sunita Chulani, Bradford K. Clark, Ellis Horowitz, Ray Madachy, Donald Reifer, and Bert Steece. *Software Cost Estimation with COCOMO II.* Prentice Hall, 2000.

[Boehm, 1999] Boehm, Barry W. "The Future of Software Processes, with Implications for Cost and Schedule Estimation," Proceedings 14th COCOMO Forum, University of Southern California, October 26, 1999.

[Brooks, 1995] Brooks, Frederick, Jr. *The Mythical Man-Month.* Addison-Wesley, 1995.

[Clark, 2000] Clark, Bradford K. "Quantifying the Effects of Process Improvement on Effort," *Software* (IEEE Computer Society), November/December 2000, pp. 65–70.

[Cusumano, 1991] Cusumano, Michael A. *Japanese Software Factories: A Challenge to U.S. Management.* Oxford University Press, 1991.

[DoC, 2000] U.S. Department of Commerce, *Industry Growth Projections,* 2000.

[Haley, 1995] Haley, T., B. Ireland, E. Wojtaszek, D. Nash, and R. Dion. *Raytheon Electronic System Experience in Software Process Improvement,* Software Engineering Institute Report CMU/SEI-95-TR-017, 1995.

[Harp, 2001] Harp, Elaine, Eva Brandt, Jim Holden, Don Reifer, and C. Doug Walters. "The Definitive Paper: Quantifying the Benefits of Process Improvement," submitted for publication.

[Jacobson, 1997] Jacobson, Ivar, Martin Griss, and Patrik Jonsson. *Software Reuse: Architecture, Process and Organization for Business Success.* ACM Press, 1997.

[Lim, 1998] Lim, Wayne C. *Managing Software Reuse.* Prentice Hall, 1998.

[McClure, 1997] McClure, Carma. *Software Reuse Techniques.* Prentice Hall, 1997.

[Paulk, 1995] Paulk, Mark C., Charles V. Weber, Bill Curtis, and Mary B. Chrissis. *The Capability Maturity Model.* Addison-Wesley, 1995.

[Poulin, 1997] Poulin, Jeffrey S. *Measuring Software Reuse.* Addison-Wesley, 1997.

[Reifer, 1997a] Reifer, Donald J. *Tutorial Software Management.* IEEE Computer Society, 1997.

[Reifer, 1997b] Reifer, Donald J. *Practical Software Reuse.* John Wiley & Sons, 1997.

[Roberts, 2001] Roberts, Bill. "The Value Equation." *Knowledge Management,* January 2001, pp. 31–34.

[SEI, 2000] Software Engineering Institute. *Process Maturity Profile of the Software Community 1999 Year End Update,* March 2000.

[Sveiby, 1987] Sveiby, Karl Erik, and Tom Lloyd. *Managing Know-how.* Bloomsbury, 1987.

[Yourdon, 1997] Yourdon, Edward. *Death March.* Prentice Hall, 1997.

Part II

The Case Studies

My goal in the next four chapters is to illustrate how we put the fundamental concepts summarized in Chapters 1 through 4 into practice using case studies. Teaching by example has proven to be an effective learning approach. It helps amplify the interplay between what is theoretical and practical within the context of an actual business setting.

5

Playing the Game of
Dungeons and Dragons
Process Improvement Case Study

*Some would argue that processes underlie all information systems.
After all, technology links and supports all organizational activities
in this information age. Directions and game plans for dealing with this
area make implementation of information systems easier for managers.*
—Alistar Davidson et al. [1997]

SETTING THE STAGE

The first case study is built on a real one that involves a company that is seeking to improve productivity via an aggressive process improvement program. I have been working with firms for over a decade. As the case unfolds, I use this firm to illustrate how to build similar business cases from situations that occur. The reason I selected the chapter title "Playing the Game of *Dungeons and Dragons*" is to show how unexpected events may influence how you justify your process improvement initiatives. My goal is help you to put the fundamental concepts that we covered in the first four chapters into practice using the case study, the game.

You are probably asking by now, "What's the object of the game, who are the players, and what are the rules?" Of course, the goal is to win the game. Winning requires you to formulate a game plan and get management to fund the investments required to pull it off. The business case provides management with the motivation they need to support you. The players include senior management, program management, the quality assurance group, the process group, and the performer organizations. These groups are organized via matrix management concepts as illustrated in Figure 5.1 [Daly, 1997]. Senior management champions the process cause and provides encouragement and support for the effort. Program management focuses on delivering acceptable products on schedule and budget. Performer organizations provide the technical talent to get the work done. The process group develops the organizational processes and helps projects tailor them for their use. Finally, quality assurance audits to ensure that projects use the approved processes. More details on these organizational roles and responsibilities are provided in Table 5.1. In my experience, these roles are standard across industries.

The organization's history of process improvement is displayed in Figure 5.2. As the figure illustrates, it began its process improvement programs

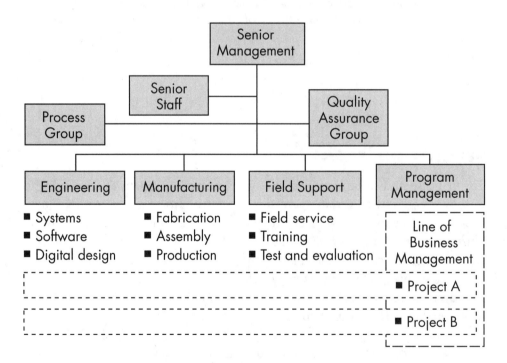

Figure 5.1: *Organizational Structure*

Table 5.1: *Organizational Roles and Responsibilities*

Group	General Role	Process Improvement Responsibilities
Senior management	Provide corporate vision and leadership. Provide oversight and direction.	Champion the overall process improvement initiative. Provide needed resources (money, talent, etc.) and support for the organizational initiative.
Program management	Manage the timely delivery of quality products that satisfy customer requirements per agreed-to budgets and schedules. Maintain customer liaison.	Sponsor process and stress its importance. Ensure that adopted process initiatives make both technical and business sense. Provide the budget needed to tailor and use the process at the program and/or project level.
Process group	Develop institutional processes and stimulate their adoption organization-wide.	Develop and roll out processes at the institutional level. Train performers in the use of the processes. Support performers as they try to use the processes. Optimize the processes and implement statistical process controls.
Quality assurance group	Ensure that performers follow approved processes.	Monitor the use of the process. If the process is not used, find out why; then recommend corrective action.
Performer organizations	Do the work needed to get the products out the door per agreed-to budgets and schedules.	Tailor the institutional process for use on their projects. Use the process to do the work. Recommend improvements based on usage experience.

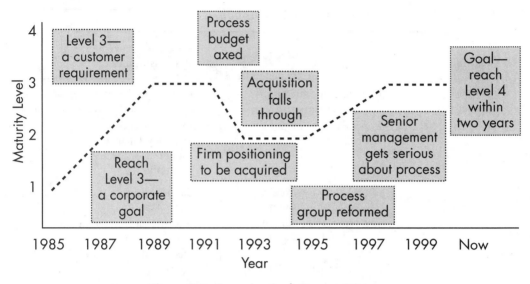

Figure 5.2: *Organization's Process History*

over a decade ago because its largest customer, the U.S. government, forced it to do so to compete on contracts. Since then, the firm has run hot and cold when it comes to process primarily due to external factors. In the mid-1990s, process took a back seat to running lean because the company was positioning itself to be purchased. The focus was on maximizing profit by minimizing overhead and capital expenses. Because money wasn't available at this time for process, the organization reverted to the way it had done business in the past. This wasn't difficult because the people who stayed on during these years were the old-timers who were familiar and comfortable with the old ways. As a result, the organization lost its momentum and regressed from CMM Level 3 to Level 2 process maturity rating.

About three years ago, things took a positive turn. Senior management loosened up the purse strings when it decided to stay in the aerospace electronics business. Managers focused on several opportunities and won several important contracts. They started acquiring firms to help infuse new talent and technology into business areas that had become stale. Most important, they recognized the importance of process and started to make an effort to recapture the improvements they had made in the past. To win several new contracts, they reformed the process group and tasked it with leading the charge to being reassessed CMM

Level 3. They took people with talent from key programs and placed them in the process group. Once a plan of attack was in place, they found the money to fund it. Senior management got serious about process improvement when customers said "good job" after independently assessing the firm at Level 3. Several of the key players in the process group were given incentive awards based on performance. Everyone seemed excited by the turn of events.

The process saga continues today unabated. While senior management remains supportive, program management is not convinced that it buys them anything. Their experience with process and other corporate initiatives has been spotty. Some have seen other corporate initiatives (e.g., total quality management [Schulmeyer, 1992]) come and go. Their reaction is either to wait and see or to stonewall the process group's efforts to enlist their support. Others recall their past experiences with process and either like it or hate it. There seems to be no middle ground. Most in the middle do not share senior management's enthusiasm for process. They say that they need to be convinced before they will spend their project funds on yet another process initiative. What being convinced means, you are not sure of. But your job is to address their concerns and convince them that spending lots of money on process is a worthy cause. Senior management supports you. They say that all you need to do is tell them what you need.

The current goal is to reach CMM Level 4 within two years. As Figure 5.2 illustrates, senior management has tasked the process group with the responsibility of leading the charge to Level 4. Senior managers are motivated again by competitive factors. Big procurements are coming up, and they believe that being at Level 4 will help their chances of winning the contracts. Their customer told them that their chief competitor is at Level 4, and they want to level the playing field.

CURRENT BUSINESS CLIMATE

Business is booming, and your people seem happy. Marketing is reporting that sales are at an all-time high this quarter. To meet the forecasts, the firm will have to double the software staff during the next year to handle all the planned upgrades and new project starts. Where the firm will get all these skilled people is a concern, and management is starting to lose sleep over the challenge. Many managers seem to be spending most of their time recruiting. As expected, the firm is also experiencing some turnover because the market for good software people, even in the face of an economic downturn, is hot.

As expected, morale is high. Management has refocused its energy to capturing market share from positioning the company to be acquired. As a result, managers have become more open to investing in process, people, and technology. However, every time they are asked for money, they respond with "I don't understand why you software guys need this." They don't seem to grasp what software people do. As a result of internal pressure, they've started to make limited strategic investments in their software competitive capabilities and capacity. Process improvement is the central theme because CMM Level 4 is believed by many to be a necessary prerequisite for winning future contracts with the government. However, every time you ask for money for process improvement, management asks for additional justification.

The software organization's four-part strategy for improvement is illustrated in Figure 5.3 [Reifer, 1997a]. As already mentioned, process improvement comes first. It is viewed as the central thrust because it provides the organizational framework for the other improvements (tool the process, train people in its tailoring and use, and so on). In parallel, the workforce is being educated and trained according to newly established career paths. The training is aimed at fanning out the process to projects. As the third thrust, open systems and architecture concepts are to be introduced into the business units. These will be the unifying concepts for developing future product lines/families. With architecture comes use of more COTS and increased software reuse. Last, a structure has been developed to enable projects to prioritize and better tap the internal research and development (IR&D) efforts. This will enable the research leads to justify continuance in next year's battle of the budget.

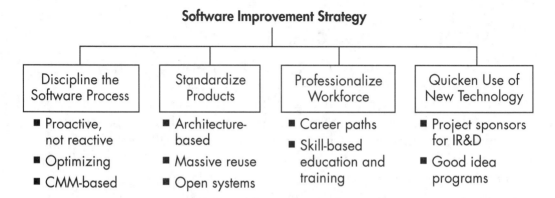

Figure 5.3: *Four-Part Improvement Strategy*

Let's complete the picture of the current business climate by looking at other factors that management believes directly contribute to software cost, productivity, quality, and staff continuity:

Overall experience   The current workforce experience averages over 20 years. The reason for this is staff attrition. During the lean years of the early 1990s, the younger engineers were frustrated as the firm downsized, and many of them left. Jobs were plentiful, and it was easy for them to find positions with other firms who were hungry for talent. Not so for the older troops. Jobs were not so easy to find for them, and they were reluctant to leave because they were vested in the profit-sharing plan.

Staff capabilities and morale   Workers are energized and enthusiastic about management's focus on process. They view positively the return to process and management's willingness to invest in them, their environment, and technology. In addition, the positions that were eliminated during the early 1990s have been reinstated, and younger and more dynamic workers are being hired. The newcomers are more open to doing things differently.

Education and training   The addition of new workers has opened up a myriad of training opportunities for the entire engineering and management workforce. In-house courses have been created to introduce non-software program managers to software. Seminars are being held in software engineering and other interesting topics. This focus on education and training has created a climate in the organization that views change more favorably.

World-class facilities and environment   Management has recently started to invest in better facilities, equipment, and tools for software workers. Managers recognize that they are undercapitalized and are trying to provide engineers with pleasant offices and powerful workstations, networks, and tools. They have justified this investment in terms of reducing turnover. By creating a conducive working environment, they hope to reduce the number of people leaving for what they perceive to be greener pastures.

Technology adoption   Internal research and development funds for software technology development have tripled this year. This turnabout resulted after a major client criticized management for not spending enough on software research. Efforts to channel software architecture, smart agent, and network security developments into the product lines were funded. The challenge is finding people to work these projects. The best people always are too busy because they are working the high-visibility, tough projects.

As part of these initiatives, your firm has tasked the process group to develop a game plan for reaching Level 4 by the end of the year. The plan will have to be sold to middle management. As already mentioned, skeptics and critics abound. While upper management is championing the effort, many in the middle are still resistant to yet another process push. They need more convincing. This situation dictates the following seven rules of engagement when the game of *Dungeons and Dragons* is played for real.

1. *Let the numbers do the talking.*   Your primary job is to figure out how to get the recalcitrant middle managers into your corner. Because their bosses support the initiative, they will talk the talk. But because of the perceived risks involved, they won't walk the walk. Your job is to get these managers to embrace joint efforts with projects aimed at reaching Level 4. You know these managers relate to numbers. They will support any believable proposal that helps them get the product out the door cheaper, quicker, and better. Your strategy for getting support must be to let the numbers do the talking for you.

2. *Don't assume that program managers understand software.*   Most of the middle managers don't come from a systems/software background. Most are old-fashioned hardware engineers who grew up during a time when software represented a problem, not a solution. Some were hired from the customer community because they understood the operational aspects of the system. Others were hired right out of college and have been with the firm for 30 to 40 years. When you talk with them, most of them tell you war stories about the good old days when there wasn't any software to worry about. Most of them need to update their knowledge of systems and software because their technical skills are outdated.

3. *Justifications must be made at a project level.*   Project management is tasked to maximize profit and keep costs to a minimum. In support of these goals, middle managers are ranked and rated on their ability to deliver quality products that satisfy agreed-on requirements on schedule and within budget. They aren't rewarded when they spend money on processes that benefit the firm at large; they receive recognition, promotions, and bonuses when they achieve project goals. To get their support and sponsorship, you must build a bulletproof business case that justifies your proposed investment of time, talent, and energy in terms of project benefits. Even though they care about their peers, they need incentives to motivate them to help others.

4. *You must address past experience, both pro and con.*   The organization has a lot of history and folklore associated with process improvement. Unfortunately, many managers view previous initiatives negatively. That's because they burned a lot of resources and generated few perceived benefits at the project level. To succeed, you must address this experience as you sell your program. Otherwise, these managers will sabotage your effort and try to steal your funding. To overcome these obstacles, you must convince these critics that your efforts will help them get their jobs done cheaper, quicker, or better. If you can't, your plan is doomed.

5. *Your plan must focus on near-term results.*   Budgets for initiatives such as process improvement are funded as overhead activities. Such budgets are developed annually. To win funding approval, you must generate near-term results. If you don't, you could lose your funding to competing projects. The budget process starts in June with proposals for both new and continuing programs. Competition for money is keen, and there is never enough money to fund everything that needs to be done. Worthy projects are screened and ranked by business area managers in September. Criteria for the final selection and funding revolve around how well you support business area objectives, projects, and new business proposals. If these managers aren't sold on reaching Level 4, you will lose out.

6. *Any software processes must be compatible with your existing management infrastructure.*   The process initiative establishes the underlying framework that you will use to pursue the remainder of your four-part software improvement strategy. To be accepted, you must make sure that the processes you come up with integrate with and into your firm's existing management infrastructure (organizational structures, decision processes, management reviews, metrics, and so on). Otherwise, the software processes you devise will be perceived as out of sync, and their usefulness will be viewed as marginal. In other words, you can't change the way middle and upper management does its job. Even if the processes it uses are flawed, changing them is outside the scope of your improvement effort.

7. *You must track and demonstrate accomplishment of goals.*   Because middle managers are goal-directed, you must crisply define your goals, justify them, track them, and celebrate their accomplishment (or note their failure). This is how you will earn respect in your organization. Although setting a goal of reaching Level 4 within two years is enough for seniors, those in the middle expect you to tell them why it is important to their bottom line. They want to know what you expect to achieve in quantitative terms. They also expect you to track and report progress and deliver what you promise. If you don't, they will probably recommend using the money allocated for this worthwhile activity elsewhere during the budget process next year.

DEVELOPING A GAME PLAN

Your process group has been devastated by turnover since you reached Level 3 two years ago. Last year, management cut the group's budget in half when it was trying to reduce overhead expenses. Then three of the five remaining engineers left to work on projects because they felt that process group assignments were parking positions. The best people in your firm seem to be put to work on projects, not overhead assignments. That's where the promotions are and what's considered fast-track. Besides you, the only people who are left in the group are two retirees who were hired as consultants to work with projects because they have credibility and two part-time courseware developers. Fortunately, you have just received permission to hire an analyst to help implement your Level 4 metrics requirements. To get the group back on track, it must be reinvented and revitalized (its mission and people's perceptions of its role must be changed). In addition, the group must be staffed with high achievers who can generate results quickly.

Besides you, the process group has four people filling the eight slots that are illustrated in the organization chart in Figure 5.4. As mentioned, two retirees are on board and acting as liaisons with projects. These two senior practitioners are held in high regard by the working troops. Your other two employees are part-timers from academia whom you brought on to develop education and training materials. The candidates for the two process developer vacancies are well-thought-of people who are between assignments. The third vacancy will be filled with the new metrics hire. Your task is to develop a game plan for reaching Level 4 as the team is being built and middle management is being convinced to support it.

Figure 5.4: *Process Group Organization Chart*

The budget for the process group for this year is $2.4 million:

- Personnel (four employees) $700K
- Consultants (two retirees) $450K
- Academicians (two part-timers) $200K
- Assessment support $200K
- Education and training $250K
- Promotion and outreach $250K
- Specialized Web tools $100K
- Web site development $250K

The budget funds the staff's developing and fanning the process out to project organizations ($1,350K), training ($250K for seminars brought in from the outside), promotion ($250K to prepare a newsletter, work with the customers, and attend conferences), and assessment support ($200K to bring in an external assessment team). The major new task to be pursued by the process group is Web site development ($350K). The group will put a process asset library on line to make their products (processes, training materials, improvement metrics) easily accessible to those who have access via the firm's network. They will continue tracking their performance using the metrics data on defects and costs that they collect as part of their process.

There is lots of pressure on you and the process group to move to Level 4 within two years. In its zeal to support the process improvement initiative, senior management took your suggestion to make process one of the factors in its middle management salary bonus scheme. Because their paychecks will be directly affected by the move to Level 4, many middle managers have suddenly awoken to the importance of process. They have started asking questions about what's involved in software process improvement. Unfortunately, the burden of success or failure falls on you because management cooperation with the process group isn't listed as one of the criteria for use in computing the bonus.

You are assuming the role of the process group manager for this exercise. Assume that you have just been promoted to fill the position. How do you get started? Do you staff the group or plan first? Who should get involved; what should they do? When do you kick off the effort? How do you build and energize the team? Where do you find qualified people for the group? What are upper management's expectations? Which program managers support you? Will they collaborate with you and permit their programs to serve as pilots? Senior management has summarized these questions in one: "What are your plan of action and milestones?" Middle managers ask a different question. They want to know, "What's in this initiative for me?" In other words, they are more interested in the business case justifications than in plans for moving to Level 4.

Before developing a game plan, some factfinding should be conducted. What is the group really being asked to accomplish? Is Level 4 the game, or is the game changing the culture as discussed in Chapter 1? Do you know? Have quantitative objectives for the effort been finalized and agreed on? If not, seek clarification. What are the measures of success for the effort, and how will they be demonstrated? How do these measures relate to the goals set for the effort? Will an outside observer be required to confirm that you've reached Level 4, or can you use someone from another division? Again, if you don't know, you should find out. You need to dig deep to discover hidden agendas.

Luckily, the real objectives have been defined using the goal–question–metric (GQM) paradigm discussed in Chapter 2. As shown in Figure 5.5, these goals and their related measures of success focus on productivity improvement to justify the expenditure of $2.4 million annually to pursue process improvement. "Where did this number come from?" you are probably wondering. When you dig, you find out that the numbers were developed by projecting productivity gains achieved three years ago into the future. Because the numbers are being questioned, you will have to determine their merit as you develop your plan and business case.

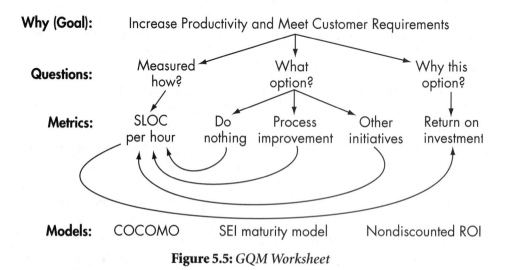

Figure 5.5: *GQM Worksheet*

You can start your plan effort in earnest. Because you're relatively new to process improvement, you have brought a management consultant on board to guide you through the planning process (for at most six months). Your boss has recommended that you pay for this expert with surplus funds. Your strategy here was to avoid political infighting by providing someone credible whom everyone could agree with (or blame) to help craft the business plan/case. The process the consultant recommends following is shown in Figure 5.6.

The process in Figure 5.6 homes in on steps 4 through 7 of the seven-step business planning process discussed in Chapter 2 (develop a business plan, prepare the case, sell the idea, and execute) (see Figure 2.4). The process in Figure 5.6 starts with vision and translates it into the work that needs to be performed via goals using activities to group tasks that are similar. Let's briefly discuss what needs to be done during each of the steps.

Start the Process by Involving Stakeholders

Start by establishing an infrastructure aimed at getting stakeholders involved in the planning process. Charter a steering committee and working groups. Invite key people and influence makers to participate. Hold your kickoff meetings as soon as you can. Build group consensus. Publish and promote the results via your Web site. Address the legitimate concerns raised by these groups. Show participants that their inputs are important by acting quickly on their suggestions. Identify stakeholder "win" conditions, and plan to use them to prioritize your work accordingly [Boehm,1998].

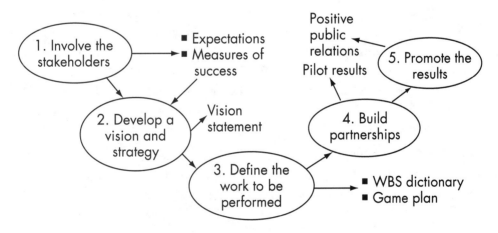

Figure 5.6: *Recommended Planning Process*

Develop a Top-Level Vision and Strategy

Building on the discussion in Chapter 2, write down what the initiative is trying to achieve (vision) and how you are going to make it happen (strategy) in simple language that anyone can understand. You will be surprised how hard it is to write such a document. Once you have your ideas on paper, review the document with your stakeholders, improve it, and have them take ownership of it. This document, which should go on your Web site, will help you explain the initiative, its goals, and how the goals are going to be achieved to anyone who asks.

Define the Work to Be Performed

Based on your GQM objectives, define the tasks that need be done in the near and long term. The work breakdown structure shown in Figure 5.7 organizes the work that needs to be performed to achieve these goals using activities and their subsidiary tasks (Figure 5.7 shows the mapping between tasks and activities). For each task, define the inputs, outputs, deliverables, and dependencies. Don't get bogged down in details when you start. Begin by identifying the most important things you must do to be successful. Cut the list to the five most critical things you need to do using stakeholder inputs and win conditions to establish priori-

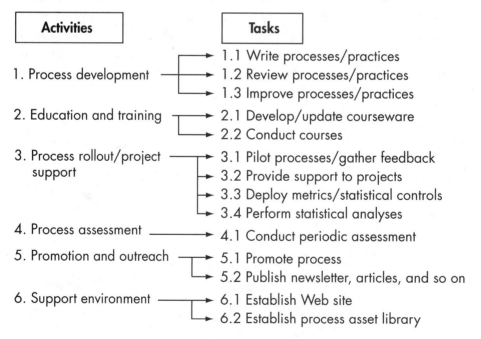

Figure 5.7: *Process Improvement Work Breakdown Structure*

ties. For example, statistical process controls must be deployed to achieve Level 4 (task 3.3). But you are not yet staffed to handle this challenge. You could correct this problem as you develop your plans by filling one of your vacancies with someone with the skills to tackle this task. The person you hire in turn can act as a mentor and focus on developing core competency in this needed area.

In Figure 5.7, each activity is broken into related tasks. A task is defined as the smallest unit of work subject to management accountability. Once properly defined, tasks generate products, consume resources (people, time, and so on), and may be related to or constrain one another. For example, the support environment provides stakeholders with timely access to process resources stored in the process asset library via your Web site. Two tasks are involved in this activity: developing the Web site and hosting the process asset library (PAL) on it. As already mentioned, the PAL is the mechanism that the process group plans on using to make its processes, training materials, newsletter, and help desk support available via the firm's network to those who have authorized access. In addition, the PAL facilitates collaboration with working projects through specialized tools such as Microsoft's NetMeeting.

As you talk with your stakeholders about implementing these steps, the consultant offers the following suggestions relative to their accomplishment:

Establish expectations or management will set them for you.   Work with your stakeholders to set realistic expectations for reaching Level 4. Otherwise, the expectations they set for you may not be achievable. Set reasonable but aggressive goals that you can live with. Use these goals to prioritize the tasks to be done by their perceived importance. As part of this effort, brief management, and get them to concur with the group's ratings. You will need everyone's support at one time or another as the initiative unfolds.

Do things that middle managers think are important.   Respond to your middle managers by completing tasks that they feel are important to the success of their projects—typically tasks that will have a positive impact on their project's ability to deliver promised products on schedule and under budget. If you help these managers, they will help you. Make them look good, and they will become your strongest supporters. Fail to deliver, and failure will haunt you forever.

Do the easy things first.   As you prioritize tasks, look for easy things that can be done quickly to generate positive effects. Completing them will help you display your initiative in a positive light. Perceptions are important. Middle managers view overhead activities such as yours negatively especially when they don't see anything of value coming from them. To counter this, promote your early successes. Make the people in the middle believe that you are a producer. Then they might be more apt to work with you when you ask them to pilot your processes on their next major upgrade.

Start with an operational concept.   Develop operational concepts for use as you kick off your Level 4 initiative. A list of concepts is provided along with a brief summary in Table 5.2. These concepts should be couched in terms of the methods and tools that you will use to deploy needed new processes, pilot them, and transfer them into use throughout the organization. Most important, these concepts should provide management with feedback about your progress and whether or not you are achieving your numbers.

Then develop an actionable plan.   Using these operational concepts and your WBS, develop a plan of action and milestones aimed at realizing the expectations you've set. Be practical: focus on the things that can be easily accomplished. Emphasize tasks in your plan that will move your Level 4 processes into project use in an ordered and systematic manner. Your challenge is to get busy people (e.g., the influence makers and the 20 percent responsible for 80 percent of the work) to use something new. That's why you need to budget to support the early adopters who agree to try the new processes.

Use available, free resources.   Try to take full advantage of the resources you have access to and are paying for as part of overhead charges. In other words, tap the expertise that exists within your firm in areas where you may need specialized help (accounting, legal/licensing, and so on). The trick is finding out where and to whom to go for help. For example, find an expert who understands intellectual property rights to help you when dealing with software licensing issues. This person can help you cut through the legal mumbo jumbo and exercise the advantage you may have when negotiating licenses with vendors. Be careful to avoid "experts" who say it can't be done. Their job is to tell you how to get it done, not to try to deter you from innovating.

After listening to the consultant's suggestions, you continue with the steps illustrated in Figure 5.6.

Table 5.2: *Operational Concepts*

Operational Concepts	Summary
Process development	Address the approach you will use to get to Level 4. You plan to exploit industry experience and best practices to expedite this job. You will hire an outside firm to help you, especially in statistical process control. This firm will play a major part in the assessment.
Transition	Get projects to use new processes. You will pilot the use of the processes to demonstrate their feasibility. You will also identify early adopters who will work with you as part of the pilot evaluation team to bridge the gap to widespread adoption.
Deployment	Determine how to deploy processes once they are released for use. You will provide a process expert as liaison with the project. Education and training will be provided on a just-in-time basis.
Configuration management	Focus on maintaining integrity and version control of process group products. You will use existing methods and tools to do this job. Your steering group will be your change control board.
Quality assurance	Make sure processes are not released prematurely. You will enlist stakeholders to do work product inspections using the process in place for software development.
Distribution management	Address how processes will be distributed as they are released/updated. Your initial thoughts focus on providing access via a Web site.
User support	Answer users' questions, and provide users with timely support. You will staff your Web site with a part-time person. You will publish frequently asked questions and capture metrics on user satisfaction. In other words, you will run the site like a business.

Build Partnerships

Plan to collaborate with those people and projects that agree to support your effort. Deal only with people you know and trust. Ask these key people to serve on steering committees and working groups and to provide you with pilot projects. Ask advice, and seek their confidence. Recognize that you have to give something to the partnership. If all you do is take, what's in the relationship for others? Volunteer to spend money to help your partners succeed. Put people on the project to off-load them so that they can satisfy their obligations. Do things on a noninterference basis so that it won't seem like their success is in jeopardy.

Plan to Sell, Sell, and Sell

Recognize that those in positions of power change as people move on for whatever cause. Just as soon as you've educated one set of executives, another set comes in the door. Don't get too comfortable. Be vigilant, and look for dragons. An overhead budget the size of yours is always a target for takeover. Remember you are a success if you are viewed as one. In response, create the illusion that you are successful in all your actions, lectures, and written work. The saying that "success breeds success" is not just a platitude; it's reality. Projects will support you when it is thought you will deliver. Ride the white horse, and people will wave as you pass by. This discussion stresses the need for you to promote your successes, even when they are small ones. Recognize that the sum of a large number of small successes is often perceived as one large success.

After several iterations, you feel comfortable with your plan of action. You've also completed a top-level business case using productivity improvement to justify your expenditures. The consultant recommends that you review the plan in its draft form with your champion to make sure that it meets the mark and you haven't forgotten anything. Your champion is busy, but his second in command assures you that he will like it.

PROCESS MATURITY: ARE THE INVESTMENTS JUSTIFIED?

During an orientation briefing, the new vice president in charge of research and development asked why the firm was spending $2.4 million a year on software process improvement. Nobody in the room, including your champion, could provide a satisfactory answer (he hadn't seen your material, so he couldn't defend you). The productivity projections that you offered as justification were torn to shreds. The debate was hot and heavy. Most of the middle managers in the room grinned and vocally took sides against you. Finally, the vice president said: "If they (the process group) can't justify this expenditure, we should spend the money elsewhere—research?" Your boss called and asked you to provide an answer the next day. You are scheduled to brief this new vice president at noon tomorrow.

Most of the information you've seen in the literature about process improvement has harped on the benefits without translating them into numbers. While interesting, such discussions don't help you make a strong business case for software process improvement. Luckily, the consultant you hired has access to justification numbers. Most of them were generated internally as a product of your Level 3 metrics activities. He points to several papers when you query him about the other sources of numbers: [Butler, 1995], [Clark, 2000], and [McGibbon, 1996]. He also identifies some internal benchmarking data that you can use to justify the projections that were originally used to justify your budgets. Your plan is to use this hard data to convince the new vice president that investment in process improvement pays off. However, because outsiders will be in the meeting, you must couch the numbers in such a way as to keep them secret. If you don't, the outsiders might leak proprietary information to your competition.

Accelerating Productivity Gains Through Process

You decide to use the published industry productivity benchmark of 100 source lines of code per staff-month (SLOC/SM) as a starting point to demonstrate the gain associated with process improvement. As stated in Chapter 4, productivity is defined as the ratio of outputs (SLOCs) to inputs used to generate them (SM of labor). The consultant supplies data that shows that the average productivity gain your firm experienced during the past five years was approximately 20 percent annually as it moved from Level 3 to Level 4. During the early years, the gain was just 10 percent annually. After considerable analysis, you believe that your firm was able to accelerate productivity gains by 10 percent per year (from 10 to 20 percent) by pursuing a process improvement strategy. These numbers correlate well with the initial business case that was developed to justify the original initiative. When the outsiders leave, you plan to show the new vice president a chart that confirms the trends. Of course, your firm pursued other improvements during this time span. For example, they made additional gains by increasing capital expenditures to acquire new equipment and tools.

For you, the acceleration results in a cost avoidance averaging $2 million annually over a five-year investment time span based on the analysis summarized in Table 5.3. When you put your real numbers in, the avoidance grows to $4 million annually. After digging some more, you find out that this is how the numbers were generated three years ago. You also learn that the trend lines used then to project benefits have held true throughout this time period. However, you will use the generic numbers for this computation to protect leakage of the numbers by the outsiders.

Table 5.3: *Savings Attributed to Accelerating Productivity from 10 to 20 Percent Annually*

	Year 1	Year 2	Year 3	Year 4	Year 5
Current productivity (SLOC/SM; 10% nominal gain)	100	110	121	133	146
Accelerated gain (20%) (SLOC/SM)		120	144	173	208
Additional number of SLOCs that can be generated via acceleration assuming 600 engineers		72,000	165,600	288,000	446,400
Cost avoidance ($50/SLOC)		$3.6 million	$8.3 million	$14.4 million	$22.3 million
Cumulative cost avoidance		$3.6 million	$11.9 million	$26.3 million	$48.6 million

It should be noted that you were very conservative in your calculations. For example, you assumed that there was no gain during the first year of the improvement strategy. As another example, you did not assume that your workforce grew as the workload did. Instead, you addressed the growth via cost avoidance in terms of SLOC that you did not have to generate. You defined productivity in terms of SLOC per staff-month because this was the metric that your firm historically captured and reported for software. You discarded newer productivity metrics based on function and applications points because they were too business system oriented [Jones, 1998]. When you asked the consultant, he stated that the SLOC/staff-month metric seemed appropriate because you could use the improvement trends to build a business case that justified your expenditures for the improvement initiative.

The $50 per SLOC assumption is also a best case. Your cost per SLOC actually ranges from $50 to $150. You took the bottom end of this range to be ultraconservative in your projections. If you had taken the $150 figure, middle management would not have believed your numbers because they would have seemed to be too good. For the internal revenue, you plan to use $100 per SLOC. This correlates well with industry benchmarks for productivity and represents a more realistic saving.

Early Defect Detection and Correction

While the productivity numbers look good, you want to show more benefits in your business case justification. When asked, the consultant points you to defect data that your process group has been collecting for several years. The defect introduction and removal rates have been tabulated, compared, and reported using data that you have captured throughout the software life cycle as a by-product of the work product inspection process that you inserted as part of your Level 3 efforts. They demonstrate convincingly that the process improvements you've made lead to earlier defect removal (before release to the field).

You now want to compute the benefits early defect detection buys you. Like yours, several firms the consultant has worked with have been capturing such data to quantify these benefits from their projects. These firms have caught defects early and avoided the costly problems associated with their propagation after the systems have been fielded. They too have used work product inspections to capture the data. As these firms moved from Level 3 to Level 4, their data showed that the average number of errors that went to the field was reduced by a factor of between 20 and 25 percent. Again, this correlates well with your experience. In addition, the majority of these defects were caught in the requirements and design phases instead of during test and integration. According to your internal data, the cost of fixing a defect when it is found during these early stages saves you as much as 40 percent of your historical repair costs (saves \$20 per defect based on 100 percent rework). For the 12 major programs that your firm has under development, these savings translate to \$1.2 million annual cost avoidance, assuming

$$(12 \text{ projects/year})(10 \text{ defects/K SLOC entering test})(500 \text{ K lines/project}) = 60,000 \text{ defects}$$

$$(60,000 \text{ defects})(\$20/\text{defect cost avoidance}) = \$1.2 \text{ million}$$

In addition, these firms found that their product quality was better than yours. The average defect density for their software products when released to the field was between 0.1 and 0.5 defects/K SLOC. Your defect densities are averaging between 5 and 8 errors/K SLOC. From your viewpoint, lower defect density translates into improved customer satisfaction. However, neither you nor your consultant knows how to quantify the impact of improved customer satisfaction and include it as part of a business case.

The consultant reported that being at Level 4 also had other advantages. He pointed to several firms that used statistical process-control U-chart reports to reallocate effort from processes that were under control to those that were more error-prone. You asked, "What is a U-chart?" The consultant explained that U-charts are statistical process-control tools that plot error trends between control limits. Using these charts, he showed you how to determine how well processes were behaving [Florence, 2001]. The results were extremely heartening because they showed that Level 4 firms were more concerned with controlling variability then writing waivers to get out of processes. You plan to use this information if needed to win arguments.

Exploitation of COTS

As you are tabulating your ROI using productivity improvement and earlier defect detection and correction figures, your consultant has a brainstorm. "Why not add the benefits we are deriving through COTS and product lines?" he suggests. As with many defense contractors, you have moved from custom hardware and software solutions to those offered off the shelf. Like others, you have found such solutions risky and error-prone. To counter these tendencies, you have adopted an inspection and licensing process aimed at improving your advantage with suppliers.

Based on the consultant's inputs, you can quantify the benefits associated with enterprise-wide software licensing. For example, Northrop saved over $2 million annually by adopting improved licensing processes [Reifer, 1999]. This saving was achieved at the project level by coordinating software license purchases to gain volume discounts via increased buying power. As part of its licensing initiative, Northrop was also able to negotiate license changes to transfer spare seats to projects other than those designated in the original license agreement. Finally, Northrop put a "try before you buy" practice into operation. Trial use enabled the company to identify defects that had to be corrected before purchasing the product. Defects often had side effects that biased their error data and were difficult to find and fix. Per these results, you believe that you can save at least $1 million annually through improved licensing.

Movement to Product Lines, Architecture, and Systematic Reuse

Now you are ready to quantify the gains associated with moving to product lines. You have limited experience here. Therefore, you must rely on the consultant's inputs relative to published data [Weiss, 1999]. Implementing architecture and systematic reuse is traditionally the hardest part of the strategy. The reason behind this is that the process guidelines used, such as the SW-CMM [Paulk, 1995] and SPICE [El Emam, 1997], offer little help in this area. Because your company is a defense contractor, other restrictions make it very difficult for you to share software across projects. For example, security provisions may force you to discard existing designs because their disclosure could provide insight into how to break into the system. Sharing is not something that your customers currently encourage or provide incentives to accomplish.

You ask the consultant for recommendations on how to bring product lines, architecture, and systematic reuse into your organization. Luckily, your firm has been pursuing architecture-based reuse for over a decade as part of your internal research and development efforts. The research team has completed a domain analysis and developed reference architectures, both hardware and software, to facilitate reuse at the system level [Bassett, 1996]. Their goal was to deploy this architecture using product line management concepts by making it part of the processes their engineers use to do their work [Reifer, 1997b]. Using their recommendations, you plan to incorporate reuse provisions into your processes as you develop them for Level 4.

The benefits the research team attributed to reuse are many and substantial. Systematic reuse saves money and time by making big jobs smaller. Table 5.4 illustrates this phenomenon using a sensor system software example. Using product line concepts effectively cuts the size of the job almost in half. Reuse in this context is planned, and the components themselves are designed for reuse. For example, alarms are instantiated from some existing alarm class by tailoring, not redesign or coding. Variability is controlled. The direct reuse of existing components previously developed to populate the selected product line architecture results in the savings shown in Table 5.4.

The benefits of cutting the size of the job in half can be quantified using a cost model like COCOMO II [Boehm, 2000]. Running the model for the example summarized in Table 5.4 results in the effort and duration estimates shown in Table 5.5. Both nominal and shortest development time options were estimated. The only cost driver varied was the process maturity (PMAT) factor that was set to reflect a Level 4 organization. Table 5.5 shows that you can cut the estimated duration in calendar months by about 20 percent and effort in staff-months by about one half in both cases (most likely or nominal and shortest duration estimate).

Table 5.4: *Size of Application with and without Reuse*

Application	Size without Reuse (in SLOCs)	Size with Reuse (in SLOCs)
Real-time executive	10,000	500
Scheduler	25,000	500
Real-time data acquisition	50,000	10,000
Sensor data processing	50,000	21,000
Data analysis and alarms	25,000	10,000
Total	160,000	42,000

Table 5.5: *Effort and Duration Estimates with and without Reuse*

	Without Reuse	With Reuse
Nominal development time (months)	30	23.4
Nominal effort (staff-months)	845.3	383.7
Shortest development time (months)	22.5	17.6
Shortest development time effort	1208.7	548.7

This example illustrates the benefits associated with systematic software reuse. It suggests that each of your projects can save as much as half its costs (about $5 million) and a year in schedule through reuse. In reality, your systems are much bigger and more complex than that shown in Table 5.4. As a result, your cost saving should exceed $5 million on each new system you generate using the product line architecture you have developed and the infrastructure you have introduced. Multiply these savings across all your product lines/families, and you estimate that you can realize savings of at least $10 million annually once the technology has been transferred into operations. However, the increased costs associated with maintaining your architecture and with designing assets for reuse need to be accounted for in your calculations. These costs are factored into the worksheet you have prepared to address the costs/benefits associated with systematic software reuse, which is shown in the accompanying box.

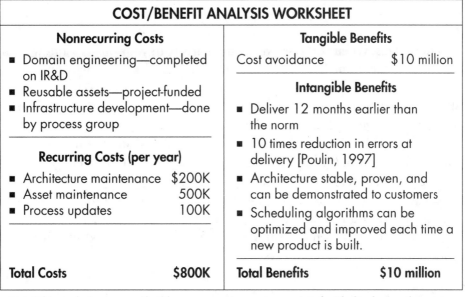

COST/BENEFIT ANALYSIS WORKSHEET	
Nonrecurring Costs	**Tangible Benefits**
■ Domain engineering—completed on IR&D ■ Reusable assets—project-funded ■ Infrastructure development—done by process group	Cost avoidance $10 million
	Intangible Benefits
Recurring Costs (per year)	■ Deliver 12 months earlier than the norm ■ 10 times reduction in errors at delivery [Poulin, 1997]
■ Architecture maintenance $200K ■ Asset maintenance 500K ■ Process updates 100K	■ Architecture stable, proven, and can be demonstrated to customers ■ Scheduling algorithms can be optimized and improved each time a new product is built.
Total Costs $800K	**Total Benefits** $10 million

Note: This analysis assumes that the nonrecurring costs associated with developing the asset population for the architecture were treated as sunk costs because they were incurred on R&D.

You believe that most of the nonrecurring investment costs as shown must be funded by projects as part of their budgets or covered by existing investments.

Your systematic software reuse initiative is just starting. It represents a major challenge because it will force you to change the way you do your business. Instead of developing products for projects, you will develop product line architectures for business units. In addition, major changes to the way you currently manage your business will be required to facilitate this changeover. Luckily, processes and tools that facilitate the change to systematic reuse exist and are starting to be used commercially [Jacobson, 1997]. But it would be unfair to assume that you will reap any benefit from this initiative during the next two years. Therefore, you have not included the incremental contribution of this reuse initiative in your ROI computation.

QUANTIFYING THE RETURN ON INVESTMENT

You still have to answer the vice president. But the consultant earned his keep by providing you the information you need to compute the return on investment. Your briefing, which is illustrated in Figures 5.8 through 5.13, is aimed at educating and convincing the new vice president of research that the money allocated to software process improvement will be well spent. The briefing is short and to the point. It assumes that the vice president doesn't want cluttered charts that get into the details. When you reviewed your charts with your boss, he threw more than half of them out. The six that survived are the charts he helped you construct. You were disappointed when he told you not to bring the consultant. But after thinking about the briefing throughout the night, you concluded that he was right. This should be an inside job.

The chart in Figure 5.8 sets the stage by emphasizing the importance of software to the firm. It lets you talk about government requirements and competitive pressures. It also lets you set expectations.

The chart in Figure 5.9 highlights your current software improvement strategy. It lets you talk about your motivation for the initiative, strategy, and past performance. It then lets you describe the four-part improvement framework you plan to use to reach Level 4 within two years.

The chart in Figure 5.10 identifies $6.2M in cost avoidance that you will realize. It shows reuse but allows you to state that you have not considered this in the ROI calculation because of timing. Because of long lead times required to change the culture, the forecasted benefits will accrue outside the two-year window you have been given to reach Level 4.

The chart in Figure 5.11 shows the process group budget and its current headcount. The bottom line on the chart allows you to emphasize importance of process as the framework for other improvements. It also lets you move to the ROI chart.

SETTING THE STAGE

- Software sells hardware and keeps our factories operating
- Software currently accounts for more than 50 percent of our engineering costs
- Our government customers fear software costs are spiraling out of control
- Our competitors have mounted aggressive software improvement programs

Figure 5.8: *Executive Briefing—Background*

WE HAVE NOT BEEN IDLE

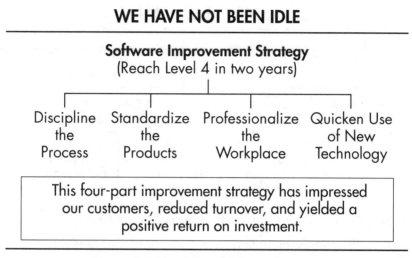

Software Improvement Strategy
(Reach Level 4 in two years)

| Discipline the Process | Standardize the Products | Professionalize the Workplace | Quicken Use of New Technology |

This four-part improvement strategy has impressed our customers, reduced turnover, and yielded a positive return on investment.

Figure 5.9: *Executive Briefing—Strategy*

STRATEGY YIELDING MANY RETURNS

Early Error Reduction
- Cost avoidance = $1.2M/year
- Increased customer satisfaction based on quality

Systematic Reuse
- Cost avoidance = $10M per year
- Faster to market
- Ten times the quality
- Just starting—expect to reap benefits within three years
- Process can be built with reuse in mind.

Exploitation of COTS
- Cost avoidance = $1M per year
- Improved maintenance
- License leverage with vendors

Productivity Improvement
- Cost avoidance = $4M per year
- Improved capabilities and capacity

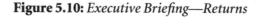

Figure 5.10: *Executive Briefing—Returns*

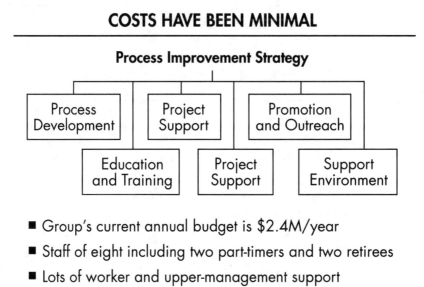

COSTS HAVE BEEN MINIMAL

Process Improvement Strategy

- Group's current annual budget is $2.4M/year
- Staff of eight including two part-timers and two retirees
- Lots of worker and upper-management support
- Process improvement provides the structure for all elements of the strategy

Figure 5.11: *Executive Briefing—Costs*

The chart in Figure 5.12 performs the ROI calculation. It takes the annual benefits in the second year and divides them by the investments necessary to pull them off. It lets you highlight both the tangible and intangible benefits. Finally, it lets you talk about software reuse as an added benefit (i.e., you don't have to bet the farm on it).

Besides setting expectations, your final chart (Figure 5.13) asks for the vice president's support. You took your boss's advice when he said: "Never brief an executive without asking for something." You asked for advice and for something you knew the vice president could help you do. Your request will endear you to him because it was designed to make him look like a hero.

As expected, the briefing went well. The vice president was inquisitive, supportive, and helpful. His parting remark was, "Count on me to help you get middle management in your camp." Your boss was pleased, and your team was thrilled at the prospects of having even more senior management support. However, you are wary. This vice president is too new to the firm to really help you pull your Level 4 initiative off in the planned time frame. All you can do is stop him from causing damage.

RETURN ON INVESTMENT

Tangibles

$$ROI = \frac{Annual\ Benefits}{Investment}$$

$$ROI = \frac{\$6.2M}{\$2.4M}$$

ROI > 250% in second year

Assumptions: Cost avoidances in Figure 5.10 realized with exception of reuse, which kicks in after we reach CMM Level 4.

Intangibles

- Better product quality
- Quicker to market
- Increased customer satisfaction
- Improved employee morale
- Responds directly to customer requirements

Figure 5.12: *Executive Briefing—ROI*

WE NEED YOUR SUPPORT

- Reaching Level 4 will take two years, assuming things go as planned.
- Our major challenge is to get those in the middle on our side (bonus is a good start). Anything you can do to help would be appreciated.
- We have a number of operational challenges:
  - Need help in staffing—getting our requisitions through the system
  - Need help in licensing—buyer support

Figure 5.13: *Executive Briefing—Finale*

The disturbing news was that only one middle manager besides your boss was present at the briefing. You invited a dozen and only one showed up. Most complained that they were just too busy to attend. You are concerned that their lack of attention signals their lack of concern.

GETTING EVERYONE INVOLVED
IN PLAYING THE GAME

You've learned to play the game of *Dungeons and Dragons* well. Just as in the real game, you've handled the unexpected. Things seem to be going well. Now's the time to shore up your executive support by putting a steering committee in place. It is also apparent that you need to do something to get more middle management involvement.

The steering committee is the easiest group to establish. In fact, it was created years ago when your predecessor kicked off the Level 3 initiatives. A charter exists, and membership is defined. Over the years, the committee stopped functioning. Now's the time to have your champion(s) call a meeting. Of course, you will have to furnish the agenda and prepare the invitations. Take advantage of the opportunity created by giving the briefing you've prepared for the vice president of research to others who might be able to provide useful advice.

Getting middle managers and workers involved is harder. Typically, this is done using an engineering council, working groups, and the like. Generating interest is not difficult. However, getting the right people to participate is a challenge. That's because the people you want are busy working projects. The key to success is to get these people involved in something they are interested in and can contribute to. If interested, they will make the time to attend and contribute to the effort. Avoid the temptation to set up a bunch of working groups all at once. I have seen this tactic fail repeatedly. Don't foster meetings for the sake of meetings. Groups such as these need the pressure of hard deadlines to come up with results. Ask your council to address transition issues. Task your working groups to solve technical problems that impede transition.

Figure 5.14 identifies the committees, councils, and working groups you believe need to be created to reach Level 4.

- *Executive steering committee*   Gets senior management involved in an advisory role to provide the initiative with oversight and direction.

- *Software engineering council*   Gets line of business management involved in coordinating product line architecture issues and reuse process recommendations.

- *Software working groups*   Gets the key performers and influence makers involved in the initiatives by having them recommend ways to support the process improvements with education and training, technology, methods, languages, and tools.

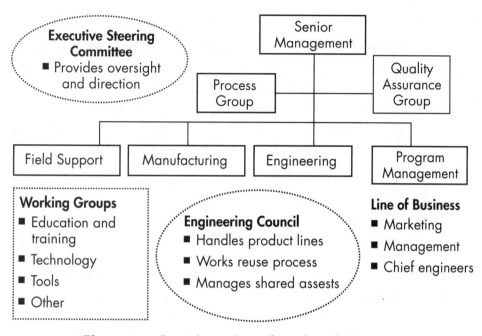

Figure 5.14: *Committees, Councils, and Working Groups*

REINVENTING AND REFRESHING THE ORGANIZATION

I think reinventing staff organizations such as process and quality assurance groups is a good idea. Engineers assigned to such staff groups get stale once they've put in more than three years of service. Being in an audit and support role, they forget how hard it is to develop and deliver quality products under extreme deadline pressures. They need to relearn what I call the humility of the trenches. That's why I believe staff groups should be populated with rotators and a small, core professional team. The rotators bring enthusiasm and fresh ideas to the table. The core team focuses the energy on the job at hand and maintains the knowledge base.

Revitalizing such staff groups is hard work [Caputo, 1998]. You are lucky. Most of the deadwood in your group has left. You can focus on bringing in the talent you need to reach Level 4. As mentioned earlier, the skills, knowledge, and abilities of these people are quite different from those needed to reach Level 3. At Level 3, you were trying to institutionalize an organizational process for software. To fully understand and be able to tailor the process, your staff had to become intimate with it. Because you were working with projects, collaborative skills were at a premium, as were teamwork abilities. In contrast, Level 4 focuses on using statistical process controls to reduce variability and increase effectiveness. Statistical analysis and metrics skills are now needed to take the data being collected and make sense of it [Wheeler, 1992]. While collaborative skills and teamwork abilities are still desirable, your staff needs to focus on using metrics data to quantify the process and making it work efficiently.

To reinvent the organization, start by crystallizing its mission. If reaching Level 4 within two years is your primary goal, try to avoid putting any of the Level 3 transition tasks in the mission statement. This will cause the organization to lose focus and become schizophrenic. To maintain emphasis, add details to your action plan as they become available. Groups tend to be shaky when their plans are vague. Don't let this happen. Continually refine your plan so that you can use it as a road map to deliver what you promise on schedule and within budget.

Refreshing a process group is fun. To succeed, the consultant recommends that you staff your process group with a core team of three and a manager as planned. The manager of the group is its chief spokesperson. This person handles the delicate interfaces with both middle and senior management. To do this effectively, you believe that this person needs to be a veteran of the organization. You are pleased because you have this qualification. The next two people are called the process arbitrators. They understand the process fully and can be called on to explain its provisions in detail. Besides writing processes, these people maintain the process knowledge base and manage the process asset library. The fourth person is the metrics analyst. This person is in charge of the metrics strategy and maintains the measurement database. You call on this person to address metrics questions and handle statistical process control issues.

To bring in fresh ideas, you plan to bring in specialists to supplement the core group on a rotation basis. The specialists will change to reflect your need for different talent at different times. Looking at the organization chart in Figure 5.4, we see that there would be four such slots in the process group. Two part-time slots are initially allocated to courseware development. The other two full-time slots are allocated to project interfaces. The technique of hiring recent retirees as consultants to work with projects is a good one. Of course, the people you hire must be knowledgeable and respected. If they aren't, their use may backfire.

SUMMARY

This chapter provides a process improvement case study. The hypothetical firm has just kicked off an effort to reach CMM Level 4 within two years. The case showed how to justify the expenditures in terms of early error detection and correction, exploitation of COTS, accelerating productivity gains, and moving to product lines, architectures, and systematic reuse.

KEY POINTS

- ✔ Managing process improvement activities is like playing a game of *Dungeons and Dragons*. To avoid the dragons, you have to anticipate when and where to make your next move. Otherwise, you might wind up in the dungeon.

- ✔ It takes a game plan, senior management support, and a solid business case to win the game of *Dungeons and Dragons.*

- ✔ When briefing senior management, always ask for something. This makes managers feel as if they are contributing to your effort.

- ✔ Most organizations have the information to build a business case. First, develop your plan of action. Then, estimate the cost for putting the plan into action. Finally, forecast the benefits, and use them to justify your planned expenditures.

- ✔ When justifying initiatives, cost avoidance is preferred to cost reduction because it deals with future expenditures.

- ✔ When determining benefits, categorize them as tangibles or intangibles. When the returns are marginal, the intangibles can be used to help tip the scales and justify the effort.

- ✔ Any combination of the four approaches discussed in this chapter can be used to pull together a business case. When using them, err on the conservative side. Nothing discredits numbers more than the perception that you are being overly optimistic with them.

- ✔ Never be casual with numbers. Define them and limit them as precisely as you can.

- ✔ Don't be afraid to suggest that organizations be reinvented and refreshed when justifying future initiatives.

References

[Boehm, 2000] Boehm, Barry W., Chris Abts, A. Winsor Brown, Sunita Chulani, Bradford K. Clark, Ellis Horowitz, Ray Madachy, Donald Reifer, and Bert Steece. *Software Cost Estimation with COCOMO II.* Prentice Hall, 2000.

[Boehm, 1998] Boehm, Barry W. "Using the Win-Win Spiral Model: A Case Study," *Computer,* IEEE Computer Society, July 1998, pp. 33–44.

[Butler, 1995] Butler, K. "The Economic Benefits of Software Process Improvement," *CrossTalk,* Vol. 8, No.7, July 1995, pp. 14–17.

[Caputo, 1998] Caputo, Kim. *CMM Implementation Guide.* Addison-Wesley, 1998.

[Clark, 2000] Clark, Bradford K. "Quantifying the Effects on Effort of Process Improvement," *Software,* IEEE Computer Society, November/December 2000, pp. 65–70.

[Daly, 1997] Daly, Edmund B. "Organizing for Successful Software Development," *Tutorial Software Management,* 5th Edition. IEEE Computer Society, 1997, pp. 275–282.

[Davidson, 1997] Davidson, Alistair, Harvey Gellman, and Mary Chung. *Riding the Tiger.* HarperBusiness, 1997, p. 106.

[El Emam, 1997] El Emam, Khaled, Jean-Normand Drouin, and Walcelio Melo. *SPICE: The Theory and Practice of Software Improvement and Capability Determination.* IEEE Computer Society, 1997.

[Florence, 2001] Florence, Al. "CMM Level 4 Quantitative Analysis and Defect Prevention," *CrossTalk,* February 2001, pp. 20–23.

[Jacobson, 1997] Jacobson, Ivar, Martin Griss, and Patrik Jonsson. *Software Reuse: Architecture, Process and Organization for Business Success.* Addison-Wesley, 1997.

[Jones, 1998] Jones, T. Capers. *Estimating Software Costs.* McGraw-Hill, 1998.

[McGibbon, 1996] McGibbon, Tom. "A Business Case for Software Process Improvement, Data & Analysis Center for Software." Contract F30602–92-C-0158, Kaman Sciences Corp., 1996.

[Paulk, 1995] Paulk, Mark C., Charles V. Weber, Bill Curtis, and Mary Beth Chrissis. *The Capability Maturity Model: Guidelines for Improving the Software Process.* Addison-Wesley, 1995.

[Poulin, 1997] Poulin, Jeffrey S. *Measuring Software Reuse.* Addison-Wesley, 1997.

[Reifer, 1999] Reifer, Donald J., George E. Kalb, and Tara Ragan. "Licensing: A Target for Process Improvement." Acquisition Management Conference, 1999.

[Reifer, 1997a] Reifer, Donald J. "The 3P's of Software Management," *Tutorial Software Management,* 5th Edition. IEEE Computer Society, 1997, pp. 10–16.

[Reifer, 1997b] Reifer, Donald J. *Practical Software Reuse.* John Wiley & Sons, 1997.

[Schulmeyer, 1992] Schulmeyer, G. Gordon, and James I. McManus. *Total Quality Management for Software.* Van Nostrand Reinhold, 1992.

[Weiss, 1999] Weiss, David M., and Robert Lai Chi Tau. *Software Product-Line Engineering.* Addison-Wesley, 1999.

[Wheeler, 1992] Wheeler, Donald J., and David C. Chambers. *Understanding Statistical Process Control,* 2nd Edition. SPC Press, 1992.

6

Quantifying the Costs/Benefits
Capitalizing Software Case Study

Mediocre people with good tools and languages will still develop mediocre systems, but good people, even when burdened with poor tools and mediocre languages, can turn out damn good software.
—Ed Yourdon [1992]

YOU'VE GOT A PROBLEM

You have recently been assigned to a new project. This is a large information technology (IT) project in a utility that recently went public. It will serve as the pathfinder for future system developments. The system, illustrated in Figure 6.1, is being developed to allow users to access information of interest from different hosts across wideband communications networks from nodes all over the state. The new system is replacing an ancient mainframe-based transaction-processing system that has outlived its useful life by more than a decade. The utility will replace the current system because it has no other alternative. The hardware vendor notified your bosses that it plans to discontinue supporting your hardware and operating system software by the end of the year.

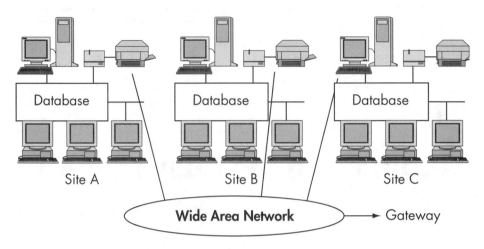

Figure 6.1: *New System Configuration*

The distinguishing features of the replacement system include the following:

- It is a client-server system with a distributed database networked locally using a local area network (LAN) and across geographical service zones (i.e., partitioned by population densities) within the state via a wide area network (WAN).

- There will be a gateway to the Internet. Plans are to open the network up for electronic commerce (EC) now and electronic data interchange (EDI) about a year later. Luckily, your initial release won't have to address these considerations. But you'll need to put the hooks into the configuration now to deal with these interfaces in the future.

- Users will generate input transactions such as queries on their workstations. Servers will service these transactions and respond with answers within minutes instead of hours.

- The amount of processing in a typical transaction is not large. However, large files, such as customer, billing, and inventory records, may be involved.

- The current office systems that do things such as order processing, billing, and reporting will be eliminated by this system. That's how the purchase was justified to the state. The old word-processing system is past its prime and must be replaced with a new one in the near term.

- Users may multiprocess as they wait for transactions to be processed (i.e., they can do other work on their workstations as they wait for responses).

The software functions have been allocated to clients/servers in this configuration, as shown in Table 6.1. Both clients and servers are connected to one another via the network. Transactions are communicated to and from clients and servers via the secure intranet and leased WAN. The client workstations perform user and office functions locally at the 250 offices that exist statewide. Records management and other functions that require access to the archival databases are handled remotely at seven regional service centers by the servers that back each

Table 6.1: *System Software Capabilities*

Client software	Server software
Systems functions	**Systems functions**
Operating system	Operating system
Communications	Communications
Security and integrity controls	Resource management
Utilities	Security and integrity controls
User applications	**Middleware**
Screen processing	Network management and security
Transaction processing	Transaction processing
File management	Database management
Report generation	Other
Office functions	**Query processing**
Word processing	SQL processing
Forms processing	Persistent database management
File management	
Applications	**Applications**
Sales and marketing	Sales and marketing
Order entry and processing	Supply chain management
Financial management	Financial management
Customer service	Personnel management and recruiting
Field service	Records management
Other applications	Other applications
Fault diagnosis	**Fault diagnosis**
Built-in testing	Built-in testing
Fault isolation and recovery management	Fault isolation and recovery management

other up to provide 24-hour operation. Regional centers handle procurements and other functions that require specialized accounting and legal expertise.

Operational concepts are new and are designed to lever the utility's buying power to keep costs low. For example, clients place an order for goods or services at their local office. Once an order is placed, it is pooled with others, and suppliers are notified of the pending procurement as part of the supply chain management application. Before a solicitation is issued, large orders are advertised to stimulate additional competition. Quotations are received at the regional center in response to the terms and conditions in the solicitation. To acquire the products and services in question, the purchasing officer negotiates a single contract that any of the local offices that participated in the procurement can cite. Financial records are kept at both regional and local offices. Plans are to migrate the entire process to the Web in the near future. Intelligent agents will be used to search the Web for additional qualified sources that can provide the required goods and services at favorable prices and terms.

The business processes employed will differ greatly from those used in the past. Each local office was autonomous in the past and under state control. For example, when cutting orders for procurements, each office negotiated contracts with suppliers directly. This resulted in duplication, inefficiency, and layers of bureaucracy. Worse than this, the state failed to take full advantage of its tremendous buying power when negotiating discounts on goods and services it used systemwide. The new public utility will use current replacement systems to streamline operations and reduce inefficiencies. The processes have been designed to reduce the bureaucracy that usually comes with centralized control. The processes will also allow the utility to use the Web to find additional suppliers and search for the best price. By design, the processes that are being developed are Web-ready. But because of the current release and cutover plan, you will not implement this option right away.

The most challenging part of the upgrade will be getting the thousands of clerical people at the local sites throughout the state to change their habits and adopt these new business processes. As mentioned, new processes are being put into place to use the system effectively. The processes are part of an ongoing push that was initiated by state management over a year ago in anticipation of going public. Products are coming out slowly, and there is a great deal of resistance to change at the worker level. If that isn't enough, the union that represents these workers is strongly opposed to the upgrade. They argue against it because they believe that the new processes and associated information systems will eliminate the need for hundreds of workers across the state. They are threatening labor actions if you go ahead with the replacement.

ORGANIZATIONAL PROFILE

Your IT group is organized as illustrated in Figure 6.2. This is a new organization, and many of its nuances are currently yet to be worked out. Your chief information officer (CIO) reports directly to the president of the public utility. The CIO is new and has brought in many of the directors from outside organizations. Many sensitivity sessions were held to get the existing staff to buy into the transition. However, the move did not go smoothly. Many of the old-timers complained when they were passed over. Several good people left to assume new positions in other IT shops. Those who adopted a wait-and-see attitude are frustrated because they do not know how to deal with the changes being made. But the younger troops seem pleased with the switch and are excited because the newcomers seem to have breathed new life into the organization.

You are assigned to the Infrastructure Directorate. Your job is to provide the processes, methods, and software engineering environment needed to support the implementation of the new information system, which is needed to support the entire organization at both regional and local office centers. Your organization is viewed as talented and progressive. You have a young, educated, and highly motivated staff. However, your programming staff has less than three years of experience with client-server applications. In anticipation of the switchover to the new system, most want to bring in new development paradigms such as the Rational Unified Process [Kruchten, 1998], object-oriented methods [Coad, 1996], use

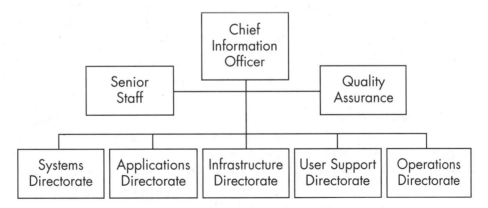

Figure 6.2: *IT Organizational Structure*

cases [Schneider, 1998], improved facilities, modern workstations, new networking gear, and modern software tools [Pont, 1996]. With regard to languages, there are two camps. One side advances the use of C/C++, while the other advocates Java. As expected, most of your staff is not skilled in the use of either language or in object-oriented methodologies, although most have read about the virtues of these new technologies. Several have taken classes after hours and want to put their new skills into practice. While some were exposed to C/C++, Java, and software engineering topics in school, their current abilities are in CICS and COBOL because those are what supports the current mainframe system. Many of the existing applications are so old that the software has been patched together to maintain operational capabilities.

In anticipation of going public (the utility is quasi-private), the utility mounted an aggressive business process reengineering effort two years ago. Teams of workers have documented existing business processes as flows. Ideas on how to improve these processes as the new system is brought into use have been taken into account. Your programmers participated in the teams to ensure that the process flows could be implemented by the client-server configuration. Of course, the reengineering process is not yet complete. While viewed positively, it is going slowly because many of the participants really don't understand the current work processes. What makes it even more difficult is that the cast of characters involved seems to change on a monthly basis. This forces the team to educate those who join the team instead of moving ahead with the improvements.

As expected, the organization has a number of unresolved issues. Its first-level managers are chosen for their technical skills and the respect shown by their peers. Little training in management is provided, although new managers are exposed to good management practices through scheduled business process reengineering workshops. Many of these good technical practitioners have difficulty making the move to management. The reengineering teams have repeatedly recommended that a new supervisor training program be implemented. Management is debating how to move ahead on this recommendation and has not yet funded the training.

A second issue has emerged relative to tools. Independent of whether the C/C++ or Java camp wins the language debate, your existing software engineering environment is horribly out of date. As the debate rages, you are being asked to recommend modern tools that support the transition to the new client-server configuration. To do this, you have formed a working group to come up with the requirements. The initial meeting of this group last week was a disaster. Instead of addressing the group's charter, the C/C++ and Java adherents went to war over language benefits. When the dust settled, little had been agreed on. While some requirements were advanced, they were so high level that they provided you only limited guidance. Luckily, you were able to get the group to scope the environment. You went into the meeting with just tools on your mind. You walked out with methodology support, equipment, and facilities as part of your charge. Both sides of the language debate rightfully argued for tools to support a full life cycle methodology. They also pushed for better facilities and equipment, arguing that what's needed to develop software is different from what's required to operate and sustain it. You agreed to increase the scope of the environment and address these concerns.

How to fund the acquisition of these facilities and equipment is your third issue. Although upgrades are needed immediately, funds have not been budgeted. A small budget for tools has been approved, but tools are treated as an expense, not as part of the capital budget. However, the needed facilities and equipment do fall under this budget. That's because expenditures for facilities and equipment are depreciated and appear on your profit and loss (P&L) statement. Because they don't want new expenses appearing on the P&L statements, the administrators at the utility don't know how to handle your requests for capital expenditures. The situation is even worse than it appears. Capital budgets are submitted annually for the next year in March. It is now April, and you've just missed the window of opportunity. Assuming that your requests for funds are approved, you will have to wait two years before you can make your purchases. Of course, senior management can reallocate funds in the current year's budget, but you'll make powerful enemies if you take money away from other groups.

Your fourth issue is vision. When building your environment, senior management wants you to support its future vision for the organization. This vision, which is contrasted against traditional prospects in Table 6.2, is too advanced for most of your programmers. They state that they are not concerned with management philosophy. They want you to make improvements in the software engineering environment now. Even though it will affect them, they have little interest in where the organization is moving as a whole. You believe you can resolve this dilemma by couching your proposals in terms acceptable to management.

Metrics is your fifth and final issue. Management has directed you to support its measurement initiatives as you build the environment. Managers want to quantitatively demonstrate that they have been successful. They have proposed 26 "measures of success" and are asking for weekly reports on progress at the worker level. Some are meaningless, and unfortunately, the metrics to support the success measures are not well defined. Major battles are being fought

Table 6.2: *Contrasting Views of the Corporation*

Characteristic	Twentieth Century	Twenty-first Century
Goals	Grow the business nationally	Grow the business internationally
Organization	Hierarchical	Collaborative
Markets	National	The world
Structure	Self-reliance	Global partnerships
Emphasis	Physical plant	Corporate infrastructure
Source of strength	People	Process and team
Strategy	Maximize efficiency	Be agile and quick to market
Tactics	High productivity and low cost	E-everything
Competition	Corporate teams	National groupings
Products	Product families	Product lines
Technology	Manufacturing-oriented	Consumer-oriented
Workforce	Domestic	International
Expectations	Security	Mobility
Major issues	– Capital costs (for growth) – Developing core competency – Motivating staff	– Conversion costs (to e-economy) – Maintaining core competency – Retaining staff
Marketplace discriminators	– Lowest possible cost – Highest possible quality	– Best value for the money – Best-of-breed in quality

over which metrics should be collected and how they should be reported. Two camps have emerged, the minimalists and the extremists. The minimalists want you to focus on quantifying one or two metrics that can be reported to management on overall improvement progress. In contrast, the extremists want to collect all 26 metrics to provide management with indicators of progress for each of its measures of success. Each side refuses to recognize the other's arguments. You need to support both camps to move ahead.

INITIAL OPERATIONAL CONCEPT

You haven't been idle. To kick off the effort, you've developed and circulated an operational concept in an attempt to reach consensus among your stakeholders. Your operational concept, illustrated in Figure 6.3, provides your engineers with

Candidate Tools

- Life cycle support
  - Requirements analysis
  - Architecture development
  - Implementation
  - Test and evaluation
- Configuration management
- Problem tracking
- Project management
- Office products
- E-mail and Web publishing
- Proposal support

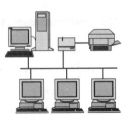

Operational Concept

- Common processes
- Common methods
- Common languages
- Common tools
- Virtual repository (repository of repositories)
- At least one workstation per engineer
- Semiprivate office per engineer
- Plenty of meeting rooms

Figure 6.3: *Environment Operational Concept*

a virtual environment consisting of the facilities, workstations, and tools needed to deploy new processes and methods organizationwide. To make sure you address each of the issues raised in your operational concept, you've developed the traceability matrix shown in Table 6.3. This table will remind you of what issues need to be covered when you move to the new environment.

Although it is notional, most of the engineers you are working with love your concept. They want you to focus on facilities and equipment first, then tools. "Let's get a workstation for every engineer" and "Let's buy such and such a tool" are the comments you hear most often. But senior management is resisting to your pleas for budget. The response is "You will have to justify what is needed thoroughly before we'll approve the expenditures." Luckily, you have a champion in the senior management camp to provide you with guidance and support. He has offered to review your business case before you submit it to senior management for approval.

CAPITAL DECISION-MAKING PROCESS

Capital decisions are made throughout the software development process. In most cases, they involve identifying alternatives and recommending a solution according to a range of factors including costs/benefits. To develop your recommendation, you would use the version of the seven-step business planning process and the GQM method introduced in Chapter 2, which is displayed in

Table 6.3: *Traceability Matrix*

Issue	Resolution Approach
Managers are techies	Project management tools will be acquired with new supervisor training and consulting support.
Which equipment, facilities, and tools?	Pilot projects using new processes will identify the requirements, assist in component selection, provide funds, and assist the working group in acquiring what the organization needs.
Budget for equipment and facilities	Corporate champions will fund needed items using discretionary and unspent capital budgets. Projects will fund any budget shortfalls.
Vision disconnect	Solutions will be architected for the long term. The initial increment will accommodate near term (in support of the pilot projects).
Which metrics?	Core metrics will be defined that support the opposing camps.

Figure 6.4. As part of this process, you would use the principles, rules, and tools we discussed in Chapter 3 to perform make-versus-buy analysis, develop cost estimates, assess the impact of depreciation, examine tax consequences, and perform cost/benefit analysis.

MAKE-VERSUS-BUY ANALYSIS

The first set of questions you have to address in your justification for additional funds revolves around make/buy analysis. As in most organizations, you have a number of in-house tools that you have developed over the years to handle things such as configuration management, problem tracking, and project management. Your engineers are skilled in the use of these tools, and your work processes have been designed around them. In addition, your IT department has interfaced these tools to its cost accounting and material management systems. If you move to alternatives, you will pay a steep price because implementing these interfaces will be a nontrivial task. You also hold licenses to a number of software products. Which do you keep, and what do you do with the others? Facilities represent a unique problem. There isn't enough room to accommodate your desire for semiprivate offices and additional meeting space. You've missed the window to impact next year's capital budget. Your champion's advice is to fight other

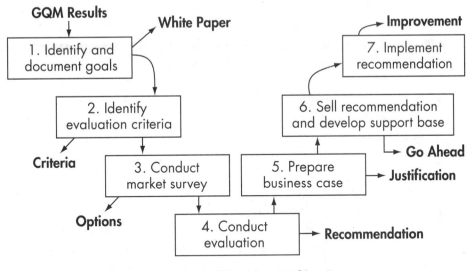

Figure 6.4: *Capital Decision-Making Process*

battles first and come back later to fight this one. Finally, most of your computer equipment is leased. However, your servers and communications gear (hubs, routers, switches, and so on) have been purchased. When you ask your contacts in accounting why they have purchased some and leased other equipment, nobody seems to have an answer. How do you handle each of these situations? What are your justification tactics?

Using In-House Tools

Most of your engineers agree that your existing software configuration management, problem tracking, and project management tools are archaic. They rely on a logical model of data that would be hard to distribute and flat-file databases that would make data extraction on the Web difficult. If the model were used, it would be almost impossible to process transactions on the Web and implement a virtual repository in your environment. When queried, the IT staff tells you that they are overwhelmed by their backlog and won't be able to take on this new task for at least a year. Of course, if management insisted, they would juggle assignments and start the interfacing work, but they wouldn't be too happy about it.

Luckily, your team has come up with an innovative solution to the problem. They suggest that you build your environment not to replace but to interface with the existing tool infrastructure. That would allow you to implement your operational concept without replacing the tools until a later time. However, there will be some additional cost to build the wrappers to mechanize the interface. When queried, the COTS vendor you have chosen to supply the infrastructure products for your virtual environment quoted six months and $800,000 (in addition to the normal licensing and support costs) to design the interface, implement the wrappers, and test the system. The vendor recommends developing an API for wrapping tools so that you can use your existing packages. Your staff likes this option because it is technically superior to what they devised.

Because the cost jeopardizes approval of your initiative, you seek an alternative solution. Your people tell you that they believe they could do the job of interfacing new tools to your custom packages in half the time and for half the money. While they historically have the ability to do a good job, you believe that they have underestimated the effort. Given the facts, there are three options you wish to evaluate:

- *Use the existing tools*   Try to adapt the existing tools so that they support your virtual environment operational concepts. Costs would be minimized. However, new tools would have to be interfaced to those that exist already.

- *Replace the existing tools*   Replace the existing tools in your environment with new ones that support your operational concept. This involves major costs because processes would have to be written and additional licenses acquired.

- *Interface your environment to the existing tools*   Implement your team's recommendation using either contractor or in-house resources.

Table 6.4 illustrates the tradeoffs between these three options. The ten-year cost ($N = 10$) is computed by taking the PV of the life cycle expenditures assuming a uniform series of cash flows (e.g., PV = $[(1 + i)^N - 1]/[i(1 + i)^N]$). The following formula uses a 6 percent cost of money (i) and assumes that the one-time costs are not discounted (i.e., occur at start of the year):

ten-year cost = PV (6%)[one-time cost + Σ annual costs]

The tradeoff analysis in Table 6.4 shows that pursuing the interface with your own staff seems preferable because its cost is considerably less than the alternatives. This tradeoff analysis also shows how life cycle cost analysis can be used to highlight the differences among alternatives. Such differences are not apparent when you casually review the raw numbers.

Table 6.4: *In-House Tool Options Tradeoff Analysis*

	Use Existing Tools	Replace Existing Tools	Interface Tools Contractor	Interface Tools In-house Staff
One-time cost	$200K	$1,600K	$800K	$400K
Annual cost	$300K	$100K	$200K	$100K
Schedule	3 months	1 year	6 months	3 months
Pluses	No changes to processes Business as usual	Get rid of archaic tools Move all at once to future	Expert devises API for tools that anyone can use	In charge of own destiny Pride that goes with job
Minuses	Would have to give up virtual environment	Rewritten processes may not work	Steep learning curve for contractor	Staff would have to be made available
Ten-year cost	$1,925K	$2,175K	$1,950K	$975K

Improved Software Tool Licensing

Licenses for existing software turn out to be an opportunity. During the past two years, your Operations Directorate members have negotiated enterprise-wide licenses with the software suppliers for commonly used software (operating systems, database management packages, and so on) for their servers and mainframes. As part of their effort, they have been able to get deep discounts and favorable terms from the software vendors for packages used across the organization. However, they have not pursued tool licenses. When asked why, they stated that tools are a project-specific choice. Furthermore, budgets for tools are approved at the project, not enterprise, level. That's why they are expensed rather than depreciated. As a result, coordination of joint needs across projects has not been pursued. When asked what it would take to tackle tool licenses, the head of the Directorate said that she just didn't have the staff to address this requirement. The Operations Directorate budget would have to be increased by about $50,000 a year if it was to coordinate needs and negotiate licenses with the vendors.

Table 6.5 shows the results of a survey you had your people conduct to determine whether you could justify this expenditure. Your leverage with the vendors seems to be very good because five to six suppliers provide 80 percent of

Table 6.5: *Improved License Coordination Dollar Savings*

	Number of Products	Number of Licenses	Nominal Discount	Improved Discount	Annual Savings ($K)
Life cycle support					
• Requirements analysis	6	28	10%	30%	50
• Architecture	3	12	10%	30%	24
• Implementation	28	147	15%	40%	58
• Test and evaluation	7	39	10%	30%	76
Existing tools*					
• Configuration management	3	5	10%	25%	3
• Problem tracking	3	4	10%	25%	2
• Project management	8	8	15%	30%	5
Office products	1	Enterprise license	NA	NA	NA
E-mail and Web publishing	1	Enterprise license	NA	NA	NA
Proposal support	1	5	10%	10%	NA
Total savings					218

*Tools justified for project use, each supplied by different vendors.

the tool licenses. The table shows that you can potentially justify the cost of the added staff for the Operations Directorate because you can save more than $200,000 by leveraging your purchasing power across projects to increase your license discount from 10 to as much as 40 percent.

The licensing initiatives you plan on pursuing would provide you some added benefits. First, vendors would be more responsive because you would become a larger client. Second, you could simplify procurement by negotiating some form of basic ordering agreement or contractual instrument. Third and finally, you could ask your legal department to negotiate improved license terms and conditions (e.g., moving spare seats from one project to another).

Facility Modifications

As noted, you don't have money to perform any capital improvements. Currently, you are stuffing people into offices. Your staff is complaining about overcrowding and the lack of meeting space. They want semiprivate offices, a lunch-room, vending machines, and meeting areas to conduct reviews and inspections. They also need more modern equipment and upgraded wiring (better ground-ing). They point to the facilities that a dotcom has next door and ask: "Why can't you provide facilities like those of our neighbors?"

You've had your facilities people draft a floor plan for the IT organization. Your 400 people are currently crammed into 100 offices on four floors. To satisfy your needs, you will need to acquire and renovate two additional floors in your building. Currently, accounting and billing personnel occupy this space. They are willing to move if someone can find nicer space for them. They too are over-crowded and seeking new facilities. Luckily, they have a capital budget of $1 million for renovation next year. The total cost for renovating your desired six floors including rewiring the space (not in the current plans) is estimated at $3 million. The good news is that the upgrade can be done in stages so that you minimize the negative impacts on productivity. Facilities recommends scheduling a floor for renovation every two months.

You can't wait two years to begin improvements. Your people expect you to work magic and get additional space now. IT has some excess space in a building about a mile away. Your plan is to move 20 of your 400 people into this space tem-porarily. The five offices you will free up in the existing facility will then be turned into meeting rooms, a lunchroom, and a liaison area for you and your people while they are on site. Luckily, the cost for the move is covered by overhead. Therefore, you can implement this plan immediately without a capital budget.

Your strategy is to find nice space that accounting and finance can move into within the year that doesn't require renovations and improvements. You can then tap whatever part of their capital budget is left to make planned improve-ments in your space. Currently, they pay $36 per square foot per year for their space in your building. This fee includes the pro rata charges for electricity, gas, maintenance, and janitorial services. Your wife is a commercial real estate broker. She has identified a newer two-story building three blocks away that seems to fit accounting's needs. The building has about 20,000 square feet of floor space. The property owner is willing to lease the entire building for $30 per square foot per year, including electricity, gas, and maintenance, if your organization is willing to sign a 5-year lease. For a 10-year lease, the property owner will lower the cost to $27 per square foot per year and make any reasonable capital improvements free. When asked, the property owner is even willing to throw in janitorial ser-vices for free if you sign the 10-year lease. The deal sounds too good to be true.

Your wife tells you that the property owner is willing to make these concessions because he likes the idea of having a single client in the building for 10 years. In the past, he has had to bear the expense of vacant space as he tried to attract new tenants, and the renovations needed to attract new tenants were expensive. He also likes having a utility like yours in the building because it won't go out of business and he can count on the rent being paid on time.

The benefits of the move to both you and accounting are tremendous. Accounting would save $5 per square foot per year, or about $100,000 a year (about $1 million over the 10-year lease). They would have their own building and room for all their people. Before the move, they would need to spend $250,000 to wire the new building for networks and phones. You would get the space you need to expand and about $750,000 of committed funds to renovate it. Your challenge is to sell the concept to senior management. Getting managers to agree to sign a 10-year lease will not be an easy task.

When you ask him, your champion advises you, "Go for it." The numbers support your case, and you've pulled a viable plan together to get the space you need. Getting signatures on the documents you need to push the idea through the system is another matter. Your only hope is to walk the document through the system.

Equipment Lease or Purchase

Again, you have no money to buy equipment. But projects have money to lease computers. However, senior management has been reluctant to lease because of the financials. Purchasing equipment allows management to depreciate the gear quickly using the declining-balance method. Unlike the straight-line method that results in a constant annual depreciation, this method applies a constant rate each year to the book value of the asset at the beginning of the year. Any declining-balance rate may be used insofar as it doesn't exceed twice the straight-line charge excluding the salvage value. The maximum rate is usually used and can be computed as $(2)(100\%/N)$, where N is the useful life of the asset.

For illustrative purposes, I've compared the results of using the straight-line and declining-balance methods to compute annual depreciation for a server valued at $20,000, assuming zero salvage value on retirement, over a 5-year period in Table 6.6. The declining-balance method permits you to write off more of the value of the asset in the early years. If you kept the asset for its full useful life, you would probably convert to the straight-line method toward the end of the depreciation schedule.

Table 6.6: *Declining-Balance versus Straight-Line Depreciation Method*

Year	Declining-Balance Book Value at Start of Year	Declining-Balance Depreciation Charge	Straight-Line Book Value at Start of Year	Straight-Line Depreciation Charge
1	$20,000	$8,000	$20,000	$4,000
2	$12,000	$4,800	$16,000	$4,000
3	$7,200	$2,880	$12,000	$4,000
4	$4,320	$1,728	$8,000	$4,000
5	$2,592	$1,037	$4,000	$4,000

However, lease costs can be expensed (your accountant says you can write off 20K maximum annually). Therefore, you can take the full cost of the equipment as an expense on your income statement. Because this has been a profitable year, an increase in expenses could have a profound positive tax consequence. Your senior management champion says the organization wishes to minimize taxes at the expense of shaving profit on its financials. This would enable the firm to carry over last year's profit without much tax penalty. The investment would also look good as a footnote in its first-to-be-released annual report and on the P&L statement. You are more than willing to help the company satisfy these goals. Table 6.7 summarizes the tax tradeoffs for the equipment purchase versus lease option for 200 PCs, 20 servers, and a range of communications and networking gear. The figures in the table are based on the assumption that the utility will be profitable for the next 5 years (i.e., must pay the 48 percent maximum corporate tax rate).

Table 6.7: *Equipment Purchase/Lease Tax Implications*

Year	Purchase Price + PV (Maintenance Costs) ($K)	PV (Tax Impact of Depreciation) ($K)	PV (Lease Cost) ($K)	PV (Tax Impact) Tax Rate = 48% ($K)
1	990.0	172.8	200.0	96.0
2	84.9	95.8	188.7	90.6
3	80.1	55.5	178.0	85.4
4	75.6	31.2	167.9	80.6
5	71.3	44.3	158.4	76.0
Total	1,301.9	399.6	893.0	428.6

The following assumptions were made for the analysis shown in Table 6.7:

- The purchase price for all the equipment including discounts is $900K.

- Annual maintenance costs for purchased equipment is 10 percent of purchase price paid in advance at the start of the year to get a discount. Assuming that there will be no price increase due to inflation, maintenance is therefore $90K/year.

- The lease cost for the same equipment is computed on a nondiscounted base price of $1M at 20 percent per year paid in advance at the beginning of the year. This cost includes an annual maintenance contract. The figures in the table reflect the PV of this $200K per year expenditure assuming the cost of money to be 6 percent.

- The effective tax rate was assumed to be 48 percent because the organization was profitable.

- The declining-balance method was used to determine depreciation expenses.

- The tax impact of the purchase option was computed by multiplying the present value of the calculated depreciation by the effective tax rate (48 percent). Depreciation was assumed to have a 5-year useful life and zero salvage value. Depreciation was posted on the books at the start of the year. The tax implications of each option were computed as shown in Table 6.8.

- The tax impact of the lease option was computed by determining the present value of the tax liability calculated by the effective tax rate (again 48 percent).

Table 6.8: *Computation of Tax Impact of Equipment Purchase*

Year	Book Value ($K)	Depreciation (DDB method) ($K)	Tax Impact (48%) ($K)	PV (Tax Impact) ($K)
1	900.0	360.0	172.8	172.8
2	540.0	216.0	103.7	95.8
3	324.0	130.0	62.4	55.5
4	194.0	77.6	37.2	31.2
5	116.4	116.4	55.9	44.3
Total	0	900.0	432.0	399.6

Note: Move to straight line after Year 5.

For example, you would take 48 percent of $200K during the first year to compute the value that appears in the table.

■ All entries in the table assume this year's value of the dollar.

Table 6.7 provides you with the ammunition you need—the facts and figures—to win the battle of the budget. However, you should do several things before presenting the numbers to management. First, you should meet with accounting to make sure that your assumptions are correct. As the experts, they know the latest tax laws and have insight into how your organization handles depreciation and taxes. For example, the tax rate may be forecast to vary or depreciation may be taken at the end instead of the beginning of the fiscal year. If this is the case, you need to reflect the correct assumptions. Second, you should meet with legal to determine whether you are entitled to take an investment tax credit for the purchase option. If you can, the credit comes directly off your tax liability. Therefore, the total amount of the credit should be added to the tax impact column as a reduction.

If everything checks out, ask your champion for advice on how to present this and the results of the other analysis you've conducted upward. You probably don't want to do everything I suggest all at once. First, fight the battles you believe you can win. Then try to win the more difficult fights. For example, getting management to agree that you need space is easy; getting management to fund your intricate plan to provide it may be more difficult.

PUTTING SOFTWARE COST MODELS TO WORK

You can also use a software cost model like COCOMO II [Boehm, 2000] to quantify the benefits of your environment initiative. Such models can provide you with the additional justification you need to get management to approve your initiatives. Often, just looking at the make/buy alternatives is not enough. You will need to make a more compelling business case to stimulate senior managers to approve your software tool, equipment, and facility investment proposals. The make/buy analysis substantiates your tactics and shows you where to find the money to pay for your recommendations. Unfortunately, it doesn't provide your senior management with a convincing reason to push ahead into new territory.

As the basis of your business case, I suggest that you create a benchmark project for your client/server upgrade. This benchmark can then be used to compute the benefits that accrue to a typical project due to your initiatives. It can also be used to assess alternatives and conduct sensitivity analyses. I suggest that you take a medium to large applications project for your benchmark. Choosing too small a project is often a mistake because results may not scale broadly. Looking at the selection options in Table 6.1, I recommend taking sales and marketing as your candidate because it is a large application and parts reside on both the client and the server. This selection has many other advantages. The application is highly visible and important to the organization. Requirements are limited, and there are many people available to help scope the needed functionality. Getting marketing to agree on the requirements in a reasonable time period is probably the only difficulty with the selection.

When using cost models, you need to understand what is and isn't included in their scope. Table 6.9 summarizes the effort that is included within the scope of the COCOMO II estimate. In-scope activities are those that are normally included as part of the model's output. Understanding what's included is important because you will have to add effort to cover work that is outside the model's scope. For example, the table shows that you will have to add about 10 percent for the requirements synthesis task and 20 percent to cover system testing because these activities are not part of the estimate. Because this benchmark estimate may establish management expectations, you need to make sure that it is complete and comprehensive.

Table 6.9: *COCOMO II Model Scope*

In-Scope Activities*	Out-of-Scope Activities**	
Requirements analysis	Requirements synthesis	Add 6–10%
Software product design	Beta testing	Add 8–10%
Software implementation	System testing	Add 10–25%
Software integration and testing	Organization level	
Project management	– Configuration management	Add 2–6%
Project configuration management	– Distribution management	Add 2–4%
Project quality assurance (QA)	– Independent QA	Add 4–8%
Normal documentation	– Independent audits	Part of QA
Standard metrics		

*Effort part of the COCOMO run

**Added effort needed because these activities are not part of COCOMO run

It is important to note that each of the popular cost models we identified in Chapter 3 has a slightly different scope. Therefore, you must be extremely careful when you compare the outputs of two models side by side. If you aren't careful, you might wind up comparing apples with trucks.

Figure 6.5 illustrates the four-step process your process group has developed for software estimating. As shown in the figure, the process calls for you to develop and compare two estimates and reconcile the differences. Because you are using this process to develop benchmarks, you really don't believe that you have to do all of this work. You can elect to use either a task-oriented estimating approach or a cost model. To do otherwise would be too labor intensive for your purposes. Independent of the technique selected, the credibility of the estimate is important. Making too many simplifications can discredit you in the minds of management. Your goal should be to achieve a balance between the many factors that influence how the estimate is perceived.

I use a cost model because I want to illustrate its power in this section. Models are credible when properly calibrated. Putting a screen shot showing the

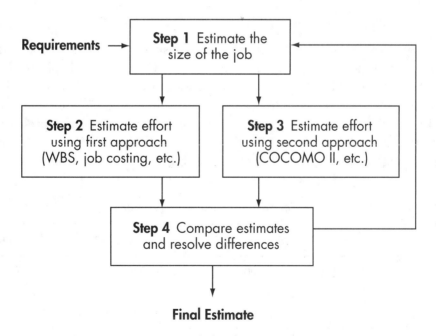

Figure 6.5: *Recommended Software Estimating Process*

model's output in your pitch to management provides what I call "face" validity. Because the model says so, people believe the numbers have to be right. Outputs are often expressed using decimal points. This implied precision, whether it is real or imaginary, further adds to their perceived validity. In other words, these mathematical models have a psychological advantage over what management perceives is nothing more than best guesses based on experience.

Let's use the process illustrated in Figure 6.5 to develop an estimate for our benchmark. To start, we need to size the job. We can use either source lines of code (SLOC) or function points to do this. Which of these two metrics is best is a hotly debated topic. I suggest that you use whichever is easiest to quantify within your organization.

Step 1: Estimate the Size of the Job

To start, we have decided to estimate the size of the job in equivalent new SLOC. Because not everything you develop as part of the application will be new, you must develop conventions to handle at least the following four types of software in these size estimates:

- New
- Modified
- Reused
- COTS

Again, you are lucky. Your process group advises you that they have taken the conventions suggested in Chapters 2 and 3 of the COCOMO II book [Boehm, 2000] to estimate these components. When asked, your chief software engineer provides you with the software size estimates summarized by these four categories in Table 6.10. He is credible to management and therefore represents a good source for these numbers. This is especially true if you portray these numbers as rough-order-of-magnitude (ROM) estimates.

Table 6.10: *SLOC Estimates for Sales and Marketing Application*

	New (SLOC)	Modified (SLOC)	Reused (SLOC)	COTS (SLOC)
Client	25,000	5,000	5,000	0
Server	13,000	15,000	10,000	7,000
Total	38,000	20,000	15,000	7,000

To convert these numbers to equivalent new SLOC, we can use the following formula:

software size (SLOC) = new + 0.5 (modified) + 0.3 (reused) + 0.2 (COTS)
software size (SLOC) = 38K + 0.5 (20K) + 0.3 (15K) + 0.2 (7K) = 53.9K SLOC

What this formula says is that it takes about half as much effort to handle the 20K SLOC of modified code because most of the design exists, not all of the code needs to be modified, and not all of the integration and testing needs to be performed. It also assumes that reused software was designed for reuse, so it doesn't need to be modified. Instead, it can be instantiated for reuse and tested. There should be no design or coding modifications. For COTS, it assumes that you don't have access to the source code. Instead, you will focus your effort on wrapping COTS (via a common API and middleware) so that it can be integrated into the application and tested. As expected, no design or code modifications will be made to COTS software.

Steps 2–4: Estimate Effort Using COCOMO II

As mentioned, you will generate a single estimate for your applications software benchmark to complete steps 2 to 4 of the process. To do this, you will use the process shown in Figure 6.6. For simplicity's sake, you will set the model's scale factors at the organizational level (see Table 6.11) and use the model's default values for the remaining cost drivers. This will allow you to vary the cost drivers to perform both parametric and sensitivity analysis. For this estimate, these values will be the benchmark numbers you will use as a point of departure for further analyses. As part of your management brief, you plan to compare what would happen on this benchmark project with and without pursuit of your initiatives. This will allow you to compare options in a way your management will understand.

You can use the COCOMO II software package (available on CD in [Boehm, 2000]) to generate an estimate once you have rated each of the model's cost drivers (both the scale factors and effort multipliers). You can generate cost and duration estimates by plugging the size estimates shown in Table 6.10 into the package and setting the scale factors to the values in Table 6.11. The nominal model output is displayed in Figure 6.7. It estimates that the project would probably take 19.8 months and 216 staff-months of effort to complete, assuming nominal ratings. To reduce confusion, you have not included the parts of the estimate that are out of the model's scope (see Table 6.9). Because you plan to use this estimate as a benchmark, you believe it doesn't have to be precise.

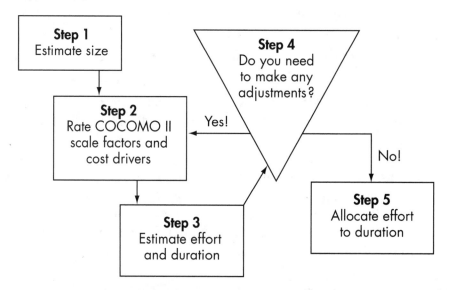

Figure 6.6: *COCOMO II Estimate Development Process*

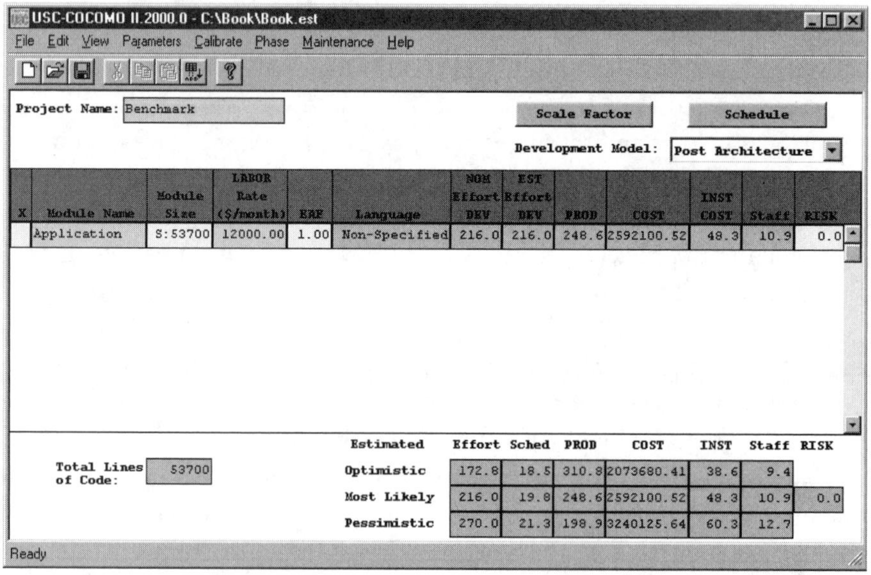

Figure 6.7: *COCOMO II Nominal Output Screen*

Note: This estimate was generated by the software package provided in [Boehm, 2000] using the size estimate in Table 6.10, default values for the EAF, and scale factors set to the values shown in Table 6.11.

Table 6.11: *COCOMO II Scale Factor Ratings for Benchmark Project*

Scale Factor	Rating	Explanation
PREC: Precedentedness	H	While the organization understands the goals of the move to client/servers, your staff has less than three years of experience working with related systems.
FLEX: Development flexibility	H	Because the organization is moving to client/server applications, there is considerable flexibility in the way it interprets how to use its process for new applications.
RESL: Architecture/ risk resolution	H	The move to client/server architecture is providing the organization with many opportunities to address risk and risk resolution using processes devised for this purpose.
TEAM: Team cohesion	N	Based on experience, you anticipate that the team will function cooperatively and work well with stakeholders. There are no outside customers, and relationships will be under your control.
PMAT: Process maturity	L	As part of your business process reengineering effort, you are putting new processes into practice. Therefore, you rate process maturity for the organization as low.

However, your estimate must be believable. Therefore, the first thing you do is to compare the estimate to folklore. Assuming $12K per staff-month, the $48.27 per SLOC estimate that results compares well with the $50 per SLOC that management assumes is valid based on experience. However, you know that you will be asked many other questions by management about your numbers. It is not that the managers don't trust you. Instead, you believe that they are inquisitive. They want to understand what the numbers mean as well as what they say. In addition, they always pose "what-if" questions to determine whether or not there are other options that should be explored. Based on your past experience, they will identify options that you have not contemplated as you conducted your analysis. In addition, politics and money will play a part in the meeting. Because there is only so much money available, everyone knows that the money to pay for your initiatives will have to come out of someone else's budget. Most of the managers in the meeting will support you when their funds are not jeopardized by your actions.

PERFORMING RISK ANALYSIS

You can do many useful things using the benchmark estimate once it has been developed. For example, you can quantify the impact of the risks listed in Table 6.3. Using hard numbers like these as your basis, you can quantify the effects of pursuing your recommended actions using the benchmark for making comparisons. The sections that follow illustrate how you could use the COCOMO II cost model to resolve the first two items in Table 6.3.

Managers Are Techies

You are surprised to learn that one of the COCOMO model's underlying assumptions is that the project is "well managed." As such, the model does not normally take situations like having good technical people promoted into managerial positions into account. You can't look at the impact of techie managers on estimated cost and duration by varying the model's personnel cost drivers—analyst capability (ACAP), programmer capability (PCAP), personnel continuity (PCON), application experience (APEX), platform experience (PLEX), and language/tool experience (LTEX). However, you can vary the scale factor associated with teamwork (TEAM) to assess a part of this risk and the sensitivity of your estimates to it. With all other factors held constant, the estimated effort will vary from 198 to 235 staff-months of effort and 18.8 to 20.9 months in duration.

The model clearly indicates that this issue is not a major swinger because the effort varies by just 8 percent and schedule by 5 percent when this parameter is varied over its full range. Figure 6.8 shows the results of setting the TEAM scale factor at its best value. Of course, these numbers assume that none of the other model factors are affected by the decision to use techies as managers. If you were still concerned, you could model the tendencies using one of the COCOMO II "user-defined" cost drivers. Of course, you would have to use "expert opinions" or actual data to calibrate this new driver before you could use it effectively.

Which Equipment and Tools

Again, you would use the parametric relationships in the model to assess the impact of different equipment and tool options using the benchmark project as your basis for comparison. Things get a little more complicated because you now have to look at a number of related cost drivers: for example, the richness of the environment (TOOL), its volatility (PVOL), and the skills of the people using it (PLEX) and (LTEX). With all other cost drivers besides these four held constant,

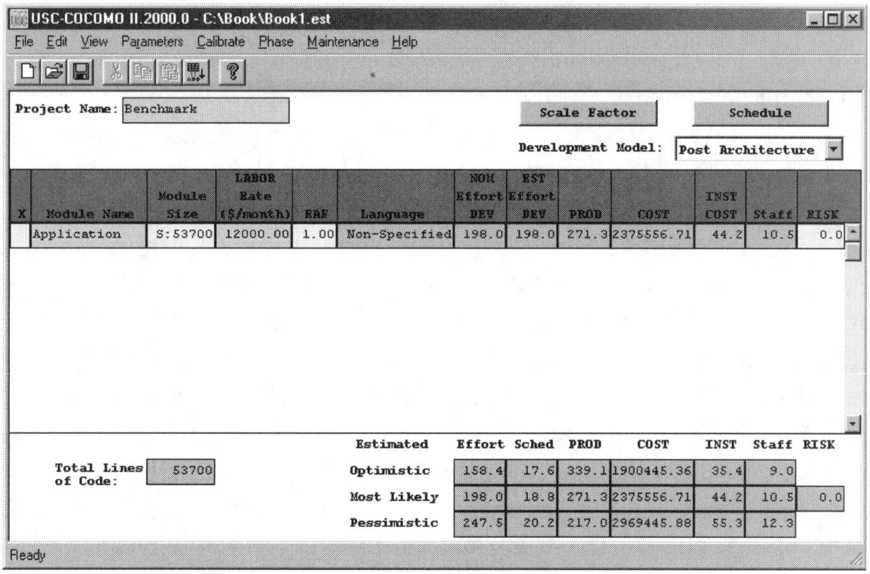

Figure 6.8: *Estimate Assuming TEAM Is Set Very High*

the estimated effort varies by a factor of about 5 to 1 as these drivers are varied over their full range. Selecting the proper setting for these drivers is what's important. For example, changing tools and equipment may improve richness at the expense of volatility and skills, based on the assumption that the environment currently in use is stable and your people are skilled in its use. If this isn't the case, variation of these cost drivers could result in a major increase in the estimate.

Quantifying risk using a cost model like COCOMO II provides you with the ability to assess and prioritize risks according to their estimated impacts. Models also let you compare options both quantitatively and qualitatively. They allow you to look at sensitivities and evaluate negatives such as learning curves and transition effects. When performing a risk analysis, you can look at many different parameters either singly or in combination. You can then select to first address items that you determine to have the greatest cost and/or duration impacts.

ADDRESSING "WHAT-IF" QUESTIONS

You can also perform many useful trade studies using your benchmark estimate as a comparative foundation. For example, you could assess the impact of using more commercial off-the-shelf (COTS) packages in the application, different languages, tools like generators and translators, and/or different paradigms on your cost and duration estimates. Let's look at adding more COTS packages as an illustrative example.

Use of COTS is attractive to many developers because existing packages can often be integrated into an application at considerably less cost and in a fraction of the time compared to developing new software. COTS packages are software applications that exist and are used as is to perform a variety of functions that are part of your application. Their primary advantage is that you don't have to maintain them because some third party provides them. Instead, you can focus your efforts on integrating the packages into your application and testing them. This can be done as part of the standard development process or in some customized version of the product. Unfortunately, you lose many of these advantages when you modify COTS. If you aren't a major customer for the package, you have little control over either its destiny or its evolution. To assess the relative benefits of increased COTS use in your benchmark, you would rerun the model assuming a larger COTS content, as shown in Figure 6.9. You would also look at the additional licensing and integration costs associated with COTS using a spreadsheet like the one in Table 6.12 to summarize the costs so you could determine the relative costs/benefits.

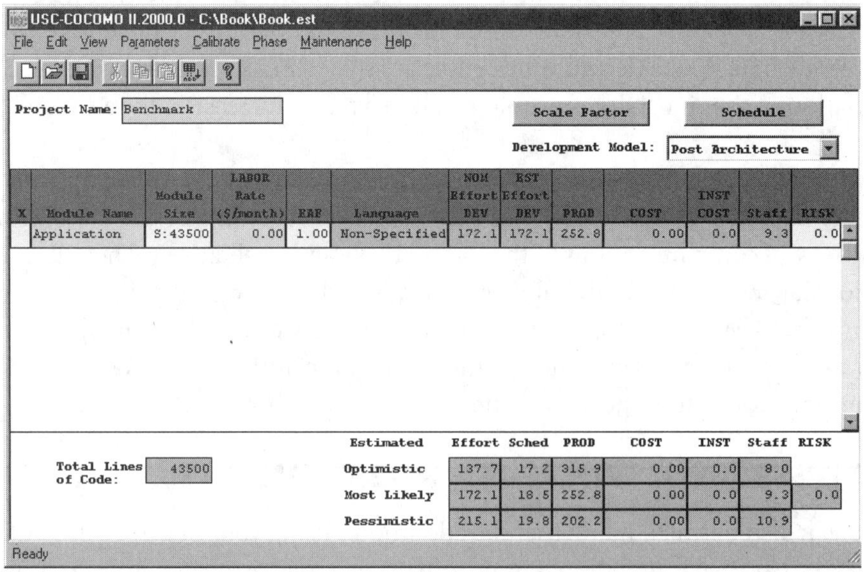

Figure 6.9: *Estimate Assuming Increased COTS*

Table 6.12: *Cost of COTS versus New Development*

Factor	COTS ($K)
Development license costs	50
Run-time license costs	50
Integration and test costs	48
Maintenance costs (5 years)	25
Total	173

Let's look at how you developed the numbers for the COTS alternative. First, you assumed that you could replace an additional 13K SLOC of new development with COTS components (the new total will be 20K SLOC of equivalent code). As a result, the new size estimate that you use in the model run, 43.5K SLOC, was derived as follows:

software size (SLOC) = new + 0.5 (modified) + 0.3 (reused) + 0.2 (COTS)
software size (SLOC) = 25K + 0.5 (20K) + 0.3 (15K) + 0.2 (20K) = 43.5K SLOC

Next, you assumed that you have to purchase a development license before you can integrate the COTS components into your product. Based on the licensing agreement, you also assumed that you would have to pay the vendor a run-time license fee of $100 each time you use the COTS in your client applications in any of your 250 offices statewide. Third, you assumed that there would be additional four staff-months (SM) of effort to integrate and test COTS software. This represents the additional effort to wrap the packages so that they interface to your API. Finally, you assumed that vendor support for the COTS packages doesn't come free. Maintenance is provided via an annual service agreement that is priced at 10 percent of the original development license fee. This standard agreement provides you with around-the-clock telephone support. It also provides you with software fixes as they become available from the vendor. New versions of the COTS packages are not included in the agreement. Upgrades to each package will have to be evaluated separately as they become available.

As Figure 6.9 shows, increasing COTS use from 7K to 20K SLOC cuts your cost by about 44 staff-months using the benchmark for comparison. But these benefits won't come free. As shown in Table 6.12, licensing, integration, and maintenance costs will add about 15 SM of equivalent labor at $12K per SM into the equation to compensate for the additional $173,000 in expenditures. Increasing the use of COTS therefore results in net savings of about 29 staff-months or $350,000. You are probably asking: "Is the move to COTS worthwhile?" To answer this, you have to look at the situation and the intangibles more closely.

The COTS trade study you completed shows that it would be beneficial to use COTS under the following conditions:

- You don't have to modify the COTS packages to provide additional functionality or to satisfy any unique API or interface requirement.

- The underlying technology associated with the COTS package capabilities is stable. The only anticipated package changes will be feature additions, not technology refreshments.

- The COTS package performs as advertised. You could live without certain features. But your users would be all over you if their applications did not perform with the speed and efficiency they are currently used to.

- The COTS vendors are established, provide you adequate support, and remain solvent. If not, you might have to take over maintenance of a COTS package to continue supporting your clients. This assumes that you have put a copy of the source code in escrow to guard against this contingency. However, you would still have to staff an effort to keep the package updated and that would be costly. Failure of the firm would quickly negate the advantages of COTS use. As part of your licensing practices, you should make sure that the vendors you deal with will be around for the long run.

With these factors in mind, you can now make a decision. As noted, use of COTS packages has both advantages and disadvantages. I've given you a brief discussion of some of the factors that should influence your decision. In addition, licensing practices and costs play an increasingly large part in your findings. As a final thought, get your process group to focus on your licensing processes and get your legal department involved in improving your licensing practices if you anticipate using COTS software in your applications. Because they know how to transfer processes into practice, they will do a credible job.

MAKING YOUR NUMBERS BELIEVABLE

In my experience, few engineers present credible business cases. Instead, they examine the engineering tradeoffs and prepare their arguments around the technical merits of the case. To survive in the business world, engineers must provide others with the business case information they are looking for to make decisions. This case has touched on some of this information. For a recommendation to be believable by nonengineers, it needs to address the following nine nontechnical considerations:

- *Cash flow*   Influence of the recommended alternative on your projected cash flow, including before- and after-tax analysis. Realize that recommendations may change once you have examined the tax consequences of the decision.

- *Cost basis*   Basis of the costs you used in your estimates—for example, how the cost of labor was computed vis à vis the projected labor mix.

- *Costs/benefits*   The costs/benefits, including a discussion of why you should pursue the recommended alternative (an analysis of both the tangible and intangible benefits).

- *Estimate fidelity*   Insurance that your numbers reflect the folklore numbers your management uses to make sanity checks on your estimates ($/SLOC, SLOC/SM, and so on). Also confidence that your models are calibrated against your company's, not general industry, experience.

- *Present value (PV)*   Value of future expenditures and relative costs/ benefits in terms of current-year dollars.

- *Profit and loss*   Influence of the recommendations on P&L in terms of items on the organization's balance sheet and income statement.

- *Risks*   Dollar value of the risks and the criteria you used to rank and stack them by priority (including their dollar impacts).

- *Source of funds*   Budgets you will use as the source of your funds and what your contingencies are if they are not available.

- *Tax implications*   Tax implications of your recommendations along with the depreciation schedules and projected tax write-offs.

As we discussed in earlier chapters, assume that members of your senior management staff will be asked to scrutinize your proposals. These people typically come from accounting, business, customer, and legal backgrounds. They are more skilled in business than engineering functions. The trick to getting their support is to ask them for help. Do this early, and do this often. If you solicit their help, they will tell you how to package the material so that it will sail through the nontechnical reviews. They will also ask the hard questions in advance of the review. This will give you time to prepare answers well in advance of the meeting. They will also provide insight into what management may be looking for. Depend on these people for support especially if your seniors rely on them for their opinions.

SUMMARY

This chapter discusses a case study involving software environment improvements. Since going public, the hypothetical utility is moving its applications from mainframes to a client/server architecture. Its Infrastructure Directorate is trying to bring in modern equipment and tools and upgrade the facilities. The case shows how to justify the expenditures primarily in terms of costs/benefits. It also looks at tax implications and capital budgeting issues.

KEY POINTS

- ✔ Major issues in this case range from deciding on tools to determining how to fund facility and equipment upgrades in light of budgetary problems.

- ✔ When performing a make/buy analysis, use the benefits that are available to justify your recommendations (e.g., the improved licensing discounts and innovative capital budgeting techniques in the case study).

- ✔ Use today's dollars to evaluate alternatives (e.g., look at the PV of projected cost/benefit cash flows).

- ✔ Don't be afraid to look for innovative solutions when faced with financial constraints.

- ✔ When comparing capital decisions, examine the tax implications of your recommendations using accelerated depreciation methods (e.g., declining-balance method) to compute the book value of the investment options.

- ✔ Develop benchmark projects using software cost models to justify investments, perform risk analyses, and address "what if" questions.

- ✔ Cost models such as COCOMO II make your numbers more believable to nontechnical managers because they create the illusion of preciseness.

- ✔ Make your numbers believable by addressing the concerns of your nontechnical proposal reviewers (legal, accounting, and so on).

References

[Boehm, 2000] Boehm, Barry W., Chris Abts, A. Winsor Brown, Sunita Chulani, Bradford K. Clark, Ellis Horowtiz, Ray Madachy, Donald Reifer, and Bert Steece. *Software Cost Estimation with COCOMO II.* Prentice Hall, 2000.

[Coad, 1996] Coad, Peter, David North, and Mark Mayfield. *Object Models, Patterns and Applications,* 2nd Edition. Prentice Hall, 1996.

[Kruchten, 1998] Kruchten, Philippe. *The Rational Unified Process.* Addison-Wesley, 1998.

[Pont, 1996] Pont, Michael J. *Software Engineering with C++ and Case.* Addison-Wesley, 1996.

[Schneider, 1998] Schneider, Geri, and Jason P. Winters. *Applying Use Cases: A Practical Guide.* Addison-Wesley, 1998.

[Yourdon, 1992] Yourdon, Edward. *Decline and Fall of the American Programmer.* Prentice Hall, 1992, pp. 27–28.

7

Making Your Numbers Sing
Architecting Case Study

*Science can amuse and fascinate us all—
but it is engineering that changes the world.*
—Isaac Asimov [Ehrlich, 1998]

THE GRAND PROPOSAL

This is an interesting time for your organization. Business is down because you seem unable to build competitive products cheaply and quickly. Every time you have gone head to head with the competition during the past year, you have lost. Your management hired a firm not too long ago to determine why you were losing business. It polled the marketplace and talked to people from your key accounts and your competition's. The findings indicated that customers viewed your products as expensive, archaic, and inflexible. Because earnings are decreasing, your investors are worried, and your board of directors has expressed concern. Management panicked after the stock price took a dive. Employees are unhappy with the situation as shown by the high attrition rate for key personnel. Everyone seems to agree that action is needed, but nobody seems to know what to do to remedy the situation.

177

Your firm makes, markets, and manufactures process control systems for medium- to large-scale manufacturing organizations. It has been in business for 50 years and is viewed as the market leader. The firm is organized as shown in Figure 7.1. The firm's current products are listed along with a brief description of them in Table 7.1. The firm's hopes were that your new data warehouse product would take the marketplace by storm. However, demand for it did not materialize as expected because the firm did not anticipate the rapid move to the Web and business-to-business (B-to-B) computing. Customers view much of what the firm has recently developed as outdated technology.

To change perceptions, management has kicked off a major initiative to move your firm to the Web. They have given you nine months to get on line and get the first wave of products out the door. This schedule is fixed in concrete because the deadline is the end of the fiscal year, and the company wants good news to report to the stockholders. Of course, the company realizes that it is playing catch-up and not everything can be accomplished at once. However, the

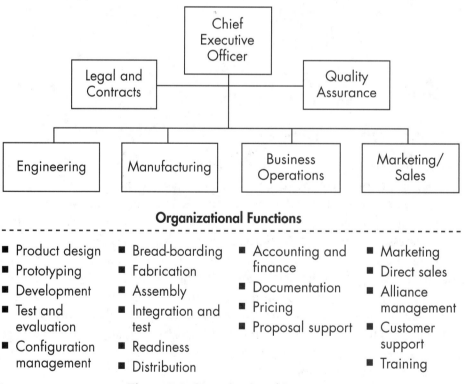

Organizational Functions

- Product design
- Prototyping
- Development
- Test and evaluation
- Configuration management

- Bread-boarding
- Fabrication
- Assembly
- Integration and test
- Readiness
- Distribution

- Accounting and finance
- Documentation
- Pricing
- Proposal support

- Marketing
- Direct sales
- Alliance management
- Customer support
- Training

Figure 7.1: *Organizational Structure*

Table 7.1: *Current Products and Product Lines*

Market Area	Products	Description
B-to-B systems	None	Means to identify, compete, and procure components using the Web instantaneously
CAD/CAM	Computer-aided design (CAD) link to your CAM systems	Means to import/export data from your computer-aided manufacturing (CAM) systems to/from client CAD packages
Data warehouse	Software package that runs on server to provide virtual data warehouse	Software that manages drawings and other documentation generated when a client uses your process control products
Inventory control	Software package that runs on server to manage inventory	Software that tracks inventory and computes reorder points by projected need
Process control	Process control systems for manufacturing production lines	Hardware and software that controls the movement of products through the assembly line and performs quality checks in real time using a customer input rule base
Production control	Software package that runs on server to control production	Software that keeps track of manufacturing lots as they step through the production process and reports where they are and what their status is to clients
Web-enabled systems	None	The ability to use the Web to track production lots and information about their components from anywhere in the world

firm wants to achieve something meaningful so that it can show it to customers at the trade show that will be held a week before the annual meeting. Your job is to decide what can be done. They want you to pitch your proposal to them tomorrow (or sooner). However, they have agreed to give you two weeks to get a plan of action and milestones together.

You are new to the organization, and this is your first major assignment. Before you begin, you start digging to learn the company's history, culture, and folklore. After about a day's research, you summarize your findings in your engineering journal as follows:

- This is a 50-year-old profitable firm that started when a larger firm rejected the founder's idea for using real-time, rule-based controls on client manufacturing lines to improve quality.
- The firm currently employs just fewer than 1,000 people.
  - Engineering (30 percent)—college educated, young, and energetic
  - Manufacturing (30 percent)—skilled and talented, primarily blue collar and unionized
  - Marketing (30 percent)—inexperienced, most feel expectations are unrealistic
  - Business operations (10 percent)—carryovers from the mainframe era (i.e., fear change)
- Products have been pursued in the past in an opportunistic manner. When a customer identifies a need, the company works with them to fill it. The client defines the requirements and provides the seed capital. The company builds the product and determines how to market it. The client acts as a beta tester and provides testimonials that the firm uses as part of its marketing campaign. The firm fields the product, maintains it, and sustains it after it is declared operational.
- For the most part, the engineering and manufacturing processes are hardware-oriented. Most managers in the firm don't realize that the majority of the engineering effort is going into software development and support activities.
  - COTS vendors supply most of the hardware, including semiconductor chips and logic boards, with the company's name stenciled into the identifiers.
  - No fabrication is required during manufacturing. Instead, hardware devices are built and tested on the assembly line as parts are assembled, integrated, and tested.
  - Client preferences are handled via proprietary technology the firm has developed that allows tailoring the firmware in the process control products to the client's needs using rules that are burned into programmable read-only memories (PROMs).
  - There has not been any technology refreshment since the products were put on the market about seven years ago. Of course, operating system

and similar updates have been incorporated as announced to maintain platform compatibility. But no new and innovative technology has been harnessed to boost the firm's perceived market position.

- Existing products are marketed using outside salespeople who push the product in exchange for a sizable commission. The company taps the sales force's existing client base and contacts at a reasonable cost. The sales force handles leads and existing clients directly.
- The firm is in a cash position and is looking to grow. Its recent stock offering resulted in an influx of capital that senior management has been debating how best to use to grow the firm per the strategy in its market prospectus.
- Senior management doesn't have a clue when it comes to software. Because all the managers hear are the troubles, they view it as a problem, not a solution.

■ Software management is from the "trust me" or "hero" school of management. Every time you ask them how they are doing, they say, "Trust me, I will finish it on time." You've tried, but are discouraged by the fact that they haven't seemed to generate anything on schedule recently.

To determine what to do, you have been reading the literature. One of your findings is the model shown in Figure 7.2. This model identifies what you believe are the components of a winning Web strategy for your business. It is organized around the three dimensions of make, market, and manufacture. You are developing the architectural elements of the model in your attempt to determine whether it will solve your problem relative to the Web.

The strategy paper you are reading suggests that you attack developing product features and quality first because you cannot succeed if you don't bring superior products to market. As you read, you are struck by several ideas. First, product lines seem to be the key to success because they enable you to build products with competitive features quickly and cheaply. Second, architecture is the key that unlocks the door to product lines. With architectures, systematic reuse is possible. Third and finally, reuse represents the silver bullet you are searching for to derive a reasonable plan of action and workable milestones for your management.

To learn more, you initiate a search and find that there are many books listed on the topics of architecture and software reuse. When you ask your chief software engineer which of these books are good, he cuts the list down to six: Bass, 1998; Jacobson, 1997; Lim, 1998; Poulin, 1997; Reifer, 1997; and Szyperski, 1999. You ask him why he picked these. He responds that each is important

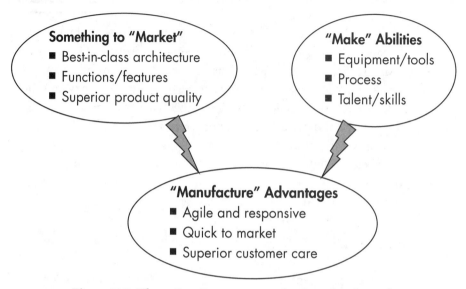

Figure 7.2: *Three-Part Improvement Strategy for the Web*

because it treats a different aspect of the product line technology. After reading each, you glean the following six important concepts.

1. *Architecture is first [Bass, 1998].*   You really like this textbook. It is readable and full of practical advice. You particularly like the numerous case studies and the lengthy discussion of product lines. Especially pertinent is the CORBA case and the discussion of World Wide Web (WWW) interoperability. You never realized that architecture development took so much effort. You don't believe that your people are sophisticated enough to perform all the work that's called out in the book by the end of the year. If possible, you'll have to find a speedier way to develop your architecture. Maybe the next text will be of some assistance.

2. *Methodology is important [Jacobson, 1997].*   This is another great textbook. It picks up where Bass leaves off. You like its detailed discussion of use cases, object-oriented methods, and layered architectures. The book's focus on processes and methodology is extremely helpful because it provides you with guidelines on how to get the job done. However, model-based software development is a stretch for your people. Again, the book tells you that there is a lot to do, and you still don't know how you are going to get it all done.

3. *Management is a challenge [Lim, 1998].*   Not surprisingly, this book complements the other two you've read. Its emphasis is management. After discussing success factors, it dives into organizational, planning, staffing, directing, and control issues. It provides the first detailed discussion you've seen on reuse costs and benefits. It surveys reuse economic models and tells you what seems to work and what doesn't. It dwells on processes and discusses process maturity issues. It provides a lot of useful information. However, your head is hurting after you read it. You continue to think: "So much to do and no time to do it." You've experienced information overload. It's time to take a break. You decide to return to your reading after your head has cleared.

4. *Measurement is possible [Poulin, 1997].*   This text talks metrics and measurement. It starts by arming you with the facts and figures that you need to justify your architecture-based reuse program. It defines metrics in detail and tells you how to use them to quantify software reuse and reuse benefits. It suggests a metrics starter set and discusses how to capture and use them to provide indicators of progress. Finally, it provides a worksheet and a reuse metrics calculator. There is no doubt in your mind that you will use this book to guide the implementation of your metrics program. However, it lets you down when it comes to architecture. You will have to use the Bass and Jacobson books to help you measure the goodness of your architecture and the activities you mount to develop it.

5. *Focus should be on infrastructure [Reifer, 1997].*   Here's another complementary text that provides you with insight into how to put what you've gleaned from the first four texts into action. Its major message is that many technical initiatives fail because not enough early focus was placed on developing the needed management infrastructure. The author amplifies these points as he provides lessons learned and guidance on implementing an architecture-based reuse initiative in the context of product line management concepts. Like the other texts, this one is full of advice that lets you build on the lessons others have learned as they tried to implement these new techniques in their organizations.

6. *Fine-grained components hold advantages [Szyperski, 1999].*   When you started reading this book, you wondered why your chief software engineer recommended it. But, you soon ascertained the reason. The technology you plan to use to move to the Web is different from that highlighted in the other texts. This book compares the Microsoft and Sun Web strategies. It gets into ActiveX, CORBA, Java, and OMA components and suggests ways to develop applications quickly using frameworks and component architectures. After reading the text, you are convinced that you should adopt a building-block approach because that is where the technology is moving in your industry. Integrating these building blocks into the architecture is the focus the experts (e.g., [Bass, 1998; Jacobson, 1997]) agree on.

You are now ready to start preparing your strategy briefing to management. You invite the following people to a meeting to help develop the first draft:

- Chief software engineer for the company
- Line of business manager for the data warehouse
- Principal investigator for your architecture R&D efforts
- Product manager for the production control software
- System engineering manager

You invite senior management to participate, but the senior managers decline because they don't think they could contribute. But your boss agrees to review the pitch as soon as you have finished it.

DEVELOPING A STRATEGY

Synthesizing a strategy turns out to be a tougher job than you expected. During the first day, the meeting bogs down primarily due to lack of consensus on goals and terminology. In addition, several of the key players leave the session for other meetings. This is disruptive and seems to happen at the worst possible time. At the end of the first day, you and the chief software engineer stay late to determine how to make things go better the second day. Three things are decided. First, you will kick off the meeting with a presentation that outlines the goals that were set for the effort by senior management. Then you will attack the terminology challenge by presenting a brief tutorial (at most 1 hour) on how your initial architecture-based approach satisfies these goals and what the jargon associated with the product line technology means. Third, you will ask those participating to clear their calendars.

Things go better the second day. After the goals are stated and the strategy explained, your approach is painstakingly scrutinized. Although there are some agonizing moments, the product that results is better than the one you started with. More important, you get consensus on the recommendations after you do some team building. The final pitch, which management has limited to six charts, is presented in Figures 7.3 through 7.8. You are anxious to get on with the presentation. But you need to clear it with your boss before you give it to the big

GOALS OF EFFORT

- Driving issue: Losing customers and market share to competition
- Perceived cause: Products lack Web and B-to-B support
- Solution
  - View as opportunity to update product strategy
  - Move our products to the Web
  - Implement a B-to-B strategy
  - Recapture market and regain customer confidence

Figure 7.3: *Architecture Pitch—Goals*

guns. During your meeting the next morning, your boss comments as you discuss each chart.

Your boss feels that a chart like the one in Figure 7.3 does a good job of summarizing the problem and the solution. He warns you to make sure that you get the facts to answer questions about how much market share has been lost and which customers have switched. He asks you to prepare backup charts to explain what is involved in moving to the Web and what implementing a B-to-B strategy is all about. Finally, he says: "Make sure you find out if any of our competitors have implemented a B-to-B strategy and, if so and if you can get the information, what their results have been to date."

Your boss warns you not to assume that those in attendance will understand what the words in Figure 7.4's chart mean. "Anticipate questions, and prepare for them," he suggests. "For example, what's involved in establishing a Web-enabled B-to-B infrastructure?" In addition, he thinks you should have a backup chart available to summarize the pluses and minuses of using third-party packages and commercial, off-the-shelf components. "Be careful. This topic might pop up, and you need to be prepared," he states.

Your boss suggests that instead of going over the tasks (see chart in Figure 7.5), you should highlight the products that will be generated by each of them. "That's what the people in the meeting will be thinking about," he says. In response to your disturbed look, he adds: "You need to do this to relieve their concerns about what will be ready for the annual meeting and the upcoming trade show."

VISION AND STRATEGY

- Vision
  - Establish a high-performance, Web-enabled architecture for our products and product lines
  - Create the Web-enabled B-to-B infrastructure needed to support our customers as they use our products

- Strategy
  - Focus on developing an open architecture that allows us to take full advantage of third-party packages and OTS components (both hardware and software)
  - Reuse our legacy so that we can build products once instead of multiple times

Figure 7.4: *Architecture Pitch—Vision*

IMPLEMENTATION

- Within 9 months:
  - Develop initial open architecture and API
  - Move customer and marketing support to the Web
  - Update business processes/move to B-to-B systems (via purchase, alliance, or partnership)
- Within 18 months:
  - Release Web-enabled virtual data warehouse
  - Release reference architecture and infrastructure components/building blocks
  - Start building Web-enabled applications

Figure *7.5: Architecture Pitch—Implementation*

Your boss looks at the continuation of the chart in Figure 7.5 (see Figure 7.6) and says: "Ditto. Don't overwhelm them with technical details. Instead, tell them how what you are doing affects their bottom line." He then questions you for 10 minutes on what the chart really says. When you look at him quizzically, he replies: "I can't support you during the pitch if I don't fully understand what you're saying."

IMPLEMENTATION *(continued)*

- Within 24 months:
  - Implement product line management concepts that will facilitate sharing of assets across products
  - Release Web-enabled applications—small packages instead of a single application—that are compatible with existing systems
  - Recapture market leadership and customer confidence

Regaining leadership will come neither easily nor quickly

Figure 7.6: *Architecture Pitch—Implementation, continued*

COSTS AND BENEFITS

Costs	Benefits
■ Nonrecurring	■ Product line management concepts
– Architecture development	– Cut costs and speed time-to-market
– Education and training	– Improve quality 10X
– Infrastructure definition	
– Process improvement	■ B-to-B applications
■ Recurring	– Reduce acquisition costs and inventory
– Continuing education	– Leverage purchasing power
– Customer support	
– Sustaining engineering	

Figure 7.7: *Architecture Pitch—Costs and Benefits*

When the next chart (see Figure 7.7) appears, your boss's interest peaks. For about an hour, he pesters you to answer seemingly hundreds of questions. When you get snappy, he says: "Be advised that my questions are tame compared to those that others will ask." As you conclude your discussion, he suggests that the approval of this program will hinge on your numbers. He wants to go over the financials before he will schedule the briefing. You tell him you haven't analyzed the details yet. His reply: "Why not?" He makes you realize that you will have to

WHERE WE NEED YOUR HELP

- Time, patience, and support
  - Can do something meaningful by year end
  - Cannot take back market leadership quickly

- To pull this off, retain focus
  - Can take advantage of near-term opportunities
  - Cannot respond to nonaligned requests for support without taking schedule hits

- If you approve, we will come back with detailed project plan and an estimate within two weeks

Figure 7.8: *Architecture Pitch—Finale*

justify the concept to go the next step. "When should we get together again to review the numbers?" you ask.

You've lost him. When you show the chart in Figure 7.8, he is still on financials. He says, "See what you can pull together over the weekend, and let's get together again Monday afternoon at 3:00 P.M. in my office." There is no doubt in your mind that the success or failure of the briefing rests on the financials.

READYING THE FINANCIALS

You have to come up with the monetary details to satisfy your boss. To develop reasonable cost estimates, you have to develop a top-level plan of action and milestones. To quantify the benefits, you have to gather cost, productivity, and market share data. Then you have to work magic with the numbers and pull together a compelling story for management.

To start the process, you develop a work breakdown structure (WBS) for the full two-year duration of the program. Luckily, the textbooks you've accumulated give you some insight into what you need to do to develop the products your management is interested in. After much thought, you arrive at the tasks summarized by major activity in the WBS shown in Figure 7.9. You've also prepared the WBS Dictionary illustrated in Table 7.2 to capture your thoughts relative to what these tasks are all about and what their products are. Because many architecture and reuse terms are foreign to your management, you have decided to rename things using words that are familiar to them (e.g., architecture devel-

Moving to the Web

1.0 Architecture development	2.0 Education and training	3.0 Infrastructure definition	4.0 Process and product development	5.0 Project management
1.1 Specify architecture	2.1 Ready organization for change	3.1 Introduce product line concepts	4.1 Update business processes	5.1 Plan
1.2 Populate architecture	2.2 Make training available as needed	3.2 Update processes, decision structure, and organization accordingly	4.2 Implement B-to-B and Web applications	5.2 Report
1.3 Make right components available as needed			4.3 Transition to their use	
			4.4 Provide support	

Figure 7.9: *Web Initiative Work Breakdown Structure*

opment instead of domain engineering). You've also eliminated some of the recommended tasks because there just isn't time to finish them. Luckily, product line concepts aren't new to either your firm or industry.

From the information in the WBS, you've also developed the high-level milestone schedule for the first 9 months illustrated in Figure 7.10. You devised this schedule by establishing desired results at the end of months 9, 12, and 24. Then you developed the dates by working backwards. You don't really know whether the tasks can be completed as planned. To complete the schedule, you have to identify the Web applications and their sequence of development. The good news is that you believe the schedule to be politically correct.

To assess whether or not you can deliver, you must estimate how much effort it will take to complete each task. In the past, you estimated using analogy. In other words, you estimated using similarities and differences based on your experience on other efforts. However, you have no experience with Web projects.. To address this dilemma, you ask the only person you know with Web experience in your firm to develop a best rough-order-magnitude guess based on the notional information supplied in the accompanying material. In addition, you are worried about your boss's warning to make sure the numbers are right. Your credibility and your future are on the line on this initiative, and you don't want to foul it up. Best guesses, even when well intentioned, are not how you would like to run your project.

Table 7.2: *WBS Dictionary*

Activity	Task	Description	Products
Architecture development	Specify architecture.	Develop open architecture to use as a framework for moving products and services to the Web.	Architecture specification
	Populate architecture.	Acquire (buy or build) components to populate the architecture using projects to drive selection.	Component list (for the architecture)
	Make right components available.	Put in place a library to make reusable components available to Web projects that need them when they need them.	Reuse library Library user's guide
Education and training	Ready organization for change.	Prepare organization for switch to the Web and to the use of product lines, architecture, and components.	Orientation briefing
	Make training available as needed.	Acquire and offer training in support of move to the Web and product lines in a just-in-time manner.	Training classes
Infrastructure definition	Introduce product line concepts.	Assess infrastructure needs. Develop a plan to bring in product line concepts using Web projects as pathfinders.	Plan
	Update processes, decision structure, and organization accordingly.	Update software development processes, practices, and decision structure to support product line concepts for Web applications.	Policy Updated process
		Make needed organizational changes and put incentives in place to stimulate the switch to product line concepts.	Development practices Incentives
Process/ product development	Update business processes.	Reengineer business processes to support doing business on the Web.	Updated business processes

Activity	Task	Description	Products
	Implement B-to-B and Web applications.	Bring in the necessary software tools and equipment to develop, host, field, and support B-to-B and Web applications.	B-to-B host Software development environment Web/B-to-B applications
	Transition to use of processes.	Test the processes and cut over to their use in a systematic manner.	Cut-over plan Test results
	Provide support.	Support customers and users once the move to the Web has been completed.	Help desk Customer care center
Project management	Plan	Develop a project plan, and use it as a road map.	Project plan
	Report	Report progress to management.	Progress reports Briefings

Activities — **Milestone Schedule**

Architecture development
- △ Specification
- △ Component List
- △ Reuse library

Education and training
- △ Orientation briefings (all hands)
- △ Training available JIT
- △ Policy
- △ Incentives

Infrastructure definition
- △ Architecture practices
- △ Web development practices
- △ Library practices
- △ CM and QA practices
- △ Updated software development process
- △ Updated business process

Process and product development
- △ B-to-B host operational
- △ Software development environment operational
- △ Web site up △ Helpdesk up
- △ Web applications
- △ Customer support center operational
- △ Cut-over plan △ Test results
- △ Project plan
- **IOC**

Project management
- Progress reports
- △ △ △ △ △ △ △ △ △

Months from start	1	2	3	4	5	6	7	8	9

Figure 7.10: *Project Schedule*

DETERMINING THE NUMBERS

You have read that migrating to product line management and architectural concepts is an extremely difficult task to accomplish in organizations like yours. Now is the time to determine how much it is going to cost and whether or not you have allocated enough time to do the job. Because you don't have experience in this area, you bring in a seasoned pro to help you develop your numbers. You agree to develop your estimates WBS item by WBS item.

WBS 1.0: Architecture Development

When he sees your project schedule, the consultant starts laughing. "There is no way you can develop an architectural model in two months," he says [Reifer, 1997]. "The rule of thumb used in the industry for architecture development is six people (i.e., three team members to develop the architecture and three domain experts to provide the experience needed to perform the task) for six months," he says. "And the same people are needed for another six months to turn this model into a reference architecture." "But I have only nine months," you respond.

The consultant finally agrees that you can probably develop a top-level layered architecture model similar to the San Francisco project [Monday, 1999] in nine months. However, the details will have to be added iteratively over your two-year planning horizon. He also suggests that you perform a commonality analysis to identify the components that are shared across applications per this model. The results of this study should be added as a milestone at the beginning of month 3, and the component list should be slipped into the beginning of month 4 (Figure 7.10). This analysis will identify the 20 percent of the components that are responsible for 80 percent of the reuse (the 20/80 rule we discussed in Chapter 4). The cost for this architecture task is estimated as follows:

$$(6 \text{ people})(9 \text{ months})(\$12K/\text{staff-month}) = \$648,000$$

The next task for estimation is populating the architecture with reusable components. The reusable components of the open architecture [Shaffer, 1996] your consultant designed during your discussions are shown in Figure 7.11. Because you are moving applications to the Web, the selection of Java and use of a Java Virtual Machine [Orfali, 1998] environment seem natural. So does the use of business components [Herzum, 2000] and object-oriented elements [Jacobson, 1997]. As summarized in Table 7.3, your consultant estimates the cost to populate the architecture at just $100,000. However, this cost wrongly assumes that your staff is skilled in the use of Java and components. To address this problem, you

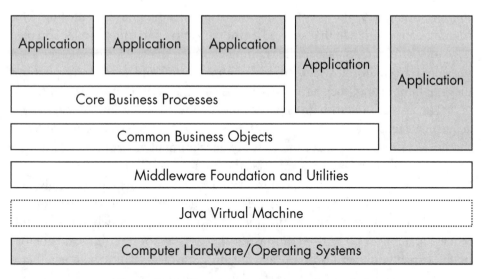

Figure 7.11: *Notional Architecture for Project*

Table 7.3: *Summary of Cost to Populate Architecture*

Architecture Element	Estimated Cost ($K)	Justification
Java Virtual Machine	25	Development license for Java toolkit and run-time environment
Middleware foundation and utilities	50	Development license for middleware
Common business objects	25	License for library of business objects available from your hardware vendor
Core business processes	0	Estimated as part of your infrastructure task
Applications	0	Estimated as part of your process/product development task
Training	25	Cost for in-house training and on-site mentoring
Total	125	

suggest adding $25,000 to cover the cost of Java training and mentoring. This training is in addition to that covered by the education and training task. You plan a five-day seminar. As part of the training contract, the teacher would come on site a day a week for four weeks to work with your staff and answer any questions they might have once they have started to use the materials that were taught.

The last task to estimate as part of the architecture development activity is acquiring a reuse library. Your consultant suggests that the cost of the software should be included as part of the software development environment. However, you also need a librarian to administer the library and library standards. "Can't the system administrator handle this?" you argue. The consultant strongly suggests a dedicated person. However, he agrees that this person can develop the standards as well as administer the library. You are surprised when the consultant estimates the cost of this administrator at $72,000. You inquire and are told by the consultant that librarians are not programmers. You debate whether a non-programmer can develop the standards for the library. Grudgingly the consultant concedes that you are right, and you up the estimate to $108,000 (9 staff-months at $12,000 each).

Table 7.4 summarizes the cost for the architecture development activity by WBS task. When the effort is put on paper, you are surprised that its magnitude is about $900,000 over nine months.

WBS 2.0: Education and Training

This set of readiness and training tasks turns out to be easy to estimate. Because you lead the effort and have to sell it to all hands, you plan to develop and conduct

Table 7.4: *Cost Summary for Architecture Development*

WBS Task	Number of Full-Time Staff	Estimated Cost ($K)	Estimated Acquisition Cost ($K)
Specify architecture	6[†]	648	
Populate architecture		*	125
Make components available	1	108	*
Total	7	756	125

*Estimated as part of other activities
[†]Includes funding for experts to participate in effort

the orientation briefings in your spare time. The consultant makes some good recommendations as you discuss this task. He suggests that you brief each line-of-business manager one on one in his or her office. These are the product line managers whom you need on your side to make change happen in the organization. This is especially true for departments in which you hope to run pilot projects. Once you have their support, you should ask them for permission to brief their immediate staff at their weekly staff meetings. Typically, it is at this level that you will encounter the most resistance. In parallel, you should conduct an all-hands education briefing. You shouldn't forget the working troops. You need to get them excited about the prospects and enlist their support to address the resistance to change in the middle. Although it sounds like a lot of work, you agree with the need to get out there and mix it with the middle.

You also need to develop skills, knowledge, and abilities in the methods and business practices that you are promoting. If you don't, your staff won't be able to accomplish the job on your aggressive schedules. But the consultant warns you to avoid a training marathon. "To train staff efficiently," he says, "firms run three or four seminars in sequence." However, the staff often forgets what they have learned because of the lag times between training and when they put the new skills into practice. "A better way," he suggests, "is to conduct the training 'just in time.'" This brings in the skills when they are needed. It also reduces the training burden because you don't have to provide classes all at once.

As you are talking, you have a brainstorm. The team reengineering the business processes already has a budget for courseware development and training. Because you are going to reenforce the use of these new business processes with your Web developments, shouldn't you be able to use this budget? But you are going to have to get your boss involved because your initial discussions with the reengineering team did not go well. They had already earmarked the money for specific efforts. Otherwise, you will have to make close to $50,000 available to develop courses that at least in part duplicate current developments. This budget does not include funds to cover the people being trained. You have assumed that those doing the work will fund the effort. If they don't, you will have to allocate another $25,000 to cover these costs.

For the purpose of completion, you will estimate the cost of contracting this courseware development and conduct task to be $75,000. However, you plan to make the case for budget relief when you meet with your boss. You believe he will be able to help you because he has an excellent working relationship with the manager of the group developing the business processes.

WBS 3: Infrastructure Development

In Chapter 4, we discussed the management infrastructure needs illustrated in Figure 7.12. The changes shown are aimed at making it easy to use the architecture and stimulate sharing of components across line-of-business groups. The philosophy underlying these changes is to make architecture and reuse natural parts of the process your software people use to do their work and to provide incentives to stimulate change to a new way of doing business. From what you've read about process improvement [Caputo, 1998], implementing changes in the infrastructure involves a lot of effort. In retrospect, you wish your boss had approved the formation of a process group last year to work many of these issues. But he didn't, and you are on the hook to pursue these developments in parallel with your architecture and process/product development tasks.

As you review the work to be done, you still like the process group model. The reason is that there are dedicated resources to both develop the processes (including the associated practices, guidelines, and metrics) and foster the changes needed to make them work operationally. But you are afraid to propose

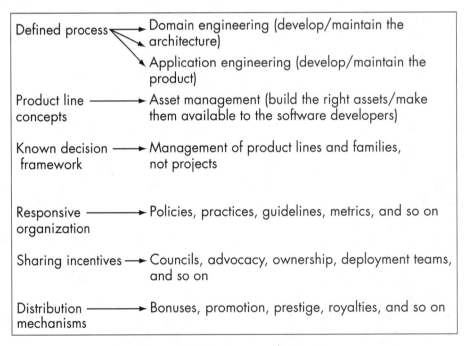

Figure 7.12: *Infrastructure Needs*

this option because management failed to approve it last year. As an alternative, you decide to pursue formation of an infrastructure group that is broader in concept. In addition to developing processes, the group would do the following:

- Develop, maintain, and sustain the architecture (the three people nominated previously would report to the chief engineer who would head this group).
- Coordinate the acquisition of reusable components to populate the architecture.
- Review the architecture for each new project proposed, and make sure that it conforms to your product line architecture.
- Assess the impact of new standards and technologies that could affect the architecture.
- Provide expert support to projects as they try to use the architecture and its components.
- Foster the concept of a standardized platform for software so that analogies can be made to hardware in order to educate management.

Your consultant suggests that you call the organization the software platform group. After much debate, you recommend staffing this group at five plus a chief software engineer. The cost for nine months would be $648,000— (9 months)(6 people)($12K/staff-month).

WBS 4: Process and Product Development

This activity is where most of the work will be carried out during the next nine months. In conjunction with updating the business processes, the following three major B-to-B applications will be placed on the Web site you plan to establish: account status, order processing, and product information. These applications were identified as critical to establishing your Web presence in a meeting held earlier this week with members of the business process reengineering team, manufacturing, marketing/sales, and business operations in attendance.

You and the consultant decide to develop estimates for these tasks by asking members of your team what they think it would take to get the job done. Your consultant likes this approach because it gets those doing the work to commit to getting the job done. Because you are sensitive to your people, you are more skeptical. Some are optimistic and estimate low, while others are pessimistic and build in safety factors. But you agree to start out using this approach. You can

Table 7.5: *Cost Summary for Process/Product Development*

WBS Task	Number of Full-Time Staff	Estimated Cost ($K)	Justification
Update business processes	0	0	Handled by another team
Implement B-to-B and Web applications	7	720	(3 applications) (300 Web objects/application)($800/Web object)
		250	Tool licenses and equipment for software environment
		100	Subcontract to design and bring up Web site
Transition to use	3	180	3 people for 5 months @ $12K/SM
Provide support	0	0	Operational support of customers after site goes operational in month 9
Total	10	1,250	

always adjust the estimates at the end of the session to take into account individual biases.

The resulting estimates and their rationale are summarized by WBS task in Table 7.5. Because applications will be developed using a mix of text, graphics, audio, and video, you have opted to use a new size metric called Web objects [Reifer, 2000] instead of either SLOC or function points as the basis of your software development estimate. The other tasks were estimated using a level-of-effort approach.

WBS 5: Project Management

The final activity addresses the planning, organizing, staffing, directing, and control tasks so important to the success of the effort. You start by developing a project plan. By design, it incorporates much of what you've prepared for your

Table 7.6: *Total Estimate*

WBS Task	Number of Full-Time Staff	Estimated Cost ($K)	Estimated Acquisition Cost ($K)
Architecture development	7	756	125
Education and training			75
Infrastructure definition	6	648	
Process/product development	10	900	350
Project management	2	216	
Total	25	2,520	550

briefing with your boss. However, you will have to add more detail when you can. You normally estimate project management by summing all other tasks and adding 10 percent. However, you are not sure that this will be enough. You have already put yourself on the line to do outreach and orientation. Table 7.6 provides an estimate for the entire project. As a result of discussions with your consultant, you decide to round the management estimate to two full-time people, you and a deputy, for the nine-month schedule.

You almost have a heart attack when you look at the total. The number your management has thrown around for this job is $1 million. Because your estimate is more than three times what they expect, you don't believe you can sell it even if you can justify the numbers.

TRIMMING THE FAT

Your consultant advises you to take it easy. "Let's look at the estimate, and see if there's any fat we can trim," he suggests. "Then we will prepare a strong justification for the expenditures." The first target of opportunity is obvious. You've set up an architecture and a process group. "Can't we combine these two groups to save some money?" your consultant says. When you think about it, combining the two teams into a single team of seven makes sense. The team developing the architecture would prepare the processes to enable the application developers to use it efficiently in parallel. The net savings would be three people for nine months or $325,000. Table 7.7 compares options and identifies the functions team members would perform.

Table 7.7: *Comparison of Staffing Options*

	Original Staffing Concept	Proposed Staffing Option
Team size and composition	Architecture team of 6 with 3 full-time members and an additional budget for 3 domain experts Librarian	Single team of 7 with the chief software engineer serving as chief architect and a junior member of the team serving as the librarian
	Process group of 6 with 5 full-time members and a chief software engineer	Additional budget for 3 experts (domain, environment, testing, etc.)
Cost	$1,404,000	$1,080,000

The second target for cost reduction is in product development. To create the architectural infrastructure to enable reuse, the plan is for the architecture team to put middleware in place along with common business objects, core business processes, and foundation-level utilities. Then the architecture group will train the developers to use the middleware to simplify application development and bring in training in the new processes. The combined estimate of $100,000 for training and mentoring seems fat. So does the transition staff of three. Assuming that the developers do their job right the first time, you probably could reduce your support staff estimate to two. You and your consultant decide to reduce the education and training estimate from $75,000 to $50,000, retain the $25,000 for training and mentoring in the architecture, forgo $50,000 in equipment purchases, and reduce the transition staff from three to two people for five months. The combined savings is $135,000.

The final target is the labor rate. You have assumed an average rate of $12,000 per staff-month. If you anticipate using junior people, this rate might be high. After reviewing each WBS entry, the only activity where the rate might be high is process and product development. But, you don't dare lower it because the rate for other activities strikes you as low. In response, you decide to leave the rate alone because you believe it reflects the total team composition.

Your new estimate is summarized in Table 7.8. Your trimming efforts have reduced full-time staff by four and eliminated $459,000 from the estimate. While not as slim as you would have liked, the new estimate is more sellable than the original option. You are still skeptical about your ability to sell this number. But

Table 7.8: *Trimmed Estimate*

WBS Task	Number of Full-Time Staff	Estimated Cost ($K)	Estimated Acquisition Cost ($K)
Combined architecture and process team	5	540	125
Education and training			50
Infrastructure definition	5	540	
Process and product development	9	840	300
Project management	2	216	
Total	21	2,136	475

your consultant advises you to wait and see if the justification is strong enough to compel management to take action on your proposal.

JUSTIFYING YOUR RECOMMENDATIONS

Now it's time for your consultant to work his magic and earn his keep. Because you have no history to compare costs against, the consultant recommends that you look at equivalent costs. You don't know how to develop a benchmark because the only cost data you have doesn't relate to the Web. You inquire if development has any Web development data, and they tell you they don't. However, they state that they solicited quotations from three major suppliers to develop a Web portal, move applications to the Web, and provide support over a 24-month period. The estimates they received and assumptions governing them are summarized in Table 7.9.

Although you feel blindsided, these quotes make your task easier. In addition, they let you know where management got the million-dollar figure. You can use these external quotes to justify your numbers. You believe you can contract part of the effort to come up with a less risky plan. Why didn't your boss show you these numbers? You are somewhat disappointed. But, there is no time to sob. You have to prepare for your Monday briefing, and there is no time to waste.

Your first task is to compare options. Table 7.10 identifies the costs of each of the choices, while Table 7.11 displays their strengths and weaknesses. For

Table 7.9: *Vendor Quotes for Developing Web Capabilities*

Firm	Quote	Assumptions Governing Quote
A	$2M	They work in house as members of your team to develop the Web portal and applications. They supply expertise and infrastructure to your specifications over a two-year period to get you up and running. You pay a license fee of $250,000 per year thereafter.
B	$1M	Hosted on a proprietary system. You use their business processes and infrastructure unmodified. You license needed applications at an annual cost of $750,000 starting at the beginning of second year. Capabilities can be added at any time for additional license fees. You support your customers by staffing a help desk. They train you.
C	$5M	They build a compliant Web system and portal to your specifications. Capability available at the end of two years with warranty. Support available for $250,000 a year once system is turned over to your staff.

Table 7.10: *True Cost of Options*

Option	Quote ($M)	First 9 Months ($M)	Year 2 ($M)	Afterward ($M/year)	Your Cost ($M) 9 Months	Your Cost ($M) Year 2	Total Cost ($M) 9 Months	Total Cost ($M) Year 2
A	2.00	1.00	1.00	0.25	1.95	1.70	2.95	2.70
B	1.00	1.00	0.75	0.75	0.324	1.08	1.32	1.83
C	5.00	2.00	3.00	0.25	0.756	1.08	2.76*	4.08
Internal	NA	NA	NA	NA	2.60	3.20	2.60	3.20

*Delivery delayed 6 months for this option

simplicity's sake, you assume that a staff-month of labor costs $12,000 independent of option or year. You know that this is incorrect but decide to adjust rates and examine the effects of different labor mixes afterwards. You make the following assumptions as you formulate the estimates.

Option A

■ The contractor will fill five of the seven developer slots for the process and product task. All other efforts and license fees estimated would remain the

Table 7.11: *Strengths and Weaknesses of Options*

Option	Strengths	Weaknesses
A	Greatly reduce risk by using new product line and architecture concepts Build core competence quickly using people with proven expertise	Getting right people often difficult because working higher priority tasks Managing contractor resources is more difficult than managing in-house people
B	Cheap and quick to develop Web capability up and running in nine months Don't have to create new groups or organizations Staff can be used by other projects	Hosted on proprietary system that provides no differentiation Totally dependent on contractor for capability Must use their processes unchanged Major changes could be costly
C	Built to your specifications (and business processes) Willing to warranty the development	Must develop specifications Capability available six months later than desired because of delays due to specification development activities
In-house	Master of your own destiny Create core competency in architectures [Prahalad, 1990] Foster a culture change that can cut cost and speed development Can adopt new business processes that offer marketplace differentiation	Expensive and time-consuming during start-up period Culture change is always risky Incentives are needed to stimulate sharing of reusable assets across organizations Much needs to be done (risky)

same except for the $100,000 for the subcontractor to design the Web site and the $25,000 training expense for infrastructure components, which would be assumed by the contractor. With these adjustments, you compute your effort for the first nine months (see data in Table 7.8) as follows:

$$\$2,611 - (5 \text{ people} * 9 \text{ months} * \$12K/\text{month}) - \$125K$$
$$= \$1,946,000$$

■ During the second year, you can reduce your costs to cover your internal team of seven (7 people * 12 months * $12K/month = $1,008K). You will also retain a budget of $400,000 to pay for licenses and purchase additional assets for the architecture. A project management team of two would be retained to provide leadership for the entire effort (add $288,000).

Option B

- The contractor will provide the needed capability at a fixed price in nine months. Once the system is operational, you will pay the license fee at the start of each calendar year.

- You assume that you will need a team of three to coordinate transition during the nine-month effort (3 people * 9 months * $12K/month).

- Because your people retain responsibility for providing customer support, you estimate that you will need a customer support team of three after the system is put into operation. You compute this cost to be $432,000 per year (3 people * 12 months * $12K/month).

- From experience, you know new features will need to be added to the system once it is operational. When you ask the contractor for a quote, he says that $500K per year should cover these changes. In addition, you believe that you will need one person full time to manage the contractor and coordinate the effort. You estimate the total annual cost starting in year 2 to be $144,000 (contractor management) plus $500,000 (to the contractor for changes) plus $432,000 (customer support), equaling $1.076 million.

Option C

- You must develop specifications before the team can contract for the effort. You estimate that it will take three of your best people a minimum of six months to prepare the specifications to the level of detail requested (at a cost of $216,000). This activity will cause you to delay the scheduled availability of your Web capability and portal a minimum of six months.

- Once the contract is let, you will need a team of five people to manage the effort. To develop your estimate for the first 15 months of the effort (9 months + 6-month delayed period), you add the cost of the specifications to the management effort as follows:

(3 people * 6 months * $12K/month) + (5 people * 9 months * $12K/month) = $756,000

- During year 2 and thereafter, two people will be added to your five-person team to take over responsibility for maintenance and customer support (7 people * 12 months * $12K/month = $1.008M).

Table 7.12 summarizes the total costs to your organization for each of the options. It was developed by adding your costs and the contracted fees for each period under examination. It paints a different picture of the options. It still shows that Option B is cheapest. But now your in-house option doesn't look so out of line with the others. To examine these options more fully, you should perform the following analyses:

- Modify your labor rate and your contractor's, and mix to reflect the anticipated costs of labor including any rises due to pay raises.

- Develop the 10-year life cycle costs, adjusting them to reflect net present value.

- Evaluate the tax implications of alternatives by including tax consequences of depreciation and tax credits.

- Look for other tax twists that might be to your advantage. For example, some states allow you to write retraining costs off against taxes when the retraining leads to new skills in the workforce. Under some circumstances, you could claim the infrastructure as a capital cost and thereby derive some tax benefit by depreciating it instead of expensing it. Of course, these are issues for your accounting people, and accounting should be brought into the picture to tell you what is legal and what is not.

Which is the best option? Of course, you believe it is in-house development. The analyses you have performed will let you demonstrate your opinion by portraying the true costs of the options and their strengths and weaknesses. But your consultant makes a good observation: "You've done a great job comparing options," he says, "but you haven't presented a business case to justify why you want to pursue any of these alternatives."

Table 7.12: *Summary of Total Costs of Options*

Option	First 9 Months ($M)	Year 2 ($M)	Thereafter ($M)	Notes
A	2.95	2.70	1.95	Technology transfer option
B	1.32	1.83	1.83	Limited flexibility option
C	2.75	4.08	1.08	Delayed specifications option
In house	2.60	3.20	3.00	Core competency option

WHY PURSUE PRODUCT LINES IN THE FIRST PLACE?

"Have I wasted my time answering the wrong set of questions for the Monday meeting?" you ponder. "Did I get sidetracked?" After you give it some thought, you strongly believe you pursued the right options. The benchmark that you used to compare options was what others thought the job would cost, not what your experience tells you it will cost. Feeling somewhat relieved, you explain your position to your consultant. He says: "You're right, but you should still prepare some backup material should management ask us what architecture and infrastructure buy us."

The easiest way to justify the infrastructure is to compare the cost of development with and without its being in place. Because the infrastructure contains the reusable building blocks for the architecture (see Figure 7.11), you could compare estimates for applications development with and without commonality. You could then compute the savings by using the applications estimates as benchmarks, as illustrated in Table 7.13.

The ROI associated with your in-house architecture option can be computed as follows:

$$\text{ROI} = \text{savings/investments} = \$2M/\$2.6M = 77\%$$

Table 7.13: *Estimated Annual Benefits Associated with a Reusable Architecture*

	Common Architecture	Unique Architecture	Notes
Size (Web objects)	300	500	Commonality reduces size
Number of applications	8	8	New developments
Total (Web objects)	2400	4000	(size)(number of applications)
Cost/Web object	$800	$800	
Applications cost/year	$1,920,000	$3,200,000	(cost/object) (number Web objects)
Maintenance cost/year	$1,008,000	$1,728,000	7 versus 12 programmers needed to maintain infrastructure/ applications
Savings/year	$2,000,000		

To generate this figure for the in-house option, you made the following simplifying assumptions:

- The savings will start in year 2 after the initial infrastructure is established. No savings are assumed during the first nine-month period.

- There is no need to compute the PV of the investment.

You are now ready to brief your boss on Monday. You feel good about your numbers. However, you won't be surprised if your boss asks you at least a dozen other questions. After all, his neck is on the line along with yours because he is supporting your pursuit of the architecture option. He wants to be comfortable with the numbers, too.

SUMMARY

This chapter presents a case study about moving to the Web. The hypothetical firm is seeking to establish a B-to-B presence on the World Wide Web. The case deals with a situation where you can't use your experience to estimate the cost of developing applications using new technology and a layered architecture.

KEY POINTS

- ✔ The literature is rich with information on product lines, architectures, and reuse. However, get help to pinpoint what's applicable because digesting and making sense of all the facts available takes a lot of time and effort.

- ✔ When you deal with new technology, it is useful to have a consultant help you prepare your business case. Be prepared to fit the advice to your problem and culture.

- ✔ When justifying something new, use a contractor benchmark as a comparative basis for your estimate. Make sure that the contractors you approach are credible sources.

- ✔ Don't be surprised when management asks you to ready financials and prepare justifications that come with hidden agendas.

- ✔ A WBS always serves as a useful structure when estimating costs task by task.

- ✔ Make the effort to trim the fat. Opportunities for reducing cost will become obvious when you review the estimate.

- ✔ When dealing with contractor estimates, dig deep and discover the hidden costs. These hidden costs and the life cycle costs will often surprise you.

References

[Bass, 1998] Bass, Len, Paul Clements, and Rick Kazman. *Software Architecture in Practice.* Addison-Wesley, 1998.

[Caputo, 1998] Caputo, Kim. *CMM Implementation Guide.* Addison-Wesley, 1998.

[Ehrlich, 1998] Asimov quote from Ehrlich, Henry. *The Wiley Book of Business Quotations.* John Wiley & Sons, 1998.

[Fortune, 1996] Ehrlich, Henry. *The Wiley Book of Business Quotations.* John Wiley & Sons, 1998, p. 192.

[Herzum, 2000] Herzum, Peter, and Oliver Sims. *Business Component Factory.* John Wiley & Sons, 2000.

[Jacobson, 1997] Jacobson, Ivar, Martin Griss, and Patrik Jonsson. *Software Reuse: Architecture, Process and Organization for Business Success.* ACM Press, 1997.

[Lim, 1999] Lim, Wayne C. *Managing Software Reuse.* Prentice Hall, 1998

[Monday, 1999] Monday, Paul, James Carey, and Mary Dangler. *San Francisco Component Framework.* Addison-Wesley, 1999.

[Orfali, 1998] Orfali, Robert, and Dan Harkey. *Client/Server Programming with Java and CORBA,* 2nd Edition. John Wiley & Sons, 1998.

[Poulin, 1997] Poulin, Jeffrey S. *Measuring Software Reuse.* Addison-Wesley, 1997.

[Prahalad, 1990] Prahalad, C.K., and Gary Hamel. "The Core Competency of the Corporation," *Harvard Business Review,* May/June 1990, pp. 79–91.

[Shaffer, 1996] Shaffer, Steven L., and Alan R. Simon. *Transitioning to Open Systems.* Morgan Kaufmann Publishers, 1996.

[Szyperski, 1999] Szyperski, Clemens. *Component Software: Beyond Object-Oriented Programming.* Addison-Wesley, 1999.

[Reifer, 1997] Reifer, Donald J. *Practical Software Reuse.* John Wiley & Sons, 1997.

[Reifer, 2000] Reifer, Donald J. "Web Development: Estimating Quick-to-Market Software," *Software,* IEEE Computer Society, November/December 2000, pp. 57–64.

8

Maneuvering the Maze
Web-Based Economy Case Study

The most important thing that must happen is the replacement of the "normal culture" for developing software with the "radical" culture embodied in death march projects. This change won't happen quickly or easily, for much of the bureaucracy will argue strenuously for the continuation of the older approaches. But, the savvy organization will acknowledge that if the first death march project succeeds, the success will be largely a matter of luck and stubbornness on the part of the team. If the organization wants subsequent death march projects to succeed with any predictability, it must change.
—Ed Yourdon [1997]

FOR OPENERS

Your boss just read an article about John Welch's push to use the Internet to slash costs of doing business at GE [Pelz, 2000]. The article reported that GE is trying to tap the Internet and the electronic commerce revolution to save millions of dollars annually. For example, changing travel practices and coordinating reservations on line netted the corporation a savings of $40 million in travel expenses in a single month compared to the same month the previous year. The article further reported,

> Welch said last month that, under the new Internet effort, GE wants
> to erase up to $12 billion from its operating costs within the next

18 months. To put that number into context, a company of $12 billion in sales would rank about 150th in the *Fortune* 500. Moreover, the $12 billion Welch wants to carve out of GE's operating costs represents about 10 percent of GE's annual revenue. It's also an astonishing one-fourth of the $46 billion that GE spent last year both to provide its goods and services for sale and for its overhead—such as travel, payroll, and advertising. These expenses are what is called its "selling, general and administrative costs," or SG&A.

The benefits reported in this article attributed to the use of this technology seemed too good to be true.

Your organization has been kicking around moving to the Web for over a year. After your boss circulates the article, senior management finally seems motivated to move out on this initiative. As the chief information officer (CIO), you are pleased that the initiative is underway. You have already developed a plan of attack for establishing your presence on the Web. Your approach is to acquire a firm with the capabilities you need to move to the Web quickly and with a minimum of disruption. This acquisition will reduce the potential delays associated with staff buildup and skills development. You thought about hiring a firm to help, but each organization you contacted said that they were just too busy to provide you with the resources you needed to fan Internet technology out to your 100 organizations worldwide. Your boss is pressuring you to recommend an option that quickly establishes your Web presence at minimum cost. You've done your homework and believe that purchasing a firm with the capabilities you need will readily respond to his needs.

Your organization, as illustrated in Figure 8.1, can easily put whatever resources you acquire to work deploying your Internet strategy to the four major development and support centers you've established worldwide. These centers support over 10,000 clients of these new systems in the field. You've introduced technology successfully before by acquiring firms with the needed capabilities. By providing the centers with the specialized assistance they need, you help them move to the Web while retaining control and maintaining cognizance over progress. This is essential because senior management will hold you accountable for the results. To minimize the financial burden on your operational groups, you will retain the budget authority for all training and support costs. That way you can provide what will be viewed as free help to the centers who commit to partner with you to pursue your strategy. Once the technology has been put into

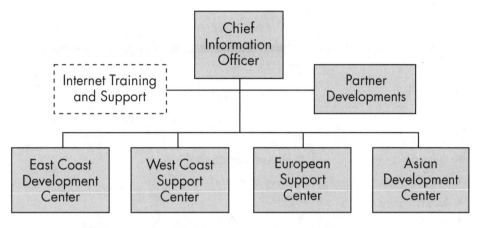

Figure 8.1: *Worldwide Organizational Structure*

practice, you plan to break up your Internet training and support group and sprinkle talent from it throughout the centers. That will eliminate the idea that you are building an empire at the expense of others.

The biggest fear expressed by the operational groups is that you will force them to use resources that are outside their control and are paid for by taxes on their bottom line. Luckily, you can demonstrate that the acquisition approach you are taking for technology transfer worked for distributed, persistent database technology; you transferred the technology within a year. To do this, you purchased a firm specializing in persistent database technology and used its resources to help develop the skills you needed internally to sustain the technology's evolution.

You recently read a great article on the benefits of adopting the SEI CMM (Chapter 5) and new IT techniques. The paper reported that Keane, Inc., was able to enhance customer service according to the e-business model portrayed in Figure 8.2 and reduce cycle times up to 80 percent. Additional benefits attributable to moving from CMM Level 1 to Level 3 are shown in Table 8.1, which analyzes 1,300 projects developing 200,000 lines of code [Hutchin, 2000]. However, the e-business model is more pertinent to what you are trying to accomplish than the statistics. This model represents a structure that you can use to manage the move to the Web and hosting of e-business and e-commerce applications on the Internet.

Each of your development centers has an active process improvement program and process group, and each has reached Level 3 on the CMM rating scale.

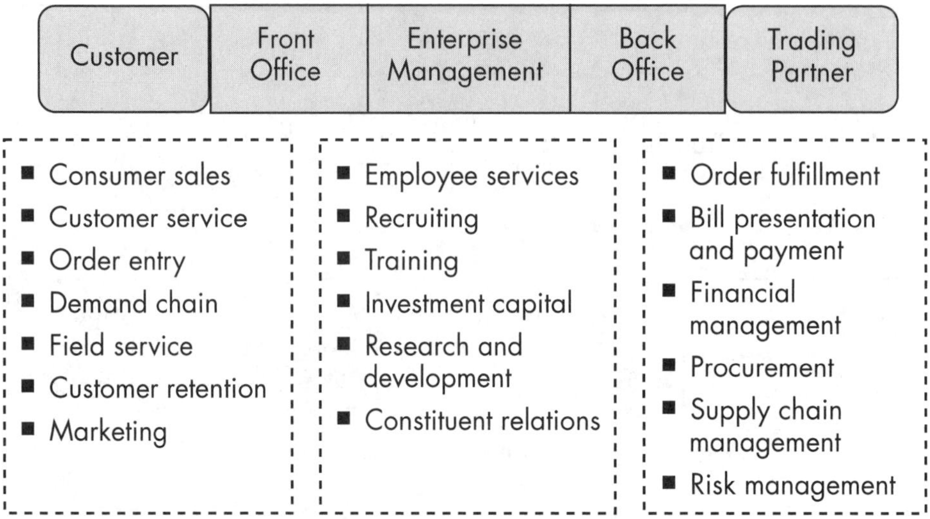

Figure 8.2: *Commercial E-business Model [Hutchin, 2000]*

Table 8.1: *Quantitative Business Benefits of the CMM*

CMM Level	Calendar Months	Level of Effort (staff-months)	Defects Shipped	Median Cost ($M)	Lowest Cost ($M)	Highest Cost ($M)
1	30	600	61	5.5	1.8	100+
2	18.5	143	12	1.3	0.96	1.7
3	15	80	7	0.73	0.52	0.93

Because they are always looking for justification for their efforts, you decide to forward the article to them. You support their efforts but don't believe that the CMM as presently structured will help you acquire a suitable firm to help you to move your applications to the Web.

FINDING A LIKELY CANDIDATE

You decide to brief your boss and get his advice on your strategy. After you present your material, your boss says that he loves the idea of acquiring a firm to do the job. He says that your organization is in a cash position and has lots of ready capital that it can use to pursue this option. But acquisitions, he warns, are major corporate decisions that receive scrutiny from many people including the accountants and lawyers. From a due-diligence point of view, he suggests that you make sure that you research the candidates thoroughly as part of your efforts to develop a recommendation and associated justification. His statements scare you because the implication is that you and you alone will be blamed if the acquisition goes sour. In response, you decide to assemble a team of business analysts who can help you find a suitable firm with solid financials and a record of growth in the area of e-business and e-commerce. Because the people involved are pros, you have confidence in the team and its ability to ferret out a winner.

You and your staff begin the search for a likely candidate. The firms that you've been in contact with are either too small or resistant to being acquired. What you need is at least a 100-person established firm that specializes in helping others move to the Internet. You are not interested in growing the business. Rather, you are interested in using the resources to train your people and support them as they deploy the technology internally to your firm. Just a few firms seem to satisfy your needs. Because these firms are busy, none is on the market. None has responded positively to your inquiries, and all seem reluctant about your takeover attempts.

You decide to identify a candidate and acquire it using whatever means you have to (hostile stock takeover, for example). With management pressuring you, you don't have any time to waste. Luckily, one of your staff has found a likely candidate. This firm, XYZ Internet Corporation, is four years old, and its sales are booming. As the box on the next page illustrates, its market capitalization is relatively small, and it has only 1 million shares of common stock outstanding. Luckily, as Figure 8.3 indicates, its stock is not doing so well, and acquisition through friendly or hostile means should be possible. But the poor stock performance alarms you. You decide to have your analysts investigate the company to determine what's amiss.

Because the firm is traded on the exchange, there is lots of information about it available on the Web. The first thing you do is access and review XYZ Internet Corporation's financials. As shown in the box on page 215, its balance sheet and income statement report that the firm actually lost money, even though its sales were over $30 million (interest isn't counted). Although this is explained in the footnotes as the result of acquiring another firm, you are concerned. You therefore ask a team of your best financial analysts to see if they can uncover the root cause of the firm's poor performance. An earnings per share (EPS) of 1 cent is far below the 75 cents anticipated by investors.

COMPANY PROFILE
Company name   XYZ Internet Corporation
Address   Anywhere, USA
Industry   Internet software solutions
Business description   Full-service provider of e-business and e-commerce solutions. Helps clients create strategic business solutions using Internet technology. Provides consulting, education, and Web software products.
Share information   ▪ Market cap ($M)—40   ▪ Shares outstanding (K)—800   ▪ Shares held by institutions (K)—200 (of the 800)   ▪ Shares held by officers (K)—200 (in addition to the 800)

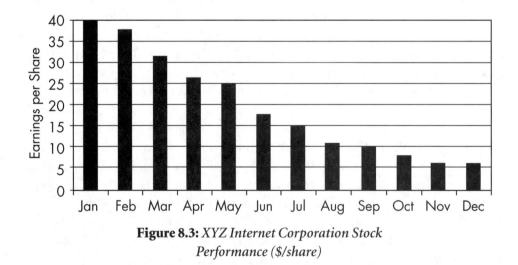

Figure 8.3: *XYZ Internet Corporation Stock Performance ($/share)*

XYZ INTERNET CORPORATION YEAR 2000 FINANCIALS		
Balance Sheet (US K)		**Income Statement (US K)**

Balance Sheet (US K)		Income Statement (US K)	
Current assets		Total revenues	31,350
– Cash	6,000	– Cost of goods sold	2,540
– Securities	0	Gross profit	28,810
– Accounts receivables	3,800		
– Prepaid expenses	100	Operating expenses	
– Inventory	0	– Salaries and wages	14,524
		– Employee benefits	5,610
Long-term assets		– Income taxes	288
– Property, plant and		– Office	1,342
equipment	3,400	– Payroll taxes	2,475
– Other	250	– Other	4,593*
Total Assets	**13,550**		
		Operating income	<22>
Current liabilities	9,900	Interest income	32
Long-term liabilities	0	Total income	10
Equity		**Earnings per Share**	**$0.01**
– Preferred stock	0		
– Common stock	259		
– Retained earnings	1,191		
– Other stockholder			
equity	2,200		
Total Liabilities and Equity	**13,550**		

*Includes $3.5M write-off taken for acquisition of a training firm last year.

Within a week, your team of analysts get back to you with the results of their investigations. They have reviewed the most current data available, including analyst reports from brokerage houses and the quarterly and annual data (10-Q and 10-K) that the firm submits to the Securities and Exchange Commission (SEC). As shown in Table 8.2, they've had a hard time determining the cause of the firm's current performance problems. Because the return on earnings (ROE) is declining compared to industry averages, the team suspects that the firm's inefficient use of resources is the reason its financial performance looks so poor. In response, you ask your team to dig deeper and do a more thorough analysis. The next day, they return with their results. As summarized in Table 8.3, these reveal little additional information on what's causing the problem. Your hunch is poor management performance, but you don't have the numbers to back up your gut feeling. All the other indicators suggest that this firm is a good buy, especially when you take revenue growth and earnings into account. The high price/earnings (P/E) ratio is of course a concern. However, the price/sales (P/S) ratio shows that investors are deriving value from this firm even though stock performance hasn't been stellar. The key is getting value for your money. That's what your management is most interested in. You will have to use value rather than financials to justify the acquisition.

As you review the data, the apparent poor management performance continues to disturb you. The declining ROE indicates that the firm is not using its assets wisely. You decide to investigate why. Typically, rising costs, poor quality, higher than expected sales costs (e.g., to close a sale), and/or runaway overhead rates cause such troubles. As expected, your financial team finds that all these factors

Table 8.2: *XYZ Internet Corporation Growth Assessment*

Factor	Rating	Analysis
Has the firm exhibited strong earnings growth?	Yes	Earnings have doubled annually over the four years the firm has been in business.
Will the firm continue its strong earnings growth?	Yes	Projections are that earnings will continue to grow at current rates assuming that sales continue to triple.
Is the firm controlling its costs?	Neutral	Not enough data to analyze. Detailed accounting data needed to fully assess.
Is management operating the business efficiently?	Neutral	While XYZ looks positive compared with the competitors, its ROE continues to decline. This indicates that rising labor costs, competition, or quality problems may be hurting the firm.
Is the potential gain at least twice the loss?	Neutral	Not enough data to analyze. Five years of data needed to make a determination.
Can the stock double in price in five years?	Neutral	Not pertinent in an acquisition. However, provides insight into potential value of the firm.

Table 8.3: *XYZ Internet Corporation Performance Evaluation*

Factor	Rating	Analysis
Growth trends	High	*Examine revenue and net income (earnings).* XYZ revenue growth rate is 45% versus sector rate of 28%. Earnings growth rate is 23% versus sector rate of 12%.
Financial health	Good	*Examine debt/equity (D/E) ratio.* Looking over three-year period, the D/E ratio looks very good, especially in comparison with competitors who are more in debt.
Management performance	Poor	*Inspect ROE and return on assets (ROA).* ROE and ROA are continuing to decline versus industry averages, indicating that XYZ is not using its assets wisely.
Market multiples	Neutral	*Examine P/E and P/S ratios.* P/E ratio is 600:1 versus industry average of 50:1. P/S ratio is 56% lower than industry average indicating that investors are buying XYZ revenue at a significant discount. However, XYZ seems valued in comparison with competitors when the write-off taken for acquisition is taken into account.
Real value	Neutral	*Examine the hypothetical value developed as the sum of factors like future earnings and intellectual capacity of the firm.* Not enough information to fully analyze.

are contributing to the predicament. Your worries diminish when you hear this because such problems can be easily fixed once the acquisition is completed. For example, cost of sales worries will be eliminated because you are acquiring the firm to provide skills, not market products and services.

DETERMINING THE "VALUE" OF A FIRM

When you investigate how market analysts determine the real value of a firm, you are amazed. Most look at existing financial indicators to develop a market value for the firm based on its net worth, future earnings, goodwill, and business reputation. For example, the quicken.excite.com securities evaluator computes value by looking at future growth and earnings. What concerns you about the process used to determine value is that most of the valuations used are subjective and don't adequately consider the firm's intellectual and production capacity. They use today's performance as an indicator of how well the firm will perform tomorrow in light of the forecasted marketplace demand and risk factors. Because you need to determine how much you will be willing to pay for XYZ Internet Corporation, you need some way to place a value on the firm's intellectual capital and production capacity.

As stated in Chapter 4, software by itself has no value. The capital to produce the software should not influence how you compute its value. Neither should its profitability or its contribution to earnings be an influence, because these variables are a function of market factors (price, promotion, and so on) that are outside your direct control. However, software by its very nature is intellectual property that gains value when used to solve a problem. Therefore, software has value when there is a "demand" for its "use" within a "target environment." XYZ Internet Corporation has value to you because it has the human skills, intuition, and wisdom to move your firm to the Web, not because it can generate products or profit.

With this framework, you could perform two very different types of analysis to compute a value for XYZ Corporation. As your first approach, you could look at the market factors, risks, competition, and the financial indicators. You could look at earnings and growth trends by assessing the future demand within the targeted market for products and services. As part of your analysis, you could examine marketplace risks and factor these into the forecasts to make them more realistic. But this approach makes little sense because you are buying this firm for its intellectual and production capacity, not its future earnings or growth.

The more challenging exercise is determining a value for the firm based on the notions that software is knowledge and knowledge is capital. For the purpose of our discussion, "knowledge capital" refers to the ideas, people, and talent used to facilitate moving applications to the Web and establishing an e-business and e-commerce presence on the Internet. To determine how much you would be willing to pay for this firm, you need to know how much the "knowledge capital" the firm owns is worth. Making such appraisals is difficult because bright people can generate great products that don't sell. They are also mobile, and retaining them when the firm is acquired will probably be a challenge.

Figure 8.4 provides a framework I developed to compute the value of "knowledge capital." This structure is characterized as follows:

- Recognizes that people are the primary resource—not tools, equipment, and machinery.

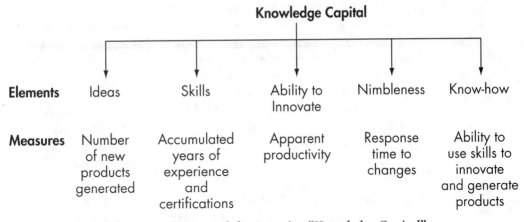

Figure 8.4: *Framework for Assessing "Knowledge Capital"*

- Further recognizes that the value of people depends on their ability to form and function as a team [Baetjer, 1997].

- Emphasizes investing in making the organization smarter, not stronger.

- Focuses on developing both the learning and the expertise needed to put available skills to use effectively in your organization.

- Realizes that innovation is as important as responding to changing markets.

- Puts a premium on generating products that are both used and useful, not on developing new ideas (the main reason your company is considering acquiring the firm in the first place).

As you will undoubtedly notice, most of the factors in the figure are hard to quantify. To rate the firm's intellectual capacity and its people resources, I suggest that you use the scheme that is summarized in Table 8.4. While still subjective, it provides you with ways of differentiating between market followers and market leaders. As expected, XYZ Internet Corporation scores high in almost all categories when rated according to this scheme. This is not surprising because it was one of the first players in the marketplace. Referrals indicate that it has also developed a good reputation for delivering quality products and services.

Table 8.4: *Rating Scheme for "Knowledge Capital" Factors*

Factor	Low	Nominal	High
Summary	Market follower: seems to be playing catch-up	Market player: launches a few products yearly	Market leader: launches many products annually
Ideas	New products evolve from existing products and product lines	New products are launched to keep up with competition	New products are launched that take advantage of windows of opportunity
Skills	Average experience is less than 2 years	Average experience is less than 5 years	Average experience is greater than 5 years
	Experience seems irrelevant	Some relevant experience	Experience relevant to task at hand
	No certifications in relevant technology	Few certifications in relevant technology	Many certifications in relevant technology
Ability to innovate	Staff productivity viewed as a problem	Staff viewed as highly productive	Staff viewed as highly productive
	Products viewed as humdrum	Products viewed as competitive	Products viewed as imaginative
Nimbleness	Seems to take forever to get them to respond	Response a function of management	Quick to market and response
	Much bureaucracy and resistance to change	Some bureaucracy and resistance to change	Limited bureaucracy and open to change
Know-how	Don't have needed skills and ability to use them on the job	Have needed skills but not ability to use them on the job	Have needed skills and the ability to use them on the job

COMPUTING HOW MUCH TO PAY

You are probably asking how you should package the results of your analysis to present to your boss. I suggest that you prepare the four charts shown as Figures 8.5 through 8.8. In a chart like Figure 8.5, you restate your goals and tell your boss why the effort is vital for your firm. You also state how you will achieve

GOALS OF EFFORT

- Create an immediate presence on the Web
  - Establish a snazzy Web site
  - Conduct e-business and e-commerce
  - Change our business practices to lever the site to save money using the Internet (like GE)

- Be viewed as a leader in our industry by our customers
  - Unlike our competitors, focus the site and our attention on e-service

Figure 8.5: *Acquisition Briefing—Goals*

RECOMMENDATION

Acquire XYZ Internet Corporation to provide experienced Web development resources

Who is XYZ?	Why XYZ?
■ 100-person, full-service provider of e-business and e-commerce solutions ■ Four-year-old firm with revenue growth of 45% versus 28% for the sector ■ Market cap of $40M	■ Earnings grow as sales forecasted to triple ■ Stock price has declined to $6, making them an undervalued firm ■ Provide value for our $ in terms of goals

Figure 8.6: *Acquisition Briefing—Recommendations*

marketplace differentiation. In a chart like Figure 8.6, you put forth your recommendation clearly and provide information about the firm you hope to acquire and its capabilities. In the chart shown in Figure 8.7, you summarize the financials and your assessment of XYZ Corporation's revenue growth and earnings potential.

FINANCIALS OF CANDIDATE

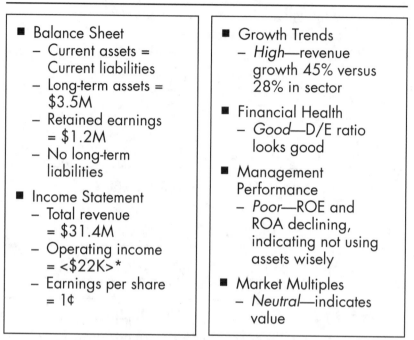

- Balance Sheet
  - Current assets = Current liabilities
  - Long-term assets = $3.5M
  - Retained earnings = $1.2M
  - No long-term liabilities

- Income Statement
  - Total revenue = $31.4M
  - Operating income = <$22K>*
  - Earnings per share = 1¢

- Growth Trends
  - *High*—revenue growth 45% versus 28% in sector

- Financial Health
  - *Good*—D/E ratio looks good

- Management Performance
  - *Poor*—ROE and ROA declining, indicating not using assets wisely

- Market Multiples
  - *Neutral*—indicates value

*Includes $3.5M write-off for acquisition of a training firm

Figure 8.7: *Acquisition Briefing—Financials*

In a chart like Figure 8.8, you describe the remaining factors and the approach you recommend for acquisition. Time utility on this chart refers to the dollar savings gained by acquiring Web skills compared with developing them. Value in this sense represents the maximum amount of money you would recommend paying for the firm. You also prepare backup charts that provide the details of your numbers, keeping them in reserve in case your boss asks for them.

To determine the maximum price you would be willing to pay for the firm, you performed the following analysis.

Price Analysis—Step 1

You compute the estimated revenue for the firm this year as follows, assuming that an average industry growth rate of 25 percent applies:

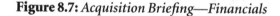

value = ($31.35M) * (1.25) = $39.2 million

CONSIDERATIONS AND APPROACH

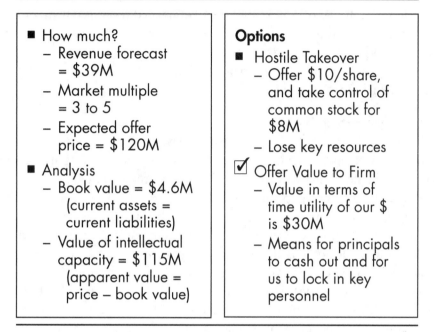

- How much?
  - Revenue forecast
    = $39M
  - Market multiple
    = 3 to 5
  - Expected offer
    price = $120M
- Analysis
  - Book value = $4.6M
    (current assets =
    current liabilities)
  - Value of intellectual
    capacity = $115M
    (apparent value =
    price – book value)

Options
- Hostile Takeover
  - Offer $10/share,
    and take control of
    common stock for
    $8M
  - Lose key resources
- ☑ Offer Value to Firm
  - Value in terms of
    time utility of our $
    is $30M
  - Means for principals
    to cash out and for
    us to lock in key
    personnel

Figure 8.8: *Acquisition Briefing—Considerations/Approach*

This amount represents XYZ Internet Corporation's projected sales for next year. Normally, firms are purchased for multiples of their projected sales. In the Internet industry, the number seems to vary between 3 and 5. This seems high to you because the firm's net worth is equal to the value of the long-term assets it owns and its retained earnings. The net worth of its current assets is zero because the firm is carrying $9.9 million in near-term liabilities on its balance sheet. In addition, current market capitalization is only $6.0 million based on the depressed common stock price of $6/share ($6 times the 1 million shares outstanding; includes stock held by officers of the company). In other words, the firm's only value rests in its intellectual and production capacity, goodwill, and reputation.

Price Analysis—Step 2

You determine the price others have recently paid for similar firms in the industry. Your research turns up five acquisitions completed during the past year. All five firms were smaller than XYZ Internet Corporation. The average size was 25. Two were in bad financial condition and were picked up cheaply. The other three were sold for multiples of 3 to 5 times their anticipated revenue. Further investigations seem fruitless because the three firms were in sound financial condition, making good profits, and growing rapidly. One by-product of your research is that you validated the rule of thumb of 3 to 5 times anticipated revenue for purchasing a firm in the Internet industry.

Price Analysis—Step 3

As an option, you estimate what you would have to spend to hire and bring a shop of 100 Web specialists up to speed on your business and its applications. This cost estimate, along with your justification, is provided in Table 8.5. You do not include the costs of personnel because you would have to spend a similar amount for any option you selected. You debate listing the business you would lose due to the lack of an e-business and e-commerce Web site as an opportunity cost. But you decide not to include these lost opportunities and the other savings that accrued in GE's case (travel savings, ability to establish supplier chains, and so on) because they would skew the numbers radically. You estimate these savings for your firm in the hundreds-of-million-dollar range. If you included such large numbers, you believe that management would question the credibility of your analysis.

Price Analysis—Step 4

You put a dollar value on the "knowledge capital" using the scheme for the ratings in Table 8.4 (see page 220), the rating matrix.

- Determine a value for each cell in your evaluation matrix per the table assuming that being a follower is a "–" and a leader a "+." Assume that each "+/–" in the rating matrix is worth $6 million (100 people @12K/ person for 5 months) in opportunity costs. This number, which represents the time utility of your investment capital, is determined by assuming that each "+/–" in the rating scale saves you 5 months of time (24 months/ 5 factors). In other words, smart people who are experienced in the application can do the job much quicker than those just learning the craft.

- For the acquisition alternative, you rate each of the five criteria a "+." Therefore, you estimate that the time value of XYZ Internet Corporation's intellectual and production capacity is worth $30 million to your firm.

Table 8.5: *Cost Estimate for Developing In-House Web Capability*

Item	Amount ($M)	Justification
Recruiting costs	2.0	Assumes 100 people @ $20K/person
Training costs	4.3	Assumes people are 20% less effective the first year and 10% less effective during the second year
Mentoring costs	2.9	Assumes hiring an extra 10 people as mentors for the two years you estimate it will take your people to get up to speed on your applications
Opportunity costs	2.1	The money you could make by placing the budget of $14.4 million in the bank at 7 percent for two years
Total	11.3	Assumes resources could be found and management is willing to delay having Web capabilities for at least a year

The following questions still need answering before you can take the results of this analysis to your boss and recommend acquisition.

- Should you suggest a hostile takeover? You could offer to purchase the outstanding shares of common stock for a premium of $10/each. The acquisition would cost at most $10 million because there are just 1 million shares outstanding (including the shares owned by the officers of the firm). This is considerably less than tendering an offer of three times revenue for a firm whose assets are worth $3 million and whose only value is the available "knowledge capital." Of course, the current staff may not look kindly on your move. They might fight you. Worse than that, the very people you are trying to bring into your group might leave just as you are taking control.

- Should you suggest an offer of $30 million? This represents a number somewhat near next year's sales forecast. The price is based on your estimate of the firm's value to your organization. You feel this is a fair offer because it is three times what it would cost you to develop a similar capability in house in two years. This option has the advantage that it would limit loss of key personnel. As part of the acquisition agreement, you could prohibit key people from cashing out their stock if they left before a specified time limit.

■ Does any other option make sense? Spending three times anticipated revenue, or $120 million, to acquire capabilities that you could build for $11 million doesn't make financial sense, even though there is much pressure to do something.

After you mull these questions over in your mind, you decide to recommend offering $30 million because this represents what you believe the true value of this firm is to your organization. As Figure 8.8 indicates, you believe that your management will support this option because it seems to make good business sense for all parties involved in the acquisition.

TO BUY OR NOT TO BUY

Your pitch to your boss went extremely well. After you answered his many questions with your backup material, he supported your recommendations. Before presenting the pitch upstairs, he asked you some additional questions:

■ What's wrong with XYZ Internet Corporation's management performance? What problems will you have to solve if you acquire this firm?

■ Who else is on the market? Do you have a fallback position should the acquisition negotiations go sour?

The questions seem reasonable, and you don't know why you didn't think of them yourself. To understand what's amiss with management, you decide to analyze XYZ's income statement more fully (see page 215). Because there is a level of detail missing from the income statement that was provided in the annual report, you get a copy of the firm's 10-K report from the SEC for more insight into its operating expenses. The detailed income statement in the accompanying box yields a lot of valuable information.

Your boss's suggestion to dig and find out more about the management performance problem has paid off. You feel you have found the cause of the firm's predicament, and you are prepared to report the following findings:

■ Apparently, the five founders of the company have been rewarding themselves at the expense of shareholders. Each principal is paid an annual salary of $1 million. In addition, each receives benefits worth $500,000 (car, expense account, and so on). The extent of the executive packages seems extravagant to you stacked up against the firm's reported performance.

XYZ INTERNET CORPORATION'S
DETAILED INCOME STATEMENT

Total revenues	US $31,350K
■ Costs of goods sold	
– In-house production	1,540
– Out-of-house production (subcontractors)	1,000
Gross Profit	**28,810**
Operating expenses	
■ Salaries and wages	
– Officers	5,000
– Employees	9,524
■ Employee benefits	
– Officers	2,500
– Employees	3,110
■ Income taxes	288
■ Office expenses	
– Rent	960
– Supplies	75
– Other	307
■ Payroll taxes	2,475
■ Other	
– Accounting	180
– Legal[1]	500
– Other	413
– Write-off for acquisition[2]	3,500
Operating Income	**<22>**
Interest Income	**32**
Total Income	**10**

[1]Large legal expense because of a lawsuit brought against the firm by temporary employees who are claiming benefits as full-timers.

[2]Acquisition was a training firm valued at $1M owned by the president's wife's brother-in-law.

- When you dig into the rent charges, you find that the founders are each receiving $75,000 annually for use of offices in their homes for the business. The firm also pays for the phone service to their homes. Again, this arrangement seems out of line to you.

- The footnote on legal expenses scares you. Recent court cases decided that temporary workers who have worked for a firm since its founding may claim compensation for benefits if they can show that they have worked only for this firm for over a year. Consequently, the potential liability for benefits compensation is in excess of $10 million.

- Finally, you get a laugh out of the footnote about the acquisition. Buying the brother-in-law's firm seems a little suspect in your mind.

It looks to you as if the founders of XYZ Internet Corporation are milking the firm. Although their actions are legal, you question their ethics. Your personal disdain aside, your analysis shows that the firm is making more money than it is reporting. If you allow the founders to cash out, you can replace them with your own team of executives, reducing annual salary and benefit expenses by at least $5 million. You can use the pending litigation during negotiations to justify why you are not offering more for the firm. You can also use the information advantageously to make the founders feel guilty.

AVOIDING THE TRAPS

The briefing your boss scheduled with the executive council goes well. He has made sure that you are prepared to handle any contingency. After some debate, the council concurs with your recommendations. They instruct you to form an acquisition team from people in the legal and contracts departments to enter into discussions with XYZ Internet Corporation and to examine its financials for any additional surprises. After several meetings with XYZ representatives and completion of a due-diligence investigation, your people are developing an agreement that outlines the terms and conditions associated with the proposed acquisition.

As the primary technical advisor to the acquisition team, you are on call to answer questions and draft clauses as the agreement is formulated. As anticipated, the chief obstacle to reaching accord with XYZ Internet Corporation is money. After considerable negotiation, the founders of the firm still want a minimum of $60 million (twice this year's revenue). You can't negotiate further because your marching orders from the executive council are to pay no more than $30 million for the firm. Everything including the details associated with agreement must be left in abeyance until the price to be paid can be settled on.

Finally there is a breakthrough. XYZ Internet Corporation suddenly agrees to take your $30 million offer. You are surprised by this turn of events. However, after making several discreet inquiries, you learn the reason for the turnaround. Apparently, the Internal Revenue Service (IRS) subpoenaed records from the president of the firm in an ongoing effort to collect disputed back taxes. When this happened, the president pressured the four other founders to take your offer because he needed the cash to settle with the IRS. They fought him at first but acquiesced when he threatened to turn them in to the IRS for tax evasion.

The acquisition team now turns to you for help in structuring the terms and conditions of the agreement. What they have included so far looks fine to you. Not surprisingly, the provisions deal primarily with legal and accounting matters. Your task is to focus their attention on the more technical considerations that need to be included in the agreement to make it work for your organization. In addition, you want to make several other suggested changes based on your experience with past acquisitions. In response to their plea for help, you recommend that they address the following seven items in appropriate legal language:

1. *Conflict of interest clause*   You suggest a clause prohibiting the current officers of XYZ Internet Corporation from establishing a competing company for a period of at least one year. Because you distrust the officers, you want to discourage them from reentering the business, soliciting customers, and raiding your organization for talent.

2. *Debt assumption*   You warn the team to make sure that your firm is not held liable for any debt that was not revealed during negotiations and is not called out in any of the financial disclosure papers. You were stung by this problem in the past in the area of equipment leasing. In that case, the firm's accounting system was on a cash basis, and the debt associated with retirement of the equipment did not appear on the books until it was paid out.

3. *Intellectual property rights*   You want to make sure that XYZ Internet Corporation passes to the acquirer the rights to the "knowledge capital" you are after as part of the deal. You suggest that the following items be called out explicitly:

- Architectural patterns, frameworks, and drawings for products and product lines
- Knowledge base of past performance, lessons learned, and project histories

- Personnel files, including merit reviews and salary histories (many firms don't provide this information because of privacy concerns)
- Software component and building block libraries
- The right to use, duplicate, copy, or disclose all technical data and software transferred in whole or in part, in any manner and for any purpose whatsoever, along with the ability to grant permission for others to do the same

4. *Key personnel clause*   You suggest a clause in the agreement that prohibits key personnel from leaving the firm within six months of the date of purchase without first securing written permission to do so for any reason except death or disablement. As part of this clause, key personnel should be listed by name and title [Marciniak, 1990].

5. *Liability limitation clause*   You want to make sure that you limit your firm's liability for past nonpayment of benefits to temporary employees. You therefore recommend a clause specifically excluding any penalties associated with labor practices that were in place before the acquisition was signed and finalized. You also suggest reviewing your own company's current labor practices to ensure that they do not violate the spirit of the law as it pertains to such benefits.

6. *Licensing issues*   All too often, the ownership of licenses and rights to use the software are not transferred as part of the rights to property during an acquisition. The right to transfer the software doesn't exist if you don't negotiate it up front as part of the original license agreement. You might need further protection because some vendors specifically exclude the ability to transfer rights to use packaged software as part of their license agreements. To address these concerns, you suggest that your team ask XYZ Internet Corporation to record all software licenses by number in the agreement along with written confirmation that current discounts, service contracts, and rights to use will pass on to your firm.

7. *Survival of warranties clause*   Finally, you suggest that the team spell out any warranties your firm will assume along with information about how they are administered. The administration details of warranties are important because they tell you how defects on property (equipment, software, and so on) transferred to your firm will be handled. You'd be surprised how many warranties are voided because this clause is not included as part of an acquisition agreement.

GOING GLOBAL

When corporate officers finally see the package, they have objections because clearance has not been received from international relations. Talking to your international staff seems like a good idea because you plan to use people from XYZ Internet Corporation to build Web capability around the world. Within high technology companies like XYZ Corporation, people and their intellectual capacity are both your biggest asset and your biggest headache [Larsen, 2000]. You ask international affairs for help in determining whether there are any legal, cultural, and trade barriers that need to be addressed in your acquisition agreement. This department is self-contained and has the expertise for these matters within your firm.

The international staff provides you with good news. They do not see any obstacles and quickly sign off on the acquisition. Because you will not be exporting products overseas, there shouldn't be any legal or trade barriers that will limit you from achieving your goals. But international is concerned that your new employees will not be well versed in working abroad. They offer to conduct orientation sessions for the people from XYZ Internet Corporation going to Europe and Asia to acquaint them with cultural, tax, and travel details. This training is important because multi-national corporations such as yours operate across national boundaries, build bridges between cultures, transfer technology, hasten change, and accelerate cooperation and growth [Fatemi, 1998].

You have plenty of internal circulars that discuss the fine points of overseas taxes and travel. But cultural issues and blunders concern you greatly. It has taken you two years and a lot of work to get people across three continents to work together efficiently. The issues that were raised during this period were primarily cultural. Because time, space, manners, and customs (norms) differ between cultures, you had to sensitize your people to the issue and increase their tolerance for one another. Behaviors acceptable in one culture are not acceptable in another. For example, the American use of nonverbal communications (eye contact, body movements, gestures) is considered insulting in China. So is the Chinese custom of belching after a good meal to Americans. The French think it funny when Americans try to speak their language and do so poorly. In response, Americans feel that the French are insulting them when they make the effort to speak their language. As another example of cultural differences, the American expectation of contractual finality is foreign to the Japanese way of doing business [Herbig, 1998]. To the Japanese, signing a contract begins rather than ends negotiations and a relationship. Moreover, they believe that the relationship created is more important than the contract. In contrast, Americans seem bound more by law than by relationships.

These are just some examples of the cultural differences that your employees must understand and address. Many others will be addressed by the orientation sessions proposed by your international relations department. The importance of tolerance for others when doing business globally cannot be overemphasized.

TIMING IS STRATEGY

You've done your homework and structured a deal that looks good for all parties concerned. However, management seems to want you to refine one issue or another every time you pitch it to them for a decision. When you think about it, $30 million is a lot of money to spend. You are not surprised that your executive staff wants to make sure that they are doing the right thing. However, you need XYZ Internet Corporation's capabilities now, not later. Independent of whether action is taken or not, management will you hold accountable if the new organization fails to quickly establish an e-business and e-commerce presence on the Web. Timing is strategy. You need help to achieve this goal as soon as possible. You need to figure out how to stimulate management to take action on your proposal as quickly as possible.

How do you get management to move forward with a $30 million acquisition? You could employ one of several strategies. You could push them until they say "yes" or "no." You could let your champion at the executive level press for a decision. You could build an even more compelling business case. The tactic that has worked best in my experience is one I call the competitive ploy. Let management know what your competition is doing in this area and pressure them for action. Arrange a demonstration of your chief competitor's Web capabilities. Send management articles emphasizing the benefits competitors are realizing. Provide excerpts from your competitors' marketing literature and financial reports. Keep the information flowing and the pressure mounting. Executives make major purchase decisions only when they believe they have to. Make them believe the time to act is now.

SUMMARY

This chapter presents a case study about acquisition. To move to the Web quickly, a large corporation is seeking to acquire a firm with the "knowledge capital" to establish an e-business and e-commerce presence. The case focuses on how to determine a value for the firm to be acquired. It also examines what to look for when analyzing the financial health of a candidate for acquisition.

KEY POINTS

- ✔ Although acquisition is a quick way to acquire intellectual capability and capacity, care must be taken to analyze candidates carefully and structure agreements well.

- ✔ A company's financial statements can give you insight into its earnings and sales growth, financial health, management performance, and how well it is doing versus its competitors.

- ✔ Because of its subjectivity, determining the "real value" of the knowledge capital a firm possesses is a difficult task.

- ✔ Knowledge capital recognizes that people are a firm's primary resource, not tools, equipment, or manufacturing capacity.

- ✔ Knowledge capital can be assessed using a framework that takes ideas, skills, the ability to innovate, nimbleness, and know-how into consideration.

- ✔ Several factors that can be easily quantifed can be used to assess a firm's financial performance.

- ✔ When analyzing the health of a candidate for acquisition, be sure to dig deep and find the root cause of any problems.

- ✔ Take advantage of the experience of others in your organization to avoid the traps that have snared others when structuring acquisitions.

- ✔ Be aware of the cultural differences that exist when working in the international arena.

References

[Baetjer, 1997] Baetjer, Howard. *Software as Capital.* IEEE Computer Society Press, 1997, p. 14.

[Ehrlich, 1998] Ehrlich, Henry. *The Wiley Book of Business Quotations.* John Wiley & Sons, p. 69 (quoting Robert G. McVicker of Kraft Foods in a speech on April 3, 1992).

[Fatemi, 1998] Fatemi, Nasrollah S., Gail Williams, and Thibaut de Saint-Phalle. *Multinational Corporations,* 2nd Edition. Thomas Yoseloff, 1998.

[Herbig, 1998] Herbig, Paul A. *Handbook of Cross-Cultural Marketing.* The International Business Press, 1998.

[Hutchin, 2000] Hutchin, Nancy L. "Electronic Commerce and Governance: A Darwinian Discussion," *CrossTalk,* Vol. 13, No. 10, October 2000, pp. 20–24.

[Larsen, 2000] Larsen, Kai R.T., and Peter A. Bloniarz. "A Cost and Performance Model for Web Service Investment," *Communications of the ACM,* Vol. 43, No. 2, February 2000, pp. 109–116.

[Marciniak, 1990] Marciniak, John J., and Donald J. Reifer. *Software Acquisition Management.* John Wiley & Sons, 1990.

[Peltz, 2000] Peltz, James P. "GE Takes to the Net to Lower Company Costs," *Los Angeles Times,* 9 October 2000, pp. C1–C5.

[Yourdon, 1997] Yourdon, Edward. *Death March.* Prentice Hall, 1992, p. 200.

Part III

Finale

The last chapter pulls things together and emphasizes that you can be successful. It is more than just a pep talk. It focuses on what you can do to change your organization using the numbers. Take heart, and make the numbers work for you!

9

Overcoming Adversity
More Than a Pep Talk

THE WARY TRAVELER

The material presented so far uses business cases to justify improvements. I also make numerous suggestions aimed at increasing the validity of your numbers and the credibility of your recommendations. Playing the numbers is dangerous, because once the numbers are made public they cannot be changed. If they are wrong, you have to live with them. Numbers have a life of their own. I remember many briefings where executives stood up and argued numbers. "They're wrong," they'd argue. "Why?" I would respond. "Because the cost is more than we had in mind," they'd reply. Executives even quote precise figures as they discuss your numbers. For example, I've recently heard the following two statements come out of the mouths of some very senior managers: "Why has our software productivity increased only 7.25 percent per year when our competition is reporting a fivefold improvement?" "Why does software continue to cost so much? Today, software costs $31.25 per source line of code. Three years ago, our costs were $26.50 per source line. That represents a meager 5 percent improvement annually." Management's ability to retain and recite numbers continues to amaze me.

The scrutiny your numbers will be subjected to is extensive. I suggest that you double- and triple-check your numbers because mistakes jeopardize trust in your work. Package your numbers with care. Always define what the numbers include and what they don't. Use industry-standard lexicons to define terms. Otherwise, you will have to explain why your definitions are different to those who want to discredit your numbers for their own purposes. Be wary of people who spew numbers without hesitation and substantiation. They probably either haven't been burnt by numbers in the past or have invented what they're saying on the spur of the moment. People who work with numbers tend to express them either in ranges or against norms. For example, they might say, "Productivity for such and such a group ranged from 2 to 5 function points per staff-month of labor during the period being questioned within these lines of business, which compares well to industry norms that range from 2 to 6."

I provide advice on how to avoid many of these problems throughout the text. Although it may seem that I am overemphasizing this issue, I'm not. Managers take numbers to the extreme. They use them and abuse them for their own purposes. They quote them when they help their cause and avoid their use when they don't. Numbers are about money, and the money game is serious business. Success with numbers is just as possible as failure. Let's look at how to succeed with them.

YOU TOO CAN BE SUCCESSFUL

Use of numbers to justify change will knock down many of the barriers in your path. Business cases that emphasize the numbers help quell the resistance to change. Through my experiences over the years, I have developed the following ten principles to guide you toward success with change:

1. *Change only if it makes good business sense.*   Frequently, proposals suggesting change are made for technical reasons. However, most firms require strong financial justification before they approve changes. Powerful business cases are needed to free up the staff, money, and other resources needed to implement changes. Unfortunately, most technical people I know haven't learned how to pull a business case together. Your job is to teach your staff how to prepare and sell their proposals upstairs. To win their trust, you must balance your desire for justification with their yearning for approval. To do so, you may have to mentor, coach, and coerce your people to provide you with the ammunition you need to win approval in the battle of the budget.

2. *Don't become enamored with the technology.* Technical people regularly become captivated by new technology because they are always looking for better ways to do their jobs. Regrettably, the investments required to bring new technology into your firm and move it into widespread use may not justified. For example, the technology may be immature or tools for mechanizing it may not yet exist. Waiting for the technology to evolve and mature may be the best option. But this may turn your people off and cause morale problems. In any case, force them to look at the options in detail, and prepare a business case justifying the use of the technology. You will be glad you did. I've seen many projects fail because they relied on technology that wasn't quite ready to support them and their mission.

3. *Get everyone involved—but not too involved.* Having people affected by a change reach consensus on how to implement it during its approval process is the right thing to do. It doesn't make sense for you to push for improvements that benefit one group at the expense of another. If you do, you will be rightfully criticized for taking sides. But reaching consensus sometimes takes more time, effort, and energy than you have. In some cases, you might have to forgo consensus to take advantage of a window of opportunity (e.g., midyear money suddenly becomes available or a project shows up that you could contribute to). Be prepared to act. Otherwise, opportunity may slip away. For your business case, you will need all affected groups to cooperate and supply information. If there is friction, it will become extremely difficult for you to build a credible rationale and win the battle of the budget.

4. *Focus changes on product developments.* Improvements that directly benefit product developments are the ones that count in most organizations. I have found that you can win most arguments if you can get a project, product, or product line manager to stand up in a meeting and say: "I need this," or "I am in full support of this option." But to gain their confidence and support, you have to convince them that your proposal directly benefits them. To portray the benefits, you have to orient your numbers to show how the proposal will help them succeed. If you don't, you may lose support. Worse, they might view you as a threat because you are trying to get at money they believe they can use for better purposes. Remember the merit increases that project and product managers receive are based on their ability to deliver products on time and within budget, not the benefits they provide to the organization at large. It has been my experience that if you show product line, product, and project managers that you can help them, they will respond in kind.

5. *Look to the future, not the past.*   When making decisions, engineers should look to the future and learn from the past. Their concern should be what it will cost to finish a project or launch a product. Past expenditures are sunk costs and don't enter into current decisions. Of driving importance to engineers is which alternative provides the best value for their money. That's the question to answer as you weave your magic in your business case. Of course, the alternatives under consideration need to be feasible. But, the future remains the focus of the analysis. Accountants look to the past, while engineers look to the future.

6. *Don't reinvent the wheel.*   In my experience, most decisions involving improvements consider alternatives that have been studied before. The difficulty is finding the results of these studies. Often, past analysis isn't documented, and business case information is spotty. But find what you can and update it; don't reinvent it. Often the alternatives have changed (a new version of the software has been recently released to fix problems, the vendor has improved its reliability, and so on), making some of the analysis irrelevant to your organization (e.g., you've switched from Unix to Windows on your servers). But, obviously, updating a past analysis normally takes less effort than performing a new one. Work study tasks to hard deadlines, and be wary of those who wish to study a problem to death.

7. *Remember Rome wasn't built in a day.*   As improvement proposals are prepared, people have the tendency to want to make many changes all at once. Because major improvements are launched every few years, they piggyback change after change in their proposal because money is finally being made available to do the right thing. Unfortunately, the push for too much causes many initiatives to fail. They try to do too much too quickly. A better approach is to be successful implementing a few good things. These changes are the ones your numbers say are important (the ones that provide the most benefit for the dollar). You should plan to demonstrate the benefits of the incremental versus the "big bang" approach as part of your business case. To address the risk, look at the cost of failure.

8. *Do the easy things first to establish credibility.*   Institute the simple and obvious changes first. This will enable you to establish your credibility by getting something that everyone deems is important done quickly. For example, bring in a cost model like COCOMO II [Boehm, 2000], and use it to improve your estimating capabilities. Others may argue that it is more meaningful to tackle the harder items.

For example, they might suggest deploying statistical process control measures as you put your new software practices into operation. I disagree. Like most action-oriented managers, I prefer short-term results to long-term reports about progress and how good it will be when you finish the job. You should plan to demonstrate the benefits of one approach versus the other in your business case. This will add even more credibility to your recommendations.

9. *Be satisfied with a 90 percent solution.*   Those stimulating change need to know when good is good enough. While I admire perfectionists, 90 percent solutions are sufficient in most situations. You don't want to leave loose ends dangling, but you do want to get something meaningful done. Results are what matters. For example, a requirements generation process can be improved considerably using an integrated product team (IPT). In contrast, achieving perfection in the requirements process is a never-ending quest. In this case, 90 percent of the benefit can be achieved using an IPT for 10 percent of the effort. In others, the percentages may vary. The important message is that you will shine when you justify your recommendations using business case analysis independent of the numbers.

10. *The sum of many small successes in business is often a big success.*   I strongly believe that success breeds success. To be viewed as successful, all you have to do is create the aura of success. This can be easily accomplished by continually making a large number of small successes visible throughout the firm. With this approach, you can even fail and be viewed as successful once the aura is established. As a side benefit, good people flock to work with those who are viewed as successful. After all, who would want to be assigned to a project that was viewed negatively? When promoting success, emphasize the numbers and the "hard" data. They will get management's attention and win you allies. They will allow you to show management how what you are doing is helping the firm succeed by lowering costs, improving quality, or reducing time to market.

CHANGE TACTICS ABOUND

Tactics to guide change operationally are also needed. As with principles, you can use tactics to shore up, spur on, and develop support for your recommendations as you deploy them operationally. I have used the following seven tactics with great success.

1. *Keep senior management informed of your progress.*   It seems that the only time you are called into your boss's office is when there is trouble. That's because he/she gets involved only when things are going amiss. Keep your boss informed to keep him/her on your side as your improvement effort unfolds. Schedule one-on-one monthly progress meetings to discuss issues, review status, and solicit advice. Use the metrics and business case data that you are collecting to assess and report your progress. This will keep your boss involved and on your side. The meeting may even provide you with some useful input, especially in the area of organizational politics and business practices. Don't wait until you get into trouble to ask your boss for help. That will result in an endless spiral of questions and answers.

2. *Build alliances with projects and people.*   The power brokers in most organizations are the influence-makers and project managers. Influence-makers are your key performers. (In most organizations 20 percent of the staff generates 80 percent of the productivity.) Their opinion counts because they are held in high regard by management and the junior members of the staff. Project managers are viewed as demigods in most organizations. They control the resources and therefore the destinies of most of the workers. Getting both camps on your side is important. Project managers ally with those who provide their projects with financial help. In contrast, influence-makers tend to support technical initiatives. Use your metrics and business case data to win the support of both camps. Both will support those who can help them justify their cause to their bosses.

3. *Mix it with the middle managers.*   Make it a practice to work with middle managers one-on-one. This allows them to ask you the questions that they can't or won't ask in public. It also allows you to exchange ideas and understand what their measures of success are for the effort. To gain their support you first have to gain their trust. Private meetings go a long way toward accomplishing this goal. During these meetings, be professional. Realize that this manager's view of software people hinges on how you present yourself. Stress the numbers and the business aspects of your initiatives in your discussions. Most middle managers are held accountable for organizational performance. You need to show them simply how what you are doing helps them deliver products to market quicker, cheaper, and better than the alternatives. If you do this, you will receive middle management trust and support. If all you do is talk about what you're doing in generalities, you will gain their animosity and be labeled untrustworthy.

4. *Don't be afraid to change courses in midstream (especially when you hit a sandbar).*   Plans are road maps. When you encounter an obstacle, you need to be agile enough to change in midstream. Metrics and business case benchmarks provide the information you need to pinpoint the problem, determine the root cause, and remedy the situation. But for this to work, you have to pay attention to the numbers and listen to what they are telling you. Frequently, I've seen managers bury their heads in the sand. They assume that if they wait, things will get better. While this may be true for certain situations, waiting too long before taking action is just as bad as acting too quickly. Timing is strategy. The optimum timing associated with each alternative should be considered as the decision is made.

5. *Deliver something you can show off and brag about.*   Business cases justify investments in improvement activities. They matter most when you realize your goals and deliver what you promise. My tactics emphasize doing the easy and visible things first. I focus my early efforts on generating products that I can take pride in and can show to people. The best way to damp criticism from any quarter is to deliver the products you promised on time and within budget. It is hard for people to find fault with your efforts when you can show them a fully functional product that you have generated successfully. It is also easy for management to justify continuance and enlargement of an effort that delivers. Too many initiatives fail because they produce nothing but paper tigers (study reports).

6. *Be perceived as important and successful.*   This tactic goes hand and glove with "the sum of many small successes in business is often a big success." People like being associated with success. Therefore, use the aura of success to build momentum and keep the bulldozer rolling. Be the project that continues to report good news to management. Reinforce the message of success using your metrics and business case data whenever possible. In most large software organizations, you'll be one of the few to be able to do this.

7. *Work with your technical staff to continually improve their capabilities and capacity.*   Many change agents focus most of their time and energy selling their initiatives to middle and upper management. They do this for the right reasons: they need their support to get money and be successful. The problem is that they do not develop the support of the working troops. In the working ranks, numbers and business case data don't mean much. Software professionals are more concerned about themselves than about the business aspects of your decisions. They want to learn new things and develop new skills, knowledge, and abilities, so make the effort to show the workers how the effort will benefit them. Highlight the benefits to their personal growth, marketability, and career advancement goals. You'll be glad you did so.

I'm trying to communicate the following three messages via the principles and tactics about being successful with change:

- Good planning and a focus on the business cases are the prerequisites to success in most improvement initiatives.

- Proper promotion and consensus are the keys to gaining trust, support, and sponsorship.

- Continual reinforcement, common sense, attention to detail, and reliance on numbers are what's needed in equal proportions to keep the effort on track.

Although you may not think so, the easy part of the effort is to develop the numbers and business cases that justify the initiatives. The hard part, in my opinion, is to get people in your organization to believe the numbers and use them operationally to make better decisions.

AVOID THE MANY TRAPS

If I've made it sound easy to succeed, it's not. All types of obstacles get in the way. As Figure 9.1 illustrates, the barriers to success include the following technical, managerial, political, and money traps.

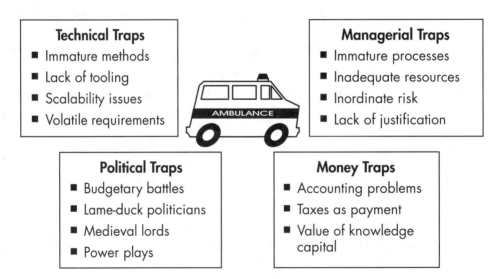

Technical Traps
- Immature methods
- Lack of tooling
- Scalability issues
- Volatile requirements

Managerial Traps
- Immature processes
- Inadequate resources
- Inordinate risk
- Lack of justification

Political Traps
- Budgetary battles
- Lame-duck politicians
- Medieval lords
- Power plays

Money Traps
- Accounting problems
- Taxes as payment
- Value of knowledge capital

Figure 9.1: *Barriers to Success*

Technical traps   Most of the books [Hall, 1998] and articles you read in the technical journals highlight the technical risks. The causes of most of these risks are listed in the figure. For example, poor choice of methods and tools often dooms the project to failure. Concerning requirements volality, we seem to continue to search for perfection when our ability to control the rapidity of requirements change is often outside our sphere of control [Reifer, 2000].

Managerial traps   Other popular texts focus attention on the managerial challenges [Pressman, 2000]. Many of the causes of failure in this category have been around for years [Brooks, 1995]. For example, we continue to schedule the impossible almost every day, especially in the world of e-business and e-commerce. No matter how you try, there is no possible way to succeed when the schedule you've agreed to is unattainable.

Political traps   The really tricky issues for most engineers revolve around politics. To survive the battle of the budget, alliances need to be formed, and treaties need to be made. Because they rely on logic, engineers have difficulty with politics because such issues are illogical by their very nature. They prefer to play by the rules of the game. But politics is often governed by an unwritten set of rules that are arbitrary and focus on power brokering [Scott-Morgan, 1994].

Money traps   The last category, money, is the cause of most problems that I have encountered. To get it, you have to penalize others by taking it from someone else's budget. As a result, there is animosity, and there are conflicts. In addition, engineers have difficulty dealing with accountants and the bean-counter mentality. This is to be expected because accountants look to the past while engineers address the future.

I don't believe that any of these barriers will bring the show to a grinding halt. If you are aware of the traps, you can avoid them. Better than that, you can use them to your advantage to win allies, overcome adversity, and get the resources you need to succeed. While nobody likes to play games, you need to understand the unwritten rules and play by them to win.

FOCUS ON THE THINGS THAT COUNT

Although there are many issues, the critical one that crops up in all my cases and discussions is dealing with people. That's not surprising because you're dealing with organizational change. You can succeed in making such changes by focusing on the business and management issues. But recognition that these issues are important depends on how your people view their world. Because software professionals frequently focus on the technical aspects of a change proposal, they typically don't recognize the importance of business cases. Many of them don't have grounding in business fundamentals. You need to change this limited viewpoint by emphasizing the significance of the business aspects of decisions. To do this, you must mentor and coach them to develop the needed skills, knowledge, and abilities. You must also teach them how to prepare a case and provide them with examples of what you think are good cases and solid justifications.

This book tries to help you accomplish these skill development tasks by reviewing the fundamentals associated with business cases and providing you with examples that others have used successfully. But business case skills alone aren't enough to succeed with change. To triumph, you must also develop the team building, collaboration, communication, and leadership skills that are needed to deploy your action plans for change. Often, engineers develop elaborate justifications and plans for change. Just as often, they then fail to follow through and deliver what they promise. As a consequence, upper management distrusts them because they have failed to make the desired changes. To achieve superior performance as you deploy your business plans, you must motivate all those who will work on the job to pull together as a team and deliver what they

Table 9.1: *Differing Needs of Stakeholder Groups*

Stakeholder Group	Needs
Software professionals	Professional growth (technical) Technical accomplishments Career advancement (typically technical) Ability to do interesting work
Middle managers	Professional growth (managerial—tactical) Project accomplishments (ability to deliver acceptable products on time and within budget) Career advancement (typically managerial) Ability to perfect their management skills
Executives	Professional growth (managerial—strategic) Corporate accomplishments (ability to earn a profit for the stockholders) Career advancement (up the corporate ladder) Ability to address strategic planning skills

promise. As Table 9.1 shows, motivating people from different backgrounds forces you to address each group's needs and conflicts that arise from differences in goals [Maslow, 1954]. Business cases help you to build bridges to reconcile these differences. To make collaboration possible, engineers must quantify the benefits of technical options in terms and language that middle managers and executives understand. This is also true for success in deployment.

OTHER INTERESTING USES OF NUMBERS

The four case studies that appeared in Chapters 5 through 8 were selected to illustrate how you can use business cases to justify improvements. They touch on how you can use numbers to make intelligent business decisions. Numbers can also help you during operations when informed decisions must be made. Let's look at three of the most common types of decisions: shutdown or continue, upgrade or replace, and whether to use risk analysis.

Shut Down or Continue

How many of you have worked on projects that seem to be going nowhere? Because of poor planning and requirements, people are spinning their wheels, and nothing seems to be happening. Project management sees the signs but doesn't seem to have the guts to take action. Their attitude is, "Let's give the team the time they need to straighten things out." Projects always tend to be in trouble in the beginning because of startup problems. But the more management delays, the more trouble the project gets into. When is enough enough?

Many factors influence the decision to shut down or continue. Because this project is generating products critical to the future of the firm, shutdown may be out of the question, so having the team develop a get-well plan is probably the best course of action. The team should determine what progress it has made and what resources are needed to complete the job more or less on schedule. Assuming that the project is using traditional project management techniques [Reifer, 1997], the team should use the management indicators (metrics, rate of progress charts, earned value and associated variance reports, and so on [Royce, 1998]) to determine the causes of the project's problems and develop a plan of action and milestones to correct them. For example, it might stop development until the requirements are solidified. Or it might reduce product functionality to achieve schedule parity. Often, taking a step backward can lead to moving two steps forward.

Shutting down a project is often a difficult decision. It is often politically fatal because few organizations are progressive enough to reward failure. From a business case point of view, it is sometimes cheaper to let a project continue than to shut it down. Of course, opportunity costs associated with alternative use of resources impacts the decision as does the out-of-pocket expenses associated with carrying on a project. Let's investigate the alternatives.

Let's assume that the get-well plan requires the current team of 20 to spend an additional six months on the project. For discussion's sake, let's assume that the team believes the plan to be achievable and that everyone has confidence in his or her ability to satisfy expectations. Besides being six months late to market, the project will therefore spend an additional $1,440,000 to generate the product (120 staff-months of labor priced at $12,000 per staff-month).

Shutdown costs are costs that are incurred when a project is terminated, for example, the costs required to close an office, relocate personnel, and/or suspend operations. Because there is not an immediate need for people, these costs also include the costs of moving people from one project to another.

You cannot shut a project down overnight. Instead, you must spend some effort to bring it a state of closure and salvage what you can. To accomplish this task, you will need a team of six for three months. The average time to place the remaining 14 people will be one month. In addition, one person will be needed to act as a caretaker for four months to administer return of equipment and coordinate closeout activities. Office space and equipment lease costs of $350,000 will also have to be paid until the end of the year. There is no way you can pay off these obligations other than finding some other project to foot the bill. Software licenses can be expensed because they can be transferred to other projects that want to use them. Finally, the opportunity costs in terms of the net revenue foregone by the shutdown is $500,000 (an estimate of the lost business). Based on these numbers, the cost of shutting down this project can be computed as follows:

total cost = labor costs + lease costs + opportunity costs
$$= (36SM @ \$12K/SM) + \$350,000 + \$500,000$$
$$= \$432,000 + \$350,000 + \$500,000$$
$$= \$1.282 \text{ million}$$

In other words, the cost of completing the project is estimated to be only $158,000 more than the cost of shutting the project down. With these numbers in hand, the choice between alternatives seems obvious. Of course, other factors may complicate the analysis. For example, the excess office space and equipment costs may be offset because you found another team that could use them. Unfortunately, such tradeoff analysis is rarely performed during get-well exercises. In addition, few textbooks on project management even bring up the tradeoff as an option that should be evaluated. I can only speculate that the reason for this is that management gets tired of troubled projects and wants to get rid of them and move on to something more upbeat.

Upgrade or Replace

The next case study looks at the decision to replace or upgrade equipment. Most of the time, the decision to replace existing systems seems to be made for morale rather than business reasons. Software engineers seem always to want the latest and greatest gear. They argue that they need the additional machine power to do their jobs quicker and better. Often, the excuses they use to rationalize the purchase of new gear are "I am running out of storage" or "I am having reliability problems with the current configuration." As discussed in Chapter 6, they may even try to justify the replacement with productivity improvements. Consequently, the upgrade of existing equipment is rarely considered a feasible option.

Let's look at an upgrade versus purchase decision. Let's assume that you have 100 workstations and three servers networked together to support development at your shop. Your staff wants new workstations that cost $3,000 each. To accommodate these new workstations, you will have to upgrade the database management software on your servers at an additional cost of $50,000. They also want to purchase $250,000 worth of new software licenses for tools to support the new methods and processes they have recently adopted.

The alternative is to upgrade the 100 existing workstations to include more memory, a larger hard disk, and a faster CPU at a cost of $1,000 each (including the labor). Operating system software for the workstations and database management licenses for servers will also have to be upgraded at a cost of $100,000. When asked if they evaluated this alternative, your programmers say "no." They did not feel it was responsive. They then argue vehemently against this option because, they say, the useful life of an upgrade is only three years versus five for new equipment. They also say that upgrading is very expensive. They justify their conclusion by showing you an analysis that takes the full book value of the equipment into account. They argue that book value is pertinent to the decision because equipment will still have to be depreciated to write the expense off against taxes in future years.

When you think about them, you find their arguments are full of holes. The first thing you realize when comparing options is that not all costs are of equal importance when making a decision. You must identify and take into account only those costs relevant to the decision. Otherwise, you might include costs that aren't applicable and bias the selection. Such costs typically don't influence the decision because they are applicable to both alternatives. In this case, the purchase of software tools is not a relevant cost because it will be made independent of which option is selected. Next, any sunk costs should be factored out of the decision. Sunk costs are costs that have already been incurred; their total will not be affected by the decision, so they are not relevant to the decision. In this case, the book value of the existing equipment should be treated as a sunk cost and be disregarded when comparing the options because it has already been expended. Finally, the suggested difference in useful life between upgraded and new equipment is bogus because equipment seems to be replaced or upgraded every two to three years, rather than every three to five years, because of technological obsolescence.

Table 9.2 compares the costs for the two options. As expected, the upgrade is considerably cheaper than acquisition of new gear; this is usually the case. Why not pursue this alternative? Having to live with unhappy programmers is probably not worth the pain. Think about it. Why do most people buy a new car? They purchase a new vehicle for status or appeal reasons, not because they need it. Then, like your people, they find some justification for the purchase, like reliability.

Risk Analysis

The final case deals with risk assessment. Although many books have been written on the topic, few if any of them adequately discuss how to quantify and compare the consequences of the alternatives. The notable exceptions are Barry Boehm's book [Boehm, 1989] and excellent paper on the topic [Boehm, 1991]. Dr. Boehm advocates the use of decision and opportunity trees to rank and rate options. Other experts outside the software field advocate use of other tools to

Table 9.2: *Upgrade Versus Replacement Cost Comparison*

Item	Replace ($K)	Upgrade ($K)
Capital expenditure (equipment)	300	100
Software licensing costs differential	50	100
Maintenance costs (annual)	15	25
Total	365	225

quantify risks and determine relative priorities [DoD, 1998; Gallagher, 1997]. Let's look at how we would quantify the risks for a typical software project situation you might find yourself in.

Table 9.3 presents a sample risk matrix developed for an actual project. The risks and related descriptions in this "top 10" list are typical of what you would

Table 9.3: *Sample Risk Matrix (Top 10 List)*

Risk	Description
1. Volatile requirements	Requirements are unstable due to marketing's seemingly daily demands to change the feature set.
2. Aggressive schedule	The scheduled time to completion is half that which was estimated. Project management forced the schedule down software's throat by threatening to kill the project if the schedule was not met.
3. Personnel turnover	The good people are pulled to work other higher-priority jobs. The resulting average experience of the team is lower than expected.
4. New processes	This will be the first project to use the new software processes the organization has devised as part of its improvement program.
5. New methods and tools	This will also be the first project to use the new methods and tools selected to support the new processes.
6. Size growth	The size in function points [Jones, 1998], on which all the software estimates are based, is growing exponentially and is out of control.
7. Testing done late	The test function is currently not staffed. Although test plans were supposed to be generated early, they will be delayed.
8. No change management	While versions are controlled, changes to them are not. Plans are for configuration management to be implemented after testing is complete.
9. New programming language	This will be the first project to use the Java programming language and its associated virtual machine environment to generate production software for picky users.
10. Managers don't manage; they program.	Managers on this project were chosen for their technical abilities. None of those performing this task has been trained in either the supervisory or the people skills needed to build and lead teams.

expect on projects observing an aggressive schedule. The risks are listed in the matrix by perceived importance. No effort has been made to prioritize the risks by dollar impact. The consequences of each risk need to be quantified in dollar terms in order to establish its priority. You could then estimate the risk exposure scientifically using the following formula:

risk ($) = (a + 4m + b)/6   **standard deviation = (b − a)/6**

where a is minimum dollar exposure, m is most likely dollar exposure, and b is maximum dollar exposure.

Taking requirements as an example, volatility means rework due to instability. You estimate that the worst case that would result would be a total redesign. The best case would be a slight modification. The most likely case would be a 40 percent modification. Using these figures as your base, you would estimate the dollar risk using the following formula, assuming that the cost of the work involved from design through release was $500,000:

risk ($) = ($25K + 4($200K) + $500K)/6 = $220,800

The problem with these numbers is that the standard deviation associated with the estimate is about $80,000. Assuming that the cost is distributed via a normal probability distribution, this means that the cost varies widely about the mean value of the statistical distribution.

WHERE'S THE TECHNOLOGY HEADING?

The approaches to preparing business cases and conducting economic analysis are stable. To my knowledge, no new breakthroughs for coping with the fundamentals have been developed during the past decade. However, new applications of methods and tools abound, as do new ways of presenting the results of the analyses performed. In addition, the Internet has taken away some of the mystique associated with business cases. More and more resources on the topic have become available as use of the Internet has gained popularity among technical folks. By invoking a search, you can find plenty of business case templates and examples. The problem is that most of these are general-purpose and not specific enough to be used as models by software organizations involved in change. But although engineering economics and business case Web sites are helpful, they don't fill the void. What's needed is a site devoted to the topic.

Table 9.4 summarizes the results of my search for materials on the World Wide Web. While lots of material on economics in general is available, few sites focus on software economics and business case analysis. The best of what's available is listed. Of course, these results will change as a function of time as will the materials within this book. That is why Addison-Wesley has permitted me to set up a Web site to provide updates on line (see the table for the address).

Table 9.4: *Economics and Business Case Web Resources*

Topic	Web Resources
Engineering economics and business cases	*www.isye.gatech.edu* (Georgia Institute of Technology) The WWW virtual library of industrial engineering with information on academic programs, conferences, courses, and publications that emphasize engineering economics
Computer economics and business cases	*http://info.berkeley.edu/resources/infoecon* (UC Berkeley) Economics of the Internet with pointers to sites on e-commerce, e-publishing, intellectual property, etc.
	www.computereconomics.com IT cost management support including industry benchmarks; also e-business strategies and market forecasts
	www.hbsp.harvard.edu (Harvard Business School) Access to case studies on e-commerce and the Internet, change management, entrepreneurship, and new technology
Software economics and business cases	*http://sunset.usc.edu* (University of Southern California) Information on cost estimating/analysis and the COCOMO suite; access to software downloads (COCOMO and code counters)
	www.sei.cmu.edu (Software Engineering Institute) Information on the Team Software Process (TSP) and Software Engineering Measurement and Analysis (SEMA) efforts
	www.software.org (Software Productivity Consortium) Practical measurement techniques, including controlled access to guidebooks, case studies, and lessons learned reports
Addison-Wesley site for this book	*www.aw.com/cseng/0-201-72887-7* Updates to this book, student exercises, and pointers to additional useful information

SUMMARY

Organizations are in a constant state of change. They are always striving to do things cheaper, better, and quicker. Software organizations are particularly subject to change because their business is getting products out the door on budget and within schedule. Enlightened software managers facilitate change by coupling sound business cases with the technical arguments for necessary improvements. They quantify the costs and benefits associated with their efforts to stimulate change and achieve superior performance by managing the improvements using metrics and "the numbers."

As the principal engineer or first-level manager responsible for stimulating such improvements, you bear the responsibility for creating, packaging, selling, and deploying business cases. Your efforts to quantify the benefits of changes and explain them to senior managers in terms that they relate to and understand do not go unnoticed. Efforts like this will nurture the perception that software professionals are finally becoming business oriented. As a role model, you will stimulate others to use business arguments to justify their technical proposals. Most important, you will change the attitudes, values, and competencies of the people you work with.

Observation

Most important, have fun when you are dealing with numbers. I like preparing business cases and dealing with all sorts of nontechnical people. Over the years, I have found my interactions with middle management, executives, and their staffs to be most enlightening. These types of interactions broaden your horizons and heighten your awareness that business is business, independent of what other engineers might try to tell you.

So in parting, good luck, and have fun preparing business cases. If you have questions or comments, please send me an e-mail message via the Addison-Wesley Web site. Don't forget to look at the site periodically for corrections, updates, pointers, and new information.

KEY POINTS IN THE BOOK

✔ Demonstrate your technical prowess by using business cases to push for improvements.

✔ Teach your people how to develop and use the numbers to justify needed changes.

✔ Encourage your people to grow professionally to fill senior management positions by stressing the business and decision-making aspects of the software job.

✔ Understand that your role as a leader is to stimulate those around you to achieve excellence using the numbers as tools.

✔ Foster an environment of collaborative teamwork in which engineers, managers, and executives work together using the numbers for the betterment of the organization.

✔ Encourage continual improvement when the numbers justify it, and when there are good technical reasons for your organization to make the desired changes.

✔ Promote the use of numbers as you conduct quantitative analysis and prepare business cases for your organization.

✔ Maintain your integrity as you use the numbers. Don't stretch the numbers to fit your case.

✔ Don't forget that the numbers will mean different things to different people. Define them carefully so that there is little confusion over their meaning.

✔ Don't be surprised when others misuse, abuse, and stretch your numbers.

✔ Finally, remember that numbers are powerful tools for decision making because they focus on determining the "value" or "benefit" for the organization.

References

[Boehm, 2000] Boehm, Barry W., Chris Abts, A. Winsor Brown, Sunita Chulani, Bradford K. Clark, Ellis Horowitz, Ray Madachy, Donald Reifer, and Bert Steece. *Software Cost Estimation with COCOMO II.* Prentice Hall, 2000.

[Boehm, 1991] Boehm, Barry W. "Risk Management: Principles and Practices," *IEEE Software,* January 1991, pp. 32–41.

[Boehm, 1989] Boehm, Barry W. *Tutorial Software Risk Management,* IEEE Computer Society, 1989.

[Brooks, 1975] Brooks, Frederick P., Jr. *The Mythical Man-Month, Anniversary Edition.* Addison-Wesley, 1995.

[DoD, 1998] Department of Defense. *Risk Management Guide.* Defense Systems Management College, March 1998.

[Gallagher, 1997] Gallager, Brian P., Christopher J. Alberts, and Richard E. Barbour. *Software Acquisition Risk Management Key Process Area (KPA)—A Guidebook.* Software Engineering Institute, CMU/SEI-97-HB-002, August 1997.

[Hall, 1998] Hall, Elaine M. *Managing Risk.* Addison-Wesley, 1998.

[Jones, 1998] Jones, T. Capers. *Estimating Software Costs.* McGraw-Hill, 1998.

[Maslow, 1954] Maslow, Abraham. *Motivation and Personality.* Harper & Row, 1954.

[Scott-Morgan, 1994] Scott-Morgan, Peter. *The Unwritten Rules of the Game.* McGraw-Hill, 1994.

[Pressman, 2000] Pressman, Roger S. *Software Engineering: A Practitioner's Approach.* McGraw-Hill, 2000.

[Reifer, 2000] Reifer, Donald J. "Requirements Management: The Search for Nirvana," *Software,* IEEE Computer Society, May/June 2000, pp. 45–47.

[Reifer, 1997] Reifer, Donald J. *Tutorial Software Management,* 5th Edition. IEEE Computer Society, 1997.

[Royce, 1998] Royce, Walker. *Software Project Management.* Addison-Wesley, 1998.

[Townsend, 1970] Townsend, Robert. *Up the Organization.* Knopf, 1970, p. 26.

Appendix A
Recommended Readings

This recommended reading list is for readers interested in learning more about the topics covered in the book. The items in the list are annotated to provide some insight into each reference.

Business Management

Hartman, A., and J. Sifonis. *Net Ready: Strategies for Success in the E-conomy.* McGraw-Hill, 2000.

This book presents a road map for profiting through e-business innovation. It helps you develop and deploy a workable strategy by guiding you through the organizing, planning, and transformation processes. It focuses on value chains and opportunity trees. Finally, it takes you through Cisco's successful experience and lessons it learned in e-conomy. A good book for those who are looking at moving their businesses to the World Wide Web.

Hoch, D. J., C. R. Roeding, G. Purkert, S. K. Lindner, and R. Müller. *Secrets of Software Success.* Harvard Business School Press, 2000.

This book reports the results of a recent survey that looked at the variables that influence results for both the product and service sides of the software industry. The survey involved more than 100 software firms and 450 top executives all over the world. Because many of the survey findings are counterintuitive, I consider this book worthwhile reading.

Waterman, R. H., Jr. *The Renewal Factor,* Bantam Books, 1987.

This management text focuses on how the best companies get and keep their competitive edge. It is a rich collection of ideas on how to renew your business and make your firm a leader. The book provides the process and tools to put its concepts into practice. The author uses many examples to show what can and has been done. This book continues to be one of my favorites because it provides insight into how to make things happen in most firms.

Change Management

Moore, G. A. *Crossing the Chasm.* HarperBusiness, 1991.

This classic discusses the issues, challenges, and experiences associated with moving technology from early adoption projects into widespread use. It is pragmatic in its orientation and full of examples. Its hypothesis is that the chasm that needs to be crossed is deep, and you must develop a realistic technology transfer strategy to bridge the gap. The book is very thought-provoking and provides insights into the barriers that make it so difficult to move promising technologies forward in most firms.

Sveiby, K. E., and T. Lloyd. *Managing Knowhow.* Bloomsbury, 1987.

I couldn't stop thinking about this book after I read it. Its message is simple yet thought-provoking. To transfer technology, you need to develop and use the know-how in your organization. As you can imagine, this is not as easy as it sounds. The book goes on to suggest ways to identify, develop, measure, and put needed know-how to work within the structure of a business idea through sound investments.

Wiegers, K. E. *Creating a Software Engineering Culture.* Dorset House, 1996.

This book discusses growing a software culture by channeling individual, team, and management behavior toward achieving shared organizational values, goals, and principles. Such cultures by their nature value individual contribution, teamwork, a passion for quality, and customer involvement. Methods, measures, and tools for fostering change are shared along with case studies and practical guidance throughout the body of the text.

Just Interesting Reading

Brooks, F. P., Jr. *The Mythical Man-Month, Anniversary Edition.* Addison-Wesley, 1995.

This well-written monograph discusses the problems and pitfalls that beset the author as he managed the development of the IBM 360 operating system. This classic is well written and full of sound advice. Most can identify with the problems that it points out. However, its solutions are somewhat dated. Its applicability across the almost four decades that it has been in print is confirmed by the fact that it is the best-selling software text on the market.

Davidson, A., H. Gellman, and M. Chung. *Riding the Tiger.* HarperBusiness, 1997.

Unlike most of the texts you'll read, this one is aimed at business managers, not software managers. It tries to arm people with a business background who are making technical decisions with the insights they need to make sound choices, especially in the areas of budgeting and scheduling. By eliminating technical jargon, the book helps managers to spot potential problem areas and make sound business decisions in the quick-paced information technology field.

Weinberg, G. M. *Secrets of Consulting.* Dorset House, 1985.

This is another of my favorite books. Besides being witty, the author knows how to deal with pampered people. The advice offered is down to earth and full of pointers on how to stimulate people to change. Focus is placed on the many psychological factors that influence success on software projects. The book provides memorable rules, laws, and principles that help you succeed in moving organizations forward even under the most trying circumstances.

Thorp, J. *The Information Paradox.* McGraw-Hill, 1998.

This thought-provoking volume tries to help businesses get their money's worth from their investments in information technology. It discusses the conflict between spending and business results. While investing in IT is thought to be a good thing by most decision makers, so is the need to demonstrate via sound business cases that IT investments yield positive returns. Through its many examples, the book shows you how to assess value and manage the on-time delivery of desired capabilities.

Yourdon, E. *Death March.* Prentice Hall, 1997.

For years, I have enjoyed reading Ed Yourdon's books. This one is no exception. It provides a survival guide to what many of us in the industry might call "impossible" or "doomed to fail" projects. The scary thing about the book is that it describes situations prevalent in many organizations today. But the book is prescriptive as it diagnoses problems. It lets you step backward to figure out how to step forward.

Software Economics

Boehm, B. W. *Software Engineering Economics.* Prentice Hall, 1981.

This tireless classic is the bible for the field of software estimation. I include it in this list because it discusses the business cases and analysis methods I refer to in my text. This book is useful because it focuses on the issues, experiences, and methods used to estimate software, perform trade studies, and manage costs throughout the life cycle. Many of the analysis methods I discuss are further amplified in this volume and it has many pertinent examples. However, the material on the original COCOMO cost model in this book is dated and has been replaced by the next reference.

Boehm, B. W., C. Abts, A. W. Brown, S. Chulani, B. K. Clark, E. Horowitz, R. Madachy, D. Reifer, and B. Steece. *Software Estimation with COCOMO II.* Prentice Hall, 2000.

This companion to [Boehm, 1981] provides a complete description of the updated COCOMO II cost model, its mathematical formulation, and its many cost drivers. I recommend the book because it shows how to use a modern estimating model for a variety of purposes (risk analysis, parametric studies, sensitivity analysis, and so on) via its many examples. The text also contains a CD-ROM with the latest free version of the software on it along with lots of applicable supporting information, manuals, tutorials, and reports.

Software Engineering

Pressman, R. S. *Software Engineering: A Practitioner's Approach,* 5th Edition. McGraw-Hill, 2001

This timeless classic introduces you the subject of software engineering and walks you through the software life cycle. As part of its coverage, it details the prerequisite knowledge for putting the discipline into practice. Topics range from conventional software engineering approaches to advanced methods. This edition puts some focus on object-oriented methods, the CMM, component-based approaches, and the move to the Web.

Software Management

Austin, R. D. *Measuring and Managing Performance in Organizations.* Dorset House, 1996.

This text introduces you to measurement issues from both the process and the people viewpoints. By referring to interviews with eight recognized experts, the author sheds light on the many measurement challenges, issues, and approaches available to combat them and yield positive results. The book provides practical guidelines aimed at building on patterns of successful organizations. Although academic at times, it is nevertheless interesting reading.

McMahon, P. E. *Virtual Project Management.* St. Lucie Press, 2000.

This book focuses on the problem of how to bring critical skills together without collocation. It discusses advances made in collaborative technology and provides practical guidance on how to put them to work to get work done without a great deal of conflict. It then presents eight practical and affordable steps to set up and succeed with a virtual project. The book then provides many resources to help you put its suggestions to work. Finally, its checklists and frequently asked questions appendix pull things together in a most usable manner.

Reifer, D. J. *Tutorial Software Management,* 5th Edition. IEEE Computer Society, 1997.

This volume provides reprints of papers organized around the five functions of management: planning, organizing, staffing, directing, and controlling. It highlights the use of proven management techniques for software. It also reprints papers on process improvement, estimating, and risk management. About a quarter of the volume is original works that highlight how to apply management concepts to making software progress visible.

Royce, W. *Software Project Management: A Unified Framework.* Addison-Wesley, 1998.

This book provides a management framework for developing software using the new paradigms (spiral, incremental, and so on), methods, tools, and technologies. I particularly like the book's emphasis on metrics, models, and quantitative methods. It provides you with the tools you need to figure out where your project is and determine its rate of progress. I also like the case study the author uses to illustrate how to use his many recommendations in practice. It is refreshing to have a software manager who has successfully managed a large project share his experiences with you in a way you can capitalize on.

Hall, E. M. *Managing Risk: Methods for Software Systems Development.* Addison-Wesley, 1998.

This well-written volume provides a comprehensive guide for successfully managing risk and creating a risk-aware culture in your firm. It focuses on process and people as it helps you establish a workable risk management infrastructure. In addition to providing pointers on how to identify risk, it takes you through the mitigation and prevention processes.

Software Process Improvement

Ahern, D. M., R. Turner, and A. Clouse, *CMMI Distilled: A Practical Introduction to Integrated Process Improvement,* Addison-Wesley, 2001.

For those of you interested in the new Capability Maturity Model for Integration (CMMI), I highly recommend this book. The authors have done an admirable job of describing the large and somewhat unwieldy new combined maturity model for systems and software in language that just about anyone can understand. The book also provides the reader with guidance on migrating to the model with information gathered from those involved in piloting its use on early adopter projects.

Caputo, K. *CMM Implementation Guide: Choreographing Software Process Improvement.* Addison-Wesley, 1998.

This book provides step-by-step guidance for those seeking to implement the Software Engineering Institute's capability maturity model. The author provides sound advice on how to get started with process improvement, points out problems you are likely to encounter, and then offers practical solutions based on experience using the techniques in large firms. The book is well written and full of practical advice on getting the job done.

Carnegie Mellon University, Software Engineering Institute (M. C. Paulk, C. V. Weber, B. Curtis, and M. B. Chrissis). *The Capability Maturity Model: Guidelines for Improving the Software Process.* Addison-Wesley, 1995.

This book defines the software capability maturity model (CMM) in terms of key process areas (KPAs). Each KPA identifies a cluster of related activities that, when performed collectively, achieve a set of goals considered necessary for improving process capability. Areas are then organized by common features, which contain key practices used as the building blocks for process improvement. Several cases are provided that serve as examples for application and computation of return on investment.

Humphrey, W. S. *Managing the Software Process.* Addison-Wesley, 1989.

This classic textbook provides practical guidelines for assessing and improving processes used for software development. It uses the five-level process maturity model popularized by the Software Engineering Institute as its framework for measurement and improvement. The author identifies key technical and managerial practices associated with each level, along with the criteria used to assess their implementation via process assessments.

Software Product Lines, Architectures and Reuse

Bass, L., P. Clements, and R. Kazman. *Software Architecture in Practice.* Addison-Wesley, 1998.

This textbook is current, readable, and full of practical advice. Besides spelling out what architecture is all about, this book provides guidance on development. I particularly like the numerous case studies and the lengthy discussion on product lines. Especially pertinent is the CORBA case and the discussion of World Wide Web (WWW) interoperability.

Jacobson, I., M. Griss, and P. Jonsson. *Software Reuse: Architecture, Process, and Organization for Business Success.* Addison-Wesley, 1997.

This textbook gets down and dirty. I particularly like its discussion of use cases and layered architectures. I find the book's focus on processes and methodology extremely helpful because it provides guidelines on how to get the job done using modern object-oriented methods and new development paradigms like the Rational Unified Process.

Lim, W. C. *Managing Software Reuse,* Prentice Hall, 1998.

This book focuses on the management challenges, issues, and experiences associated with software reuse. After discussing success factors, it dives into organizational, planning, staffing, directing, and control issues. It then provides a detailed discussion on reuse costs and benefits. It surveys reuse economic models and tells you what seems to work and what doesn't. It dwells on processes and discusses process maturity issues.

Poulin, J. S. *Measuring Software Reuse: Principles, Practices, and Economic Models.* Addison-Wesley, 1997.

This text talks reuse metrics and measurement. It starts by arming you with the facts and figures you need to justify your architecture-based reuse program. It then defines recommended metrics in detail and tells you how to use them to quantify software reuse and reuse benefits. It suggests a metrics starter set and discusses how to capture and use metrics to provide indicators of progress. Finally, it provides a worksheet and a reuse metrics calculator. This book is a useful guide for implementing a reuse metrics program.

Reifer, D. J. *Practical Software Reuse*. John Wiley & Sons, 1997.

This text provides you with insight into how to put together a software reuse initiative. Its message is that many technical initiatives fail because they don't place enough focus on developing a workable management infrastructure. The author amplifies these points as he provides lessons learned and guidance on implementing an architecture-based reuse initiative in the context of product line management concepts. Like the other texts, this one is full of advice and examples that let you build on the lessons others have learned the hard way.

Szyperski, C. *Component Software: Beyond Object-Oriented Programming*. Addison-Wesley, 1998.

This book compares the Microsoft and Sun Web strategies and provides insight into how to put them to work in your organization. It gets into ActiveX, CORBA, Java, OLE, and OMA components and suggests ways to develop applications quickly using frameworks and component architectures. After reading the text, you are convinced that you should adopt a building-block approach because that is where the technology is moving.

Statistics and Engineering/Managerial Economics

Cook, R. D., and S. Weisbert. *An Introduction to Regression Graphics*. John Wiley & Sons, 1994.

It is not often that I recommend a mathematical textbook. But this one is different from the ones you used in college. Instead of focusing on probability theory and statistics, this book provides access to a wide array of graphical tools for visualizing regression data and extracting meaningful summaries. A CD-ROM provides a copy of the R-code regression software that permits you to replicate every graph and perform every procedure described in the text.

Fleischer, G. A. *Capital Allocation Theory*. Appleton-Century-Crofts, 1969.

This classic, written by one of my professors, has been a useful friend for many years. I have used it repeatedly to answer questions concerning engineering economics. The book provides a detailed treatment of the mathematics involved in economic evaluation, the effects of uncertainty and taxes, and capital decision theory.

Juristo, N., and A. M. Moreno. *Basics of Software Engineering Experimentation*. Kluwer Academic Publishers, 2001.

This textbook's experimental design clearly and cleverly discusses how to analyze and make sense of the data. I like its focus on empirical studies and its emphasis on trying to understand what the numbers really mean. Although not for the novice, it is a good book for the practitioner to read.

Shim, J. K., and J. G. Siegel. *Managerial Economics.* Barrons Educational Series, 1998.

When I wanted a refresher on the topic of managerial economics, I searched for a text that was easy to follow and had business examples I could relate to. After reviewing several volumes, I settled on this one because it allowed me to quickly get up to speed on the topic. This well-written book is aimed at providing the basics of economic theory and its mathematics to professionals working in the field.

Appendix B

Compound Interest Tables

PRESENT VALUE

This table computes the present value (PV) of $1 for N periods using the following interest rate (i) compounding formula:

$$PV = 1/(1 + i)^N$$

Periods	2%	4%	6%	8%	10%	12%	15%	18%	20%
1	0.9804	0.9615	0.9434	0.9259	0.9091	0.8929	0.8696	0.8475	0.8333
2	0.9612	0.9246	0.8900	0.8573	0.8264	0.7972	0.7561	0.7182	0.6944
3	0.9423	0.8890	0.8396	0.7938	0.7513	0.7118	0.6575	0.6086	0.5787
4	0.9238	0.8548	0.7921	0.7350	0.6830	0.6355	0.5718	0.5158	0.4823
5	0.9057	0.8219	0.7473	0.6806	0.6209	0.5674	0.4972	0.4371	0.4019
6	0.8880	0.7903	0.7050	0.6302	0.5645	0.5066	0.4323	0.3704	0.3349
7	0.8706	0.7590	0.6651	0.5835	0.5132	0.4523	0.3759	0.3139	0.2791
8	0.8535	0.7307	0.6274	0.5403	0.4665	0.4039	0.3269	0.2660	0.2326
9	0.8368	0.7026	0.5919	0.5002	0.4241	0.3606	0.2843	0.2255	0.1938

Periods	2%	4%	6%	8%	10%	12%	15%	18%	20%
10	0.8203	0.6756	0.5584	0.4632	0.3855	0.3220	0.2472	0.1911	0.1615
11	0.8043	0.6496	0.5268	0.4289	0.3505	0.2875	0.2140	0.1619	0.1346
12	0.7885	0.6246	0.4970	0.3971	0.3186	0.2567	0.1869	0.1372	0.1122
13	0.7730	0.6006	0.4686	0.3677	0.2897	0.2292	0.1625	0.1163	0.0935
14	0.7579	0.5775	0.4423	0.3405	0.2633	0.2046	0.1413	0.0985	0.0779
15	0.7430	0.5553	0.4173	0.3152	0.2392	0.1827	0.1229	0.0835	0.0649
16	0.7284	0.5339	0.3936	0.2919	0.2176	0.1631	0.1069	0.0708	0.0541
17	0.7142	0.5134	0.3714	0.2703	0.1978	0.1456	0.0929	0.0600	0.0451
18	0.7002	0.4936	0.3503	0.2502	0.1799	0.1300	0.0808	0.0508	0.0376
19	0.6864	0.4746	0.3305	0.2317	0.1635	0.1161	0.0703	0.0431	0.0313
20	0.6730	0.4564	0.3118	0.2145	0.1486	0.1037	0.0611	0.0365	0.0261
25	0.6095	0.3751	0.2330	0.1460	0.0923	0.0588	0.0304	0.0160	0.0105
30	0.5521	0.3083	0.1741	0.0994	0.0573	0.0334	0.0151	0.0070	0.0042

FUTURE WORTH

This table computes the future worth (FW) of $1 for N periods using the following interest rate (i) compounding formula.

$$FW = 1(1 + i)^N$$

Periods	2%	4%	6%	8%	10%	12%	15%	18%	20%
1	1.020	1.040	1.060	1.080	1.100	1.120	1.150	1.180	1.200
2	1.040	1.082	1.124	1.166	1.210	1.254	1.322	1.392	1.440
3	1.061	1.125	1.191	1.260	1.331	1.405	1.521	1.643	1.728
4	1.082	1.170	1.262	1.360	1.464	1.574	1.749	1.939	2.074
5	1.104	1.217	1.338	1.469	1.611	1.762	2.011	2.288	2.488
6	1.126	1.265	1.419	1.587	1.772	1.974	2.313	2.700	2.986
7	1.149	1.316	1.504	1.714	1.949	2.211	2.660	3.185	3.583
8	1.172	1.369	1.594	1.851	2.144	2.476	3.059	3.759	4.300
9	1.195	1.423	1.689	1.999	2.358	2.773	3.518	4.435	5.160
10	1.219	1.480	1.791	2.159	2.594	3.106	4.460	5.234	6.192
11	1.243	1.539	1.898	2.332	2.853	3.479	4.652	6.176	7.430

Periods	2%	4%	6%	8%	10%	12%	15%	18%	20%
12	1.268	1.601	2.012	2.518	3.138	3.896	5.350	7.288	8.916
13	1.294	1.665	2.133	2.720	3.452	4.363	6.153	8.599	10.699
14	1.319	1.732	2.261	2.937	3.797	4.887	7.076	10.147	12.839
15	1.346	1.801	2.397	3.172	4.177	5.474	8.137	11.974	15.407
16	1.373	1.873	2.540	3.426	4.595	6.130	9.358	14.129	18.488
17	1.400	1.948	2.693	3.700	5.054	6.866	10.761	16.672	22.186
18	1.428	2.026	2.854	3.996	5.560	7.690	12.375	19.673	26.623
19	1.457	2.107	3.026	4.316	6.116	8.613	14.232	23.214	31.948
20	1.486	2.191	3.207	4.661	6.727	9.646	16.367	27.393	38.338
25	1.641	2.666	4.292	6.848	10.835	17.000	32.919	62.669	95.396
30	1.811	3.243	5.743	10.063	17.449	29.960	66.212	143.37	237.38

PRESENT VALUE OF UNIFORM SERIES OF CASH FLOWS

This table computes the PV for N periods assuming a uniform series of cash flows of $1 using the following interest rate (i) compounding formula:

$$PV = \frac{1[(1 + i)^N - 1]}{i(1 + i)^N}$$

Periods	2%	4%	6%	8%	10%	12%	15%	18%	20%
1	0.980	0.962	0.943	0.926	0.909	0.893	0.870	0.847	0.833
2	1.942	1.886	1.833	1.783	1.736	1.690	1.626	1.566	1.528
3	2.884	2.775	2.673	2.577	2.487	2.402	2.283	2.174	2.106
4	3.808	3.630	3.465	3.312	3.170	3.037	2.855	2.690	2.589
5	4.713	4.452	4.212	3.993	3.791	3.605	3.352	3.127	2.991
6	5.601	5.242	4.917	4.623	4.355	4.111	3.784	3.498	3.326
7	6.472	6.002	5.582	5.206	4.868	4.564	4.160	3.812	3.605
8	7.325	6.733	6.210	5.747	5.335	4.968	4.487	4.078	3.837
9	8.162	7.435	6.802	6.247	5.759	5.328	4.772	4.303	4.031
10	8.983	8.111	7.360	6.710	6.145	5.650	5.019	4.494	4.192
11	9.787	8.760	7.887	7.139	6.495	5.938	5.234	4.656	4.327

Periods	2%	4%	6%	8%	10%	12%	15%	18%	20%
12	10.575	9.385	8.384	7.536	6.814	6.194	5.421	4.793	4.439
13	11.384	9.986	8.853	7.904	7.103	6.424	5.583	4.910	4.533
14	12.106	10.563	9.295	8.244	7.367	6.628	5.724	5.008	4.611
15	12.849	11.118	9.712	8.559	7.606	6.811	5.847	5.092	4.675
16	13.578	11.652	10.106	8.851	7.824	6.974	5.954	5.162	4.730
17	14.292	12.166	10.477	9.122	8.022	7.120	6.047	5.222	4.775
18	14.992	12.659	10.828	9.372	8.201	7.250	6.128	5.273	4.812
19	15.678	13.134	11.158	9.604	8.365	7.366	6.198	5.316	4.843
20	16.351	13.590	11.470	9.818	8.514	7.469	6.259	5.353	4.870
25	19.523	15.622	12.783	10.675	9.077	7.843	6.464	5.467	4.948
30	22.396	17.292	13.765	11.258	9.427	8.055	6.566	5.517	4.979

Acronyms

ACAP	Analyst capability cost driver
APEX	Application experience cost driver
API	Application program interface
B-to-B	Business to business
CAD	Computer-aided design
CAIV	Cost as an independent variable
CCB	Change control board
CIO	Chief information system officer
CM	Configuration management
CMM	Capability maturity model
CMMI	Capability maturity model integration
CMMI-SE/SW	Capability maturity model integration— system engineering/software
COCOMO	Constructive cost model
CORBA	Common object request broker architecture
COTS	Commercial off-the-shelf
CPLX	Product complexity cost driver
CTO	Chief technology officer

DATA	Database size cost driver
DBMS	Database management system
DOCU	Documentation matched to life cycle needs cost driver
D/E	Debt/earnings ratio
EAF	Effort adjustment factor
e-business	Electronic business
e-commerce	Electronic commerce
EPS	Earnings per share
ESLOC	Equivalent source lines of code
EV	Expected value
FCIL	Facilities
FLEX	Development flexibility cost driver
FW	Future worth
GUI	Graphical user interface
IBM	International Business Machines
IEEE	Institute of Electrical and Electronics Engineers
IOC	Initial operational capability
IPO	Initial public offering
IRS	Internal Revenue Service
IR&D	Internal research and development
ISO	International Standards Organization
IT	Information technology
KPA	Key process area
LAN	Local area network
LCA	Life cycle architecture milestone
LCO	Life cycle objectives milestone
LTEX	Language and tool experience cost driver
MBASE	Model-based (system) architecture and software engineering
MIS	Management information systems
N/A	Not applicable
NPV	Net present value
OLE	Object linking and embedding
P&L	Profit and loss
PAL	Process asset library
PC	Personal computer
PCAP	Programmer capability cost driver
PCON	Personnel continuity cost driver

PLEX	Platform experience cost driver
PMAT	Process maturity cost driver
PREC	Project precedentedness cost driver
PROM	Programmable read-only memory
PTO	U.S. Patent and Trademark Office
PV	Present value
PVOL	Platform volatility cost driver
P/E	Price/earnings ratio
P/S	Price/sales ratio
R&D	Research and development
RAD	Rapid application development
RCI	Reifer Consultants, Inc.
RELY	Required software reliability cost driver
RESL	Architecture and known risk resolution cost driver
ROA	Return on assets
ROE	Return on earnings
ROI	Return on investment
ROM	Rough-order magnitude
RUSE	Developed for reusability cost driver
SCED	Required development schedule cost driver
SEC	Securities and Exchange Commission
SEI	Software Engineering Institute
SEMA	Software engineering measurement and analysis
SITE	Multisite development cost driver
SLOC	Source lines of code
SM	Staff-month (of labor)
SPICE	Software process improvement and capability determination
STOR	Main storage constraint cost driver
SW-CMM	Software capability maturity model
TEAM	Development team cooperation cost driver
TIME	Execution time constraint cost driver
TOOL	Use of software tools cost driver
TSP	Team software process
USC	University of Southern California
WBS	Work breakdown structure
WWW	World Wide Web

Glossary

The following terms are used in the text. I have tried to supply simple definitions to make the terms understandable. Although they would be more precise, I have avoided definitions from management or statistical texts.

Accounting profits   Difference between total revenue and the cost of producing the goods and services.

Activity   Major unit of work to be completed. An activity has a precise starting and ending date, includes a set of tasks, consumes resources, and results in generation of work products [Reifer, 1997a].

Applications software   Software that provides a set of services or solves some type of user problem [Reifer, 1997b].

Application engineering   Processes/practices used to guide the disciplined development, test, and life cycle support of applications software.

Appreciation   Increase in the market value of an asset over time.

Architecture   Structure of components, their interrelationships, and the principles and guidelines governing their design and evolution over time [Reifer, 1997a].

Asset   Something of value that a firm owns and can capitalize.

Authority   In project management, the right to give direction and allocate resources [Reifer, 1997b].

[Reifer, 1997a] Reifer, D. J. *Practical Software Reuse.* John Wiley & Sons, 1997.

Balance sheet   Document that summarizes the financial health of the firm, as measured by its assets and liabilities, at a particular time.

Barometric forecast   Use of economic indicators to predict turning points in economic activity.

Baseline   Work product that has been formally reviewed and agreed on and that can be changed only through strict change control procedures. A baseline work product may form the basis for further work activity [Reifer, 1997b].

Benchmark   Standard against which measurements or comparisons can be made.

Best practice   Engineering or management activity that directly addresses the purpose of a particular process and contributes to the creation of its output. In SPICE, a software best practice is an essential activity of a particular process [El Emam, 1997].

Book value   Difference between original cost (or other basis) and the accumulated depreciation to date.

Breakeven analysis   Analysis performed to compute the value at which the solution will recover expenditures when comparing alternative use of resources.

Budget   In management, a statement of expected results expressed numerically [Reifer, 1997b].

Business area   Coherent market created by consumers who have similar needs and purchasing tendencies. Business areas may be organized by customer, geography, product, or some other characteristic [Reifer, 1997b].

Business area manager   Person or organization responsible for managing the definition, use, and evolution of products within a business area or line of business [Reifer, 1997b].

Business case   Materials prepared for decision makers to show them that the business idea under consideration is a good one and that its numbers make financial as well as technical sense for the organization.

Capability maturity model (software) (SW-CMM)   Description of the stages through which software organizations evolve as they define, implement, measure, control, and improve their software processes. This model provides a guide for selecting process improvement strategies by facilitating the determination of current process capabilities and the identification of the issues most critical to software quality and process improvement [Paulk, 1995].

Capital   Total funds available to a firm from all sources, debt and equity.

Capital budgeting   Process of making long-term capital expenditure decisions.

Case study   Example used to communicate lessons learned from trial use of a concept or idea.

Cash flow   Receipt and expenditure of money over time.

Champion   High-level member of the senior management team who supports your idea and assists in selling it to other executives.

[Reifer, 1997b] Reifer, D. J. *Tutorial Software Management*, 5th Edition. IEEE Computer Society, 1997.

[IEEE, 1990] *IEEE Standard Glossary of Software Engineering Terminology*. IEEE Std 610.12–1990.

Commercial off-the-shelf (COTS) software Software that is supplied by a third party who retains responsibility for its continued development and life cycle support. COTS software is used as is; the version is not changed to address the unique needs of the user [Reifer, 1997a].

Commitment Obligation to expend resources at some future time, such as a purchase order or travel authorization, which is charged against a budget even though it has not yet been paid [Reifer, 1997b].

Competency Skills, knowledge, and personal attributes that enable effective work performance [El Emam, 1997].

Component-based development Process of building software systems by combining and integrating pretested and preengineered fine-grained software objects using an established framework [Reifer, 1997b].

Compounding Adding the interest to the principal during an agreed-to period.

Contingency In management, an amount of design margin, time, or money used as a safety factor to accommodate future growth or uncertainty [Reifer, 1997b].

Core competency Capabilities of the firm deemed essential for its continued survival [Reifer, 1997b].

Costing In management, the process of developing a cost estimate for an item, task, or activity. Costing and pricing are separate but related activities typically done by different people at different times during the software life cycle [Reifer, 1997b].

Cost/benefit analysis Analysis performed to compute the net benefits (can be plus or minus) resulting from an investment decision.

Cost center Organization to which control over resources and to which budgets and profit goals have been assigned [Reifer, 1997b].

Cost of capital Rate of return that investors expect to receive from an investment.

Cost of goods sold Direct cost associated with producing the items sold during a specified time period.

Critical path Series of dependent tasks for a project that must be completed as planned to keep the project on schedule.

Critical success factors Characteristics, conditions, or variables that have a direct influence on customers' satisfaction with the products and services that a firm offers to the marketplace [Reifer, 1997b].

Delegation In management, the empowerment of another with the authority to act or represent someone else in the performance of responsibilities [Reifer, 1997b].

Deliverable Product developed, packaged, and provided to satisfy documented customer needs/requirements.

Depreciation Systematic system of accounting that aims to distribute the cost or other basic value of tangible assets, less salvage value (if any), over its estimated useful life.

[El Emam, 1997] El Emam, K., J. N. Drouin, and W. Melo. *SPICE*. IEEE Computer Society Press, 1997.

[Paulk, 1995] Paulk, M. C., C. V. Weber, B. Curtis, and M. B. Chrissis. *The Capability Maturity Model: Guidelines for Improving the Software Process*. Addison-Wesley, 1995.

Development time Time required from the planned start of a task to its finish expressed in calendar months.

Direction Management activities conducted to energize, motivate, and guide personal behavior for the purpose of achieving organizational goals [Reifer, 1997b].

Discounted cash flows Method for expressing a projected stream of cash flows as a present worth.

Dispute Disagreement giving rise to a claim under a contract or agreement.

Earned value Measure of budgetary performance that relates actual expenditures to technical achievements as determined by milestone completions.

Earnings Net income or profit earned by a firm during an accounting period.

Econometric models Statistically based models where relationships among economic variables are expressed by mathematical formulas and then estimated using such techniques as regression.

Economic profits Difference between total revenue and total opportunity costs.

Economies of scale Lowering of costs achieved by spreading fixed costs over large volumes.

Education Communication of knowledge to interested parties. Quite different from training, whose goal is developing the skills and abilities needed to perform a task [Reifer, 1997b].

Effort Work required to complete a task expressed in staff-months of labor.

Escrow Condition when a deed is held conditionally by a third person, to be released or returned if the seller defaults.

Estimate Most knowledgeable forecast of the resources needed in the future to complete a task.

Expected value Weighted average using probabilities to determine weights.

Fixed costs Costs that remain constant regardless of changes in activity.

Forecasting In management, the prediction of future events. Forecasts differ from estimates in the means used to derive them and their accuracy.

Framework Semicompleted software system designed to be used to generate or create a new instance of itself from a template.

Functional organization Organizational form that groups people by skill or specialty (such as software or hardware engineering) in one department, reporting to a single manager [Reifer, 1997b].

Future worth Cash value of a decision measured using some future date as the common point of reference.

Hyperlink Device that drives intuitive navigation on the World Wide Web. Click on a hyperlink, and you will jump to a related page.

Hypertext Markup Language (HTML) Coding method used to format documents on the World Wide Web. Browsers display text, graphics, and links on Web pages by translating HTML tags that appear in the file.

Incremental tax rate Effective tax rate paid by a firm. Because tax rates are graduated, this rate typically varies as a function of income earned.

Information technology Broad category of products and services based on digital technologies for the creation, storage, and use of information. Computer hardware, software, communications media and content, and telecommunications equipment and services are manifestations of information technology.

Infrastructure   Underlying framework of an organization or system, including organizational structures, policies, standards, training, facilities, and tools, that supports its ongoing performance [Paulk, 1995].

Intangible benefits   Benefits that cannot be easily quantified.

Intellectual property   Intangible output of the rational thought process that has some intellectual or informational value.

Interest   Money charged for use of borrowed assets.

Investment tax credit   Deduction taken directly from the tax liability of a firm for qualified investments (research and development, etc.).

Key process area   Cluster of related activities that, when performed collectively, achieve a set of goals considered to be important for establishing process capability [Paulk, 1995].

Know-how engineering   Ability to transfer the know-how associated with a new technology and achieve a set of goals considered to be important for establishing needed capability.

Knowledge base   Codification of the organization's engineering experience in building and sustaining similar systems [Reifer, 1997b].

Leadership   In management, the ability to influence the behavior of others and focus it toward the achievement of accepted goals [Reifer, 1997b].

Least-square method   Statistical method in regression analysis aimed at finding the regression line with the best fit to the actual data.

Legacy   Software developed on one project that has potential for reuse on another.

Liabilities   What a firm owes.

Life cycle   See **Software life cycle**.

Line organization   Part of the functional organization that is responsible for performing tasks and delivering products [Reifer, 1997b].

Management   Getting things done through the work of other people [Reifer, 1997b].

Management reserve   In project management, time and budget set aside for contingencies.

Market share   Size of firm's revenues compared to the size of the firm's market.

Matrix organization   Combination of functional and project forms of organization, in which the line is responsible for providing skilled people and the project is responsible for managing performance [Reifer, 1997b].

Maturity level   Well-defined evolutionary plateau in achieving a mature software process [Paulk, 1995].

Mean squared error   Average sum of the variations between two variables (e.g., forecasts and sales) for corresponding periods.

Measurement   In management, the process of collecting, analyzing, and reporting metrics deemed useful in assessing status, progress, performance, and/or trends.

Metric   Quantitative measure of the degree to which a system, process, or component possesses a given attribute. Error density, for example, provides an indicator of software reliability [Reifer, 1997b].

Middleware   Layer of software that sits between the operating system and application that provides computing services through a simple programming interface [Reifer, 1997b].

Milestone   Schedule event for which some person is held accountable and that is used to gauge progress.

Minimum attractive rate of return   Minimum rate of return that is attractive to investors (e.g., interest rate cash could earn if the funds were in a bank account).

Model   Representation of a real-world process, device, or concept.

Motivation   In management, the act of influencing the behavior of others through the combined use of incentives and rewards [Reifer, 1997b].

Net income   Amount of resulting profit computed by subtracting expenses from income.

Opportunity costs   Net benefits forgone when pursuing an alternate use of resources.

Optimum price   Typically, the price at which profit is maximized.

Organizing   Management activities conducted to structure the efforts of people to optimize collaboration and communication.

Paradigm   Modeling approach for the software development process.

Payback period   Amount of time required to recover the costs of the initial investment.

Pareto analysis   Analysis based on the premise that most effects are generated from relatively few causes (the 80/20 rule).

Peak pricing   Pricing that charges a higher price during peak times than is charged in normal periods (the consumer pays a premium).

Performance   In management, a measure of a manager's ability to achieve agreed-on goals and deliver what's promised on time and within budget.

Planning   Management activities conducted to establish future courses of action at all levels of an organization. At the top, plans tend to be strategic. At lower levels, plans tend to be tactical. At all levels, plans set the standards against which progress is measured [Reifer, 1997b].

Power   In management, the perceived ability of one person to influence the actions of others [Reifer, 1997b].

Practice   Engineering or management activity that contributes to the creation of output of a process or enhances its capability [El Emam, 1997].

Present value   Cash value of a decision measured using the present date as the common point of reference.

Pricing   In management, the process of determining how much to charge a customer or user for products and services. Costing and pricing are separate activities. Organizations can price services for less than their cost and still make a profit because of economies of scale [Reifer, 1997b].

Process   Sequence of steps performed for a given purpose, for example, the software development process.

Process maturity   Relative assessment of an organization's ability to achieve its goals through the technical and managerial processes it uses to develop its products and services.

Product   Software and all its associated work products.

Product line   Family of similar products developed to service the market needs of a particular business area or line of business [Reifer, 1997a].

Product line management   Business function that manages the definition, development, evaluation, use, and evolution of assets that can be shared across projects and/or products over time [Reifer, 1997a].

Project   Organized undertaking that uses human and physical resources in one effort to achieve a specific goal [Reifer, 1997b].

Project management   System of management established to focus resources on achieving project goals.

Project organization   Form of organization in which all the people on the project report to the project manager [Reifer, 1997b].

Proposal   Provider's offer to deliver products or services to a prospective client.

Profit and loss (P&L) statement   Document that summarizes the financial success of the enterprise measured by its income and expenses over a specified time period.

Quantitative control   Any quantitative or statistically based technique appropriate to analyze a software process, identify special causes of variations in the performance of the software process, and bring the performance of the software process within well-defined limits [Paulk, 1995].

Rate of return   Interest rate at which the present worth of receipts resulting from the project is equal to the present worth of the disbursements.

Reference architecture   Software architecture defined to serve as a point of departure for a product line or family of similar systems [Reifer, 1997b].

Regression analysis   Statistical procedure used for estimating the mathematical relationship between dependent variables (e.g., sales) and one or more independent variables (e.g., price, market segment).

Resources   Intellectual and financial possessions available to an organization.

Return on investment   Measure of how much profit an investment earns computed by dividing net income by the assets used to generate it.

Reusable software   Software designed and implemented to be reused without modification.

Risk   In financial circles, exposure to loss.

Risk management   Process of identifying, analyzing, quantifying, and developing plans to eliminate or mitigate risk before it harms a project [Reifer, 1997b].

Salvage value   Amount realized, by sale or other dispositions, when the asset is retired from service.

Schedule   Actual calendar time budgeted for accomplishing goals established for activities or tasks [Reifer, 1997b].

Scheduling   In management, the process of allocating and interrelating tasks within the schedule. This activity is like figuring out a jigsaw puzzle, especially when many of the tasks must be done in parallel [Reifer, 1997b].

Sensitivity analysis   Analysis conducted to determine to which of the input parameters the solution is sensitive.

Software license   Revocable right to use software in specified places or specified platforms in specified ways.

Software life cycle   Period of time that begins when a software product is conceived and ends when the product is retired from use [Reifer, 1997b].

Staff   Persons assigned to an organization to do the work.

Staffing   Management activities conducted to acquire, develop, and retain staff in an organization [Reifer, 1997b].

Standard deviation   Measure of uncertainty computed as the square root of the mean of the squared deviations from the expected value.

Sunk cost   Expense that has occurred before an investment decision is made.

Tangible benefits   Benefits whose advantages can be quantified.

Task   Smallest unit of work subject to management accountability. A task contains a well-defined work assignment for one or more team members. The specification for the work to be performed is documented in a work package. Related tasks form activities.

Technology transfer   Process used to prove, transfer, and put technology into widespread use in an organization.

Terms and conditions   Legally sufficient descriptions of rights and responsibilities, as well as the conditions associated with them, if any.

Time value of assets   Changing value of assets from one time period to another.

Trend analysis   Statistical procedure used for estimating the mathematical relationship between the dependent variable (e.g., sales) and time.

Tracking   In management, the process of identifying the cost and schedule variances by comparing actual expenditures with projections [Reifer, 1997b].

Training   Planned development of skills and abilities needed by personnel to perform their jobs.

Uncertainty   In management, the degree of entropy associated with the information used to make a decision [Reifer, 1997b].

Useful life   Period over which an asset can be reasonably used in trade or business. The Internal Revenue Service has established minimum useful lives along with methods for computing depreciation for various classes of assets.

Value   Tangible worth of an asset being appraised.

Variable costs   Costs that vary in total in direct proportion to changes in activity.

Warranty   Representation given by a provider to a customer that the goods and services purchased will perform as promised or a refund will be given, a repair made, or a replacement made at no charge.

Work breakdown structure   Family tree that organizes, defines, and graphically illustrates the products, services, and tasks necessary to achieve project objectives.

Work package   Specification of the work to be accomplished in completing a function, activity, or task. A work package defines the work product(s), the staffing needs, the expected duration, the resources to be used, the acceptance criteria for the work product, the name of the responsible individual(s), and any special considerations for the work [Reifer, 1997b].

Work product   Artifact associated with the execution of a practice (e.g., test case, requirement specification, or code) [El Emam, 1997].

Index

281

Register
Your Book
at www.aw.com/cseng/register

You may be eligible to receive:

- Advance notice of forthcoming editions of the book
- Related book recommendations
- Chapter excerpts and supplements of forthcoming titles
- Information about special contests and promotions throughout the year
- Notices and reminders about author appearances, tradeshows, and online chats with special guests

Contact us

If you are interested in writing a book or reviewing manuscripts prior to publication, please write to us at:

Editorial Department
Addison-Wesley Professional
75 Arlington Street, Suite 300
Boston, MA 02116 USA
Email: AWPro@aw.com

Visit us on the Web: http://www.aw.com/cseng